W9-DGW-672

JOHN DEERE
QUALITY FARM
EQUIPMENT

50
Power Steering

JOHN DEERE

A HISTORY OF THE TRACTOR

RANDY LEFFINGWELL

Voyageur Press

This edition published in 2006 by Voyageur Press,
an imprint of MBI Publishing Company,
Galtier Plaza, Suite 200, 380 Jackson Street,
St. Paul, MN 55101-3885 USA

MBI Publishing Company titles are also available at discounts in bulk quantity for industrial or sales-promotional use. For details write to Special Sales Manager at MBI Publishing Company, Galtier Plaza, Suite 200, 380 Jackson Street, St. Paul, MN 55101-3885 USA

ISBN-13: 978-0-7603-2677-0
ISBN-10: 0-7603-2677-0

On the cover: *Bob Pollack's 1953 Model 630 Hi-Crop towers over western Iowa corn stubble. Corn, cotton, and sugar cane were some of the crops Deere & Company had in mind when engineers developed these increased ground clearance tractors.*

On the frontispiece: *The John Deere symbol has been an instantly recognizable icon of agriculture throughout America and the world for over 150 years.*

On the title page: *Walter Keller's 1955 Model 50 Wide Front stretches out across a neighboring field in a slightly exaggerated wide-angle lens perspective. Deere produced the 27.5-drawbar-horsepower Model 50s from 1952 through 1956.*

On the back cover: *Deere produced around 32 of these LPG-gas powered Model 3010s. This well-restored 1962 model stands out sharply against the Keller family's unrestored GP behind it.*

Editor: Peter Schletty
Designer: Katie Sonmor

Printed in China

CONTENTS

Dedication

For Lorry Dunning and for Guy Fay

These two friends, great thinkers, and consummate historians have taught me much of what I know and understand about the history of mechanized agriculture. Lorry first challenged me to "do it right," back in 1990, and he and Guy have been working hard since then to help me do just that. My respect for these two men goes beyond words and it is most easily summed up by dedicating this book to them.

ACKNOWLEDGMENTS

First and foremost, I wish to thank Les Stegh, former archivist for Deere & Company, for his careful read of my text and his thoughtful (and thought provoking) questions.

I must thank historian, researcher, and friend Lorry Dunning of Davis, California, for his tireless efforts on behalf of this book. Lorry read Theo Brown's diaries and found the "treasures." After finishing the 15,800 pages that Brown wrote over his 40 years with Deere & Company, Lorry decided the entire diary was a treasure. The excerpts that you enjoy here are just a few of the jewels from Brown's record of his history and that of Deere and the world during this amazing period.

In addition, I thank my other friend, researcher, and historian, Guy Fay of Madison, Wisconsin. Guy unearthed Theo Brown's diaries but other obligations prevented him from getting through the pages. Meanwhile, Guy uncovered Deere's history through its patents. These engineering and legal documents include not only fascinating drawings to illustrate the inventions but also the explanations of their inventors, engineers, and designers.

I am most grateful to Rodney Gorme Obien, Archivist and Special Collections Librarian of the George C. Gordon Library at Worchester Polytechnic Institute in Worchester, Massachusetts, for his help and cooperation in making available Theo Brown's diaries. Without his assistance, much of the information in the first half of this book would have been much more difficult to locate and use.

I wish to express my deepest gratitude to Harold Brock, retired Chief Engineer for Deere & Company, for his countless recollections of his days designing, testing, developing, and perfecting ever and ever better tractors.

Further, I want to thank Matt Monaghan and Dirk Hummel at OMNI Micrographics in Sacramento, California, for their assistance in reproducing drawings and other images from Theo Brown's diaries. Microfilm and digital conversion specialists, their equipment is top-notch and their skills and techniques are positively wizard-like, and wizard-quick!

To illustrate Deere's tractor history took the great cooperation of a number of enthusiastic collectors. To each of these individuals, I owe immeasurable thanks for their willingness to change plans, take days off, and even interrupt harvests to pull a variety of machines from their sheds, barns and garages.

Bruce Aldo, Westfield, MA; Steve and Sylvia Bauer, Hastings, MN; Frank Bettencourt, Vernalis, CA; Jim Blomgren, Grand Meadows, MN; John Boehm, Woodland, CA; Otis and Bettina Chandler, Ojai, CA; John Craig, Mentone, IN; Paul Cook, Yakima, WA; Tony Dieter, Vail, IA; Sue Duggan, Ostrander, MN; Kenny Duttenhoeffer, El Cajon, CA; Todd Erickson, Cannon Falls, MN; Fairfield Equipment, Fairfield, IA; Martin Gonzalez, Ojai, CA; Rod & Becky Groenewald, Director, Antique Gas & Steam Engine Museum, Vista, CA; Junior Heim, Glidden, IA; Bruce Henderson, Vail, IA; Mike and Pat Holder. Owosso, MI; Travis Jorde, Rochester, MN; Wendell and Mary Kelch, Bethel, Ohio; Walter and Lois Keller, Forest Junction, WI; Bruce and Judy Keller, Brillion, WI; Jason Keller, Greenbay, WI; Mary Jane Keppler, Director, Froelich Foundation for the Preservation of Tractor History, Froelich, IA; Dax and Karen Kimmelshue, Durham, CA; Jack Kreeger, Omaha, NE; Harland and Kenny Layher, Grand Island, NE and the collection of the late Lester Layher, Wood River, NE; Brent & Eileen Liebert, Carroll, IA; Larry and Melanie Maasdam, Clarion, IA; Frank McCune, Newport Beach, CA; Don and Charlene Merrihew, Greg and Kathy Merrihew and their sons Tyler and Mitchell, Mount Pleasant, MI; Cecil Morton, Vista, CA; Paul Ostrander and Mike Ostrander, Columbia City, IN; Bob and Mary Pollock, Vail, IA; Dave Robinson, Audubon, IA; Jim and Fay Slechta, Vail, IA; Virginia Schultz, Gary and Charlene Schultz, Ollie, IA; Jared and Jeri Schultz, Cedar Rapids, IA; Roger and Ruth Swanson, Froelich Foundation for the Preservation of Tractor History, Froelich, IA; and Roy Volk, Vista, CA.

I want to thank Darwin Holmstrom, my editor at MBI Publishing Company, for his on going efforts to make me a better writer and for his suggestion that I do this book in the first place. I owe ongoing gratitude to Zack Miller, MBI's publisher, for his continuing faith in my ability to do these great projects. I am most sincerely grateful to Peter Schletty for his thoughtful edits, and his incredible care in bringing together all the disparate elements that made up this book. And I wish to thank Katie Sonmor for her gorgeous design of this book.

Lastly, I am grateful to my partner in life, Carolyn, for her love and encouragement and for so much more.

INTRODUCTION

In central Illinois, soil conditions were perfect to frustrate even the most talented blacksmith. While horses' shoes stayed on their feet, and wagon wheel rims remained in place once the smithy had hammered them into position, that staying power was exactly the problem with the dirt. It stuck to the plow share, the curved plate that cut into the earth and slipped under it to flip it over.

In the early days of the United States, ideas and technologies moved west across the new nation as memories in the minds, or products in the wagons, of the pioneers. Upon reaching new homelands, the settlers looked around at conditions, re-examined what they'd brought with them, and over time, improved upon what they knew. Such was the case with John Deere and his plow.

Deere was born on February 7, 1804, in Rutland, Vermont. His parents, both English, had stayed in the new colonies after America's Revolutionary War. When his father William died, John and his mother Sarah moved to Middlebury where she carried on William's tailoring business. Just eight years old at the time, John apprenticed himself to a local tanner while he continued school. After taking some classes at Middlebury College, he lost interest in book learning and went to work for Captain Benjamin Lawrence where he learned to become a blacksmith.

RIGHT: 1935 MODEL GP WITH 3-ROW CORN PLANTER
Theo Brown's General Purpose "GP" models were nearly perfect by 1935 when this example was assembled. This controversial 3-row tool system appeared first for the standard tread GP tractors. Then Brown supplemented it with a 4-row arrangement for the GP-Wide Tread tricycles that followed.

Blacksmiths did more than shoe horses and mend wagon wheels. They also served as the local community inventor and fabricator. Lawrence taught Deere all the skills needed to make anything from iron. By 1825, he was on his own as a journeyman to two local smiths and in 1827, he married Demarius Lamb. His most popular and well-regarded product was a hay fork on which he

OHN DEERE

polished the tines with files and a grinding wheel. The shiny smooth tines slipped through the soil effortlessly and gathered mown hay quickly and efficiently.

In late 1836, Deere left Demarius and their children temporarily and headed out to Illinois. Leonard Andrus, a fellow Vermonter had founded the town of Grand Detour about 100 miles west of Chicago. Deere settled there. With no local blacksmith, it took him just two days to get his forge and a new business running. Plows in Vermont were cast iron and that was what Deere produced first in Grand Detour. But they were not ideal for the soil in the area. Central Vermont is sandy but Illinois' clay stuck to the plows like glue.

Andrus owned one of the local saw mills and he relied on Deere to sharpen its blades. One day when Deere was working at the mill, he spied a broken steel saw blade that had been heavily polished by the passing timbers. Recalling the way his hay fork tines moved through soil and mown hay, he reasoned that the polished steel might have the same effect through soil. In early 1838, he completed his first polished share plow and sold it to a local farmer named Lewis Crandall. Crandall told his neighbors about the ease of working with Deere's slick plow and two of them soon placed orders. By 1841, he was manufacturing 75 a year, and a hundred came out of his growing facility in 1842.

In 1843, he teamed up with Andrus, the sawmill owner, in a three-year long partnership. Together they enlarged Deere's production facility and added steam power to run grinders that polished the molded steel. In 1843, they sold 400 plows. But information that the new railroad was going to bypass Grand Detour forced Deere to relocate. He was getting his steel from England, taking months to cross the Atlantic, steam up the Mississippi and go by wagon 40 miles inland to Grand Detour. By 1846, his steel came from Pittsburgh and he was shipping his completed plows around the Midwest. He and Andrus dissolved their partnership and in 1848, Deere moved 40 miles west to Moline. He formed Deere & Tate with Robert Tate, the steam engineer who had installed the new engine in Deere and Andrus's shops.

Deere soon hired John Gould to manage the accounts. He took over sales and the shipping responsibilities himself, and he left Tate to supervise manufacture. The new plant, a 24-by-60 foot building, turned out its first ten plows on September 26. In the first five months of 1849 they made, sold, and shipped 1,200 plows. Moline not only had its railroad but the city sat on the banks of the Mississippi River.

By 1851, Deere & Tate manufactured 75 plows a week in a variety of sizes. The company also sold cultivators, grain drills and other implements that they marketed for outside manufacturers. But in 1853, Deere, Tate, and Gould went their separate ways. The former blacksmith-now successful businessman renamed his company John Deere. Then in 1858, a decade after settling in Moline, and 20 years after producing his first steel plow, Deere sold his business to his son Charles and his son-in-law, Charles Webber. Within another few years, John was back in, earning one patent after another in 1864 and 1865. Some of the company's tools, its Hawkeye riding cultivator and the Gilpin sulky plow began winning local and national awards for innovation and quality. Deere's daughter Emma had married Stephen Velie in 1860 and by 1868, when they incorporated as Deere & Company,

Velie became corporate secretary and joined John and Charles Deere, Webber, and George Vinton as founding shareholders. In 1869, the new corporation sold 41,133 plows, cultivators, and harrows, earning $646,543 (about $13.5 million today).

Over the next decade, Deere & Company introduced, revised, improved, and updated plows, gang plows (those with 2 or more plow bottoms), riding cultivators, and harrows. Within another few years, they added planters to the product line up using a "rotary drop" system that placed seeds in the soil in precisely measured increments. This allowed check-row cultivation by running the cultivators back and forth as well as up and down the fields.

John Deere died on May 17, 1886, leaving behind a large manufacturing facility that had grown to nine acres under one roof with electric lights throughout. The company manufactured 180 types of plows and it also marketed wagons for hauling produce and buggies for carrying farmers and their families. By 1895, the company had caught onto the growing bicycle craze. It sold the Leader, the Roadster and the Moline Special models. Deere & Company even hosted a 20-mile bicycle race in August 1895.

Supplying farmers with the equipment they needed had become big business by 1900. The country's population had swelled. Large cities attracted ambitious young workers. The demand to feed and dress a nation of urban workers who no longer grew their own crops became pressing. Farmers wanted more work out of their horses and tools. As Deere's board of directors watched Chicago's International Harvester Corporation move out into other areas of farm equipment, the Moline company cautiously followed behind. It merged with, founded, or acquired companies that made products that Deere's board felt matched their quality. Deere and Mansur offered some of the best corn planters anywhere. Dain Manufacturing produced fine hay tools, and Moline Wagon Co. provided farmers with superior carrying capacity. Kemp & Burpee offered efficient manure spreaders, Van Brunt Manufacturing lead the world with its grain drill planters, and Marseilles Manufacturing Company was the pioneer of automatic corn shellers.

In the first decade of the new 20th Century, the United States government took on International Harvester. Washington accusing IHC of saturating major markets with duplicate dealers to starve out competitors. The government invoked the Sherman Anti-Trust act, accusing IHC of monopolistic behavior. Industry observers feared the government would demand that the Chicago industrial giant must fracture back into individual companies. Deere & Company and others watched and waited for a final judgment. When it came, it was not as brutal as most had feared. The ruling did force IHC to eliminate dealer duplication. Yet it was clear to all spectators that in the government's eyes, big industrial production was not bad.

In 1910, then, Deere's board embarked on a program to bring under its corporate umbrella the best of its outside suppliers. Some 22 manufacturing and selling companies joined Deere & Company to provide a full line of implements with a nationwide sales, distribution and service system. As the dust settled, Charles Deere and Charles Webber looked around at what they had formed, they saw only one piece lacking from making them a true full-line competitor against International Harvester and anyone else who might have superior ambitions: Deere did not yet have a tractor.

CHAPTER 1
1912–1915

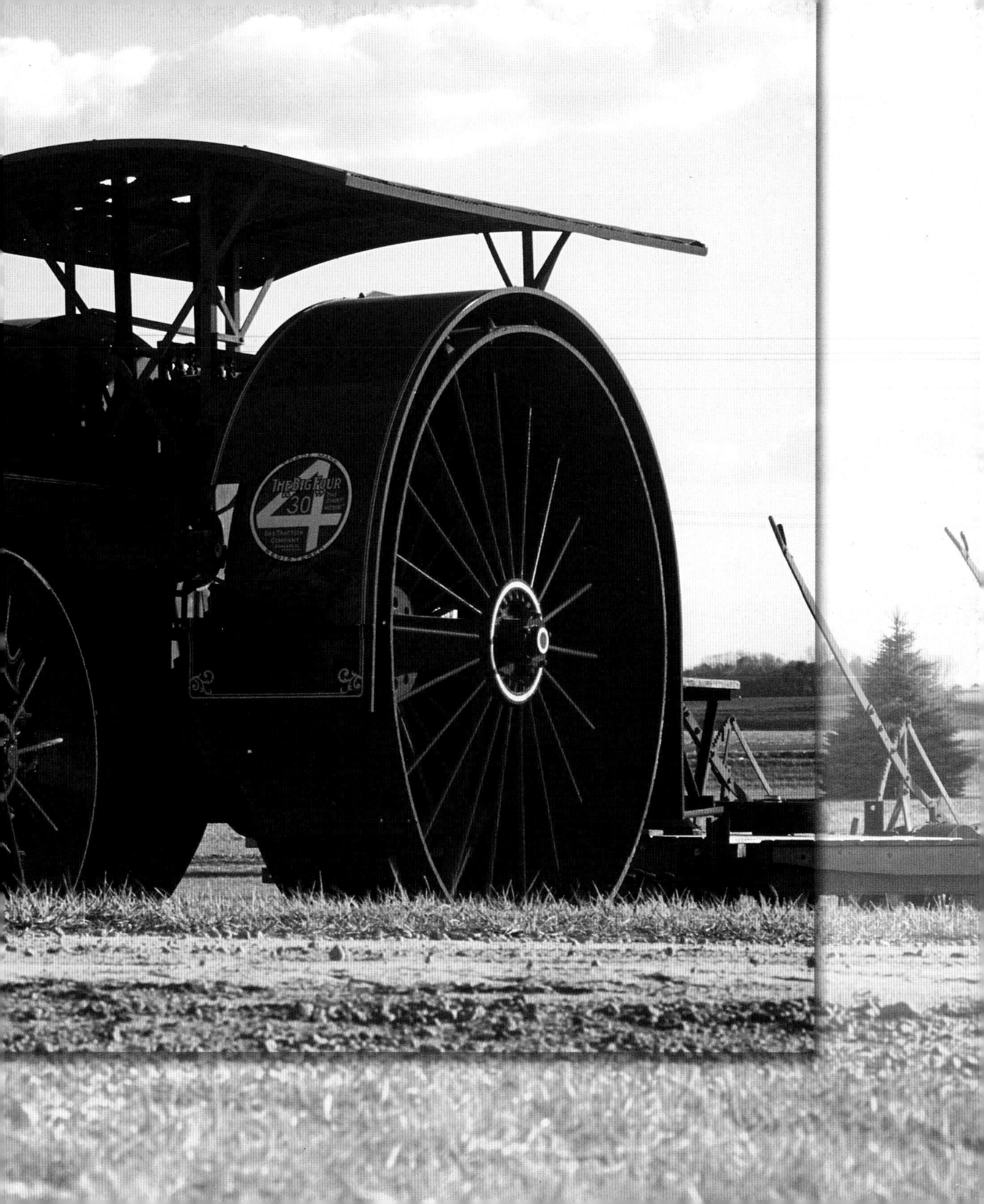
THE BIG FOUR
30
4

A WARY MANAGEMENT

FACES THE FUTURE

For Deere & Company, one of its historically most significant dates never has appeared on any calendar. It began inauspiciously. It was just another day in the mid-1950s.

At that time, Deere offered its new number-series tractors, the 40, 50 and 60 models and its diesel engine Model 70. The company had just introduced its newest powerhouse, the Model 80 Diesel. Engineers were already finalizing the Hundred Series replacements for these tractors. The current models presented numerous improvements over their predecessors, the already-legendary letter series tractors, the D, GP, A, B, G, H, M, L, LA, and R models. Deere's production, marketing, and sales departments each dutifully recorded the introduction dates for every new tractor model and series.

This particular event, even though it held much greater importance, escaped notation.

Another significant date had already passed. On that particular day, Bill Hewitt, Deere's first-ever executive vice-president, and, at age 40, its youngest senior executive yet, received a phone call. It was his ailing father-in-law, Colonel Charles Deere Wiman. The older man was offering Hewitt the most important job at Deere & Company.

Hewitt remembered that special day in May 1955. He knew the date, the hour, the minute, and his response.

"Well sir," he recalled telling Wiman politely, "I'm very grateful and very flattered. It's quite an honor. What I'd like to do is to talk to Tish about it." Tish was Hewitt's wife. She was born Patricia Wiman. Although she had married Hewitt, she always would be the Colonel's daughter.

PREVIOUS: 1912 GAS TRACTION COMPANY "BIG FOUR 30"
The Transit Thresher Company of Minneapolis, MN, later renamed the Gas Traction Company, introduced this four-cylinder model in 1904. Deere & Company admired the powerful machine's reliability and endorsed it for farmers in the upper Midwest who had to break open virgin prairies.

RIGHT: *Deere's own advertising boasted the tractor's potential. Here at Little Log House Pioneer Village in Hastings, MN, owner Steve Bauer sometimes pulls a Deere 14-plow gang behind the Big Four during show weekends.*

JOHN DEERE

RIGHT: *Most tractor designers at the time still produced two-cylinder models with 15 or 20 horsepower. D. M. Hartsough was among the earliest to design a four cylinder tractor, this particular model with 4x5 inch bore and stroke.*

"I already have," the Colonel replied, almost interrupting Hewitt. He expected an equally rapid response from the younger man. Without further hesitation, William Alexander Hewitt accepted the offer and became Deere & Company's fifth chairman. Deere's board agreed and on May 26, it unanimously elected him its president.

But that was not this day.

This particular incident, which almost passed by unnoticed, happened some months after all this had transpired. Hewitt could recall only that it began with a piece of routine inter-office mail that arrived on his desk.

"It was a press release, from one of our competitors," he recalls.

Hewitt was a man of great warmth and near-regal bearing. After retiring from Deere, he served as a U.S. ambassador to Jamaica. However, he was not at all intimidating to those he worked with, or to those whom he encountered later in life. He died in May 1998 at age 84, but several years earlier he had recounted the rest of the story of this unique day.

"It announced some new product or other, nothing really of any threatening significance. But at the bottom of the sheet of paper was printed a kind of corporate slogan, a logo almost.

"'Not content to be runner-up.' That's what it said. I think it was even in red ink."

That was the day.

"It started me thinking. Until that time, we *had* been content, even willing, to be runner-up. Always a steady, reliable, consistent number two behind International Harvester.

OPPOSITE: *Emerson-Brantingham Implement Co, in Rockford, IL, also liked D. M. Hartsough's well-designed Big Four 30 tractor. In 1912, Hartsough and company owner Patrick Lyons sold out to E-B, which continued to produce the 21,000-pound machine through 1916.*

A plow guide wheel projects about 15 feet ahead of the front wheels. This massive tractor, selling for $2,800 in 1916 (about $60,000 today), ran on 99-inch tall, 30-inch wide rear wheels.

40

ABOVE: *Steering took great arm strength. These big machines weighed 25,550 pounds and in 1917, they sold for $4,500, almost $100,000 today.*

LEFT: 1916 TWIN CITIES 40
Minneapolis' Joy-Willson Co. developed this machine for Minneapolis Steel & Machinery Co. (MSMC) in 1910. After assembling five prototypes using this 7-inch bore, 10-inch stroke four-cylinder engine, MSMC ordered 200 to begin selling in 1912.

Minneapolis kept this final version of the 40-65 tractor in production from 1913 through 1924, long after technology had left it behind. By then, farmers could buy four tractors for the money.

"And it made me wonder about being number one. What would it take? How long would it require? What kind of products did we need to introduce? What did we need to change? Was it anything more than just our own thinking, our own perception of Deere & Company?"

Early Efforts

When the board of directors agreed in early 1912 to produce a tractor, they succumbed to strong pressure from inside and out. The need for a tractor in Deere's lineup had been apparent to their competitors for years. North America's first gas tractor competition had taken place four years earlier in 1908 in Winnipeg, Manitoba, Canada. The shows continued through 1912 and each year these events offered demonstrations of plowing, hauling, tractor maneuverability and engine power output. But the rules were inconsistent from one year to the next. True, these trials gave farmers and observers a chance to see machines succeed or fail in practical tests. Yet there was no objective way to evaluate one tractor as better than another.

Still, the tests and their results generated stories in leading farm journals of the day. It was the first generation of the information age. Successful farmers were progressive, and read a variety of publications, most of which advocated "power farming." The reports from Winnipeg spurred interest among farmers who weren't there to see for themselves.

By 1912 International Harvester and J. I. Case competed against more than 50 other firms that manufactured self-propelled farm tractors. Farmers across the United States owned and operated an estimated 10,000 gas tractors (and still ran more than 72,000 steam engines). Deere's own branch managers had appealed to the board long before then to recognize their customers' growing interests. While the U.S. Census reported that there still were 20.5 million horses and mules on American farms, regional managers saw sales of implements following buyers out of their showroom doors, down the road, and into their competitors' retail outlets where the farmers found tools they could hook up to tractors they could buy.

In Atlanta, St. Louis, and elsewhere, Deere's branch managers incorporated into their own sales catalogs a large 30-horsepower machine manufactured in Minneapolis, the Gas Traction Company's Big Four 30. This tractor was typical of the more powerful gasoline engine machines of the time. It weighed nearly 10 tons and operated on 8-foot diameter spoked-steel rear wheels. One Big Four had pulled a seven-bottom 14-inch Deere gang

plow to win a gold medal at Winnipeg during the 1910 trials. The branch managers sought to capitalize on the Big Four's performance. They vigorously promoted its front plowing-guide wheel mounted 20 feet ahead of the tractor. Its linkage to the front axle kept the tractor aligned in the furrow for accurate plowing. Deere's advertising and sales brochures began referring to the machine as "our tractor." This presumed arrogance, and the actual profits that Deere reaped on each Big Four sale, soured Gas Traction Company's management. When Deere approached them, they rebuffed Deere's purchase offer and turned instead to Emerson-Brantingham. Deere quickly developed a less possessive and somewhat less lucrative agreement with Minneapolis Steel & Machinery Company, and soon Deere promoted Minneapolis' new Twin Cities models, also offered with a plow guide option.

Twin Cities' big engine developed 40 horsepower at the drawbar but 65 on its belt pulley. This made it a potent machine both for plowing through unbroken soil and threshing grain.

RIGHT: 1954 MODEL 70 HIGH CROP

Deere originally conceived its high clearance models to work in cotton and cane fields. Iowa corn farmers used the tractor for cultivating young corn plants.

INSET: 1954 MODEL 40 HIGH CROP

Deere's Dubuque plant produced only 284 high crop model 40s. This was the first.

Within two years Twin City tractors appeared regularly in Deere's catalogs. These catalogs, meant for export to South America, showed a Model 40 tractor demonstrating a 10-bottom gangplow. Reluctantly, the board accepted what their dealers saw as inevitable. After nearly a decade of looking warily at the future of the self-propelled traction engine, be it steam or gasoline powered, board members took tenuous steps forward. On the first of July 1912, they assigned staff engineer C. H. Melvin to produce a tractor.

Theophilus Brown, Deere's superintendent for the previous year at its Marseilles spreader works in East Moline, watched the development and later reported on Melvin's three-wheel tractor. Brown, born in April 1879, and named after his grandfather, earned a degree in mechanical engineering in 1901 from Worcester Polytechnic Institute in Massachusetts. He had joined Deere in late 1911 when he was 32. Within a year Deere's board named him plant superintendent. There Brown came to supervise 725 laborers producing more than 20,000 manure spreaders annually. By 1916, the board promoted him again to become head of the Plow Works experimental department, working closely with Deere chief engineer Max Sklovsky. Sometime after Brown retired at age 73 in 1952, he summarized all of Deere's earliest tractor development attempts in an internally published confidential report that appeared in 1953:

1956 MODEL 60 ORCHARD

By the mid-1950s, Deere's work with Henry Dreyfuss Associates yielded collaborations that worked well in all specialties and looked smart enough to appeal to farmers of either gender. The full sheet metal protected trees from damage and operators from injury.

"March 5, 1912, Deere & Company Executive Committee resolved that 'A movement to produce a tractor plow should be started at once, having in view constantly, that the success of the same would be enhanced if not assured, were it possible to divorce the tractor from the plow and to thus make it available for general purposes.'"

Brown continued, "On July 1, 1912, Melvin was transferred from the Experimental Department at John Deere Plow Works to the General Company and given the assignment of designing and building an experimental tractor plow. A room in the plow works was provided."

C. H. Melvin's three-wheeler went through field tests from late 1912 through early 1914. Melvin apparently had based his concept and design on that of an existing competitor, Hackney Manufacturing Company of St. Paul, Minnesota. The resemblance was too great to be accidental. Hackney's Auto-Plow had power enough to pull three plows, which Hackney placed below the operator between the axles. In its tricycle configuration, farmers

JOHN DEERE
70

1955 Model 50

The Dubuque factory fitted this wide-front model with rear axle extensions. Deere offered power steering as an option.

could run the Auto-Plow in either direction. With its two drive wheels leading, it plowed. With its single steering wheel leading, it could tow wagons from its drawbar. The operator shifted from one seat to the opposite facing one, straddling the controls and steering wheel.

Melvin's tricycle was quite similar. However he moved the operator's position farther from the engine. The farmer sat at the extreme rear end while plowing or nearer to the engine in drawbar applications.

It appeared that Melvin never received that part of the board's message that spoke of removable plows. Or else he ignored it. On his experimental machine, such versatility was not possible. However, one benefit accrued from this error as Melvin perfected a power lift mechanism for his plows that appeared again and again in later experiments. Deere eventually incorporated it into production machines.

Theo Brown recorded that the company spent nearly $6,800 in developing and testing Melvin's three-wheeler. (That would be nearly $125,000 in 2003.) Yet Melvin built only one of them and by 1953 when Brown summarized all the early efforts, no test records remained in existence in Deere's archives. Perhaps this was because it was a failure.

LEFT: *It's one of the most recognized faces in the agriculture industry. These tractors introduced Deere's independent power take-off (PTO) allowing equipment to operate properly even while the tractor operator stopped or changed gears.*

BELOW: *That's what farmers like to see: a clear gasoline fuel bowl. Farmers also could order the Model 50 to run on liquefied petroleum gas (LPG) or All-Fuel.*

During this period, Joseph Dain Sr. joined Deere & Company as a board member when the company acquired Dain Manufacturing Company in Ottumwa, Iowa, in 1910. Dain had been something of a tinkerer who began producing agricultural implements from the atypical background of a successful furniture manufacturer. (Many more implement makers had blacksmithing in their background.) He had developed hay harvesting and handling tools. International Harvester Corporation vigorously pursued Dain Manufacturing in late 1903 despite its alliance with Deere. Initially IHC sought licensing agreements, but the closer it looked at Dain's products and their quality, the more IHC wanted outright ownership. With the machinery that Joe Dain invented for Deere in later years, it's fair to wonder how farm tractor history might have changed had IHC succeeded.

Deere's Heirs Take Over the Business

Throughout the first years of the 20th Century, John Deere's son, Charles, ran the company. Charles was working fast to secure his own long-term marketing agreements and in some cases, he acquired his former outside suppliers in order to thwart International Harvester's ambitions. After Charles Deere died in late October 1907, William Butterworth, his successor, further consolidated the company's far-flung agreements. Dain joined Deere on the last day of October 1910. He received his full asking price and a corporate vice-presidency.

1954 Model 40 C

Deere's 40 series crawler replaced the M and Dubuque introduced them with three track rollers or idler wheels along the bottom of the track for support. This model also has Deere's hydraulic bulldozer blade.

Dain's position on the board and his fascination with machines drove his awareness of the farmer's and the company's interest in tractors. As Theo Brown compiled his 1953 summary, he quoted Dain's conclusions on Melvin's attempt. "Joe Dain recalls it was a failure. Field performance—and trouble keeping it from breaking down— were problems."

"In 1914," Brown summarized, "development was stopped on the Melvin. The transition from heavy tractors moving slowly and pulling twelve or sixteen plows was giving way to smaller tractors which could pull three. Melvin had attempted to fit three plows underneath his tractor, like the Hackney Motor Plow [sic] which Leslie Hackney had applied for patent in 1910. Neither was a great success."

The company still was nervous about tractors, however, the board realized the machine was a necessary evil. It turned next to Joe Dain. Minutes of a meeting on May 27, 1914, tell all:

"Mr. Dain was asked to report to the Executive Committee whether or not a tractor could be built to sell at about $700 and in the meantime to suspend work of development until his report is made." (The $700 price is about $12,850 in 2003.)

Days later, more board minutes followed:

"June 9, 1914: Mr. Dain said he was working on a plan which he would submit as soon as completed. It was Mr. Webber's idea that we should decide very soon whether or not a light tractor could be built to sell to the farmer for about $700. Mr. Dain further stated that the tractor he is planning would operate a three-bottom plow."

While the concept of a crawler is simple, the execution is complex. The hefty yellow linkages here raise and lower the optional bulldozer blade.

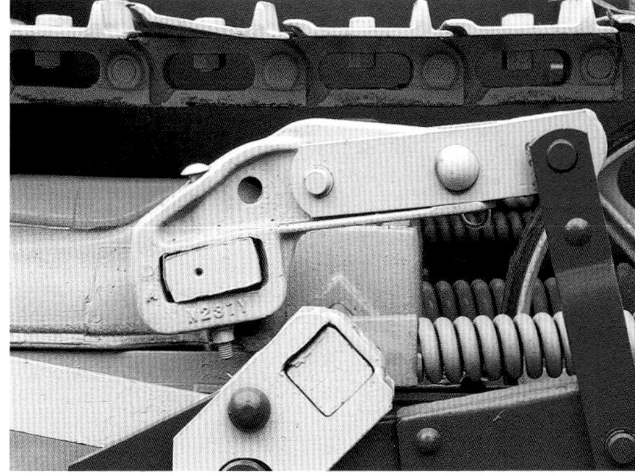

Board member Charles C. Webber was another Deere & Company vice-president. He was the former owner of Deere & Webber, the company's Minneapolis sales branch. He also was a grandson of John Deere.

A fortnight later came a decision:

"June 24, 1914: Resolved: That the preliminary work of designing an efficient small plow tractor be continued under the auspices of Mr. Dain and the Experimental Department."

Just after Labor Day, Dain updated his progress. "September 8, 1914: Mr. Dain reported that [more than] $6,000 had been expended in connection with work done by Mr. Melvin and further stated he thought he could build a light tractor for experimental purposes for about $3,000.00 [$55,000 today]. Approved."

Dain worked through the winter adapting ideas from other makers including some from his predecessor, Melvin. Dain's new prototype was a tricycle fitted with a four-cylinder Waukesha engine. Unlike Melvin's tractor, where two wheels took the power, Joe Dain used driveshafts and chains and powered all three. His two front wheels straddled the engine and also steered the tractor while the wide, single, center-mounted rear wheel supported implement weight and transferred engine traction to the ground.

Outside politics slowed testing and development on every new project through the fall of 1914. Germany's declaration of war on Russia, and England's subsequent declaration

1955 Model 70 with 1958 Model 22
Single row cotton harvester
An experienced, ambitious individual picking cotton could harvest half-an-acre in a long day. Deere's mechanical high-drum harvester would do more than 10 acres in the same day.

against Germany and Austria in August, brought widespread ramifications to U.S. industry. By late fall, the threat of war slowed orders, and Deere cut back to four-day work weeks.

Six months later, Dain again advised the board of his progress. Now caution and skepticism confronted him.

"February 13, 1915: Mr. Dain has developed a small experimental tractor and it is questionable whether we should enter into the manufacture of this machine."

Butterworth and others did not hesitate to express their concerns. Deere & Company was not a tractor-maker, they argued, and becoming one would require a huge investment. Yet others spoke louder. Branch managers reported ever-increasing customer inquiries and interest.

"Now, Therefore, Be It Resolved," the minutes continued, "That Mr. Dain continue his work with the tractor now built until he considers it perfected, and that it be ascertained at that time the amount we have invested, for the purpose of fixing a basis upon which we would sell the same to a separate company for its development and sale. Also, that Mr. Dain advise the basis upon which his transmission can be used in said tractor." (Elsewhere within Deere, Dain had supervised development of other products for the company, including a friction-drive transmission.)

C. H. Melvin designed this machine as a reversible tractor. It pulled plows when its engine led the way, and towed wagons when its engine was at the rear. The design bore some resemblance to the Hackney brothers' Auto Plow, introduced in 1911. Deere tested Melvin's tractor from late 1912 through early 1914 before dropping the idea. Deere & Company Archives

While Dain continued to work on his prototype tractor in Deere's experimental department, away from the mahogany executive offices, William Butterworth reexamined his concerns. His own inclinations were to follow faithfully the paths first defined by his predecessor, Charles Deere: Proceed slowly, consolidate the company's holdings, and convert assets to cash whenever possible.

When Dain's tractor came up at an executive committee meeting three weeks later, Butterworth's cautions were apparent. But once again he did not prevail. Again, Brown quoted the minutes:

"March 9, 1915: it was the sentiment of the Board:

"That Mr. Dain should continue his work in connection with the tractor, give it a thorough trial in the field and continue its development;

"That the present was not the time for Deere & Company to decide whether it should go into the tractor business or not;

"That it might seem wise later and it might not;

"That the wise thing for the Company to do was to watch the development of this business, and also to watch and develop the tractor, in order that the Company might be ready for any emergency."

The committee minutes concluded with one further piece of information. Up to that date, Joe Dain had spent just about $2,890 on his present experimental tractor. With his spending cap at $3,000, Dain was coming right in on target.

CHAPTER 2

1915–1916

N DEERE

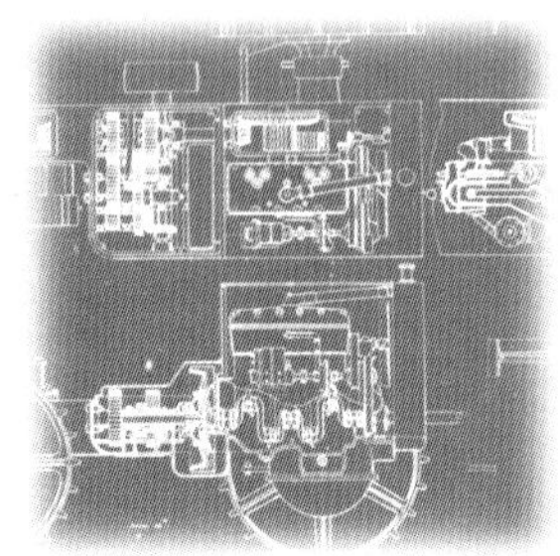

HALTING MISSTEPS LEAD TO INNOVATION

During the next six weeks, William Butterworth walked a tightrope. He had emphatically assured Deere's bankers that his company was not in the business of making tractors, nor was it interested in that business. Now he wondered how the bankers and other investors would react when they learned he had authorized further investment in tractor "experiments."

Butterworth felt pressure. His predecessor had populated the board with men who had been presidents of their own firms. They were independent contractors and suppliers outside of Deere & Company, men accustomed to making the hard decisions that affected their own businesses directly. They were reliable enough to maintain business relationships that, in some cases, went back to John Deere himself. These were businesses that were so efficient and successful that Charles Deere, and now Butterworth, had acquired them to keep from losing them to fierce competitors. The men who ran those companies were accustomed to reacting quickly to market pressures. Their stake in their companies had been substantial; they had achieved their successes within their own lifetimes. Now these men sat on Butterworth's board where decisions came slowly and where the chairman expected them to be patient.

Deere's board had appointed Butterworth as the second caretaker of a company grown vast beyond its namesake's imagination. William saw himself as conservator rather than innovator. Men with less at stake in this company than he held were now suggesting moves that were more rash than what he wanted. Yet Butterworth knew these men, many as friends, some even as Deere family relatives. Did these men have a better feel for the future of the agricultural implement business?

PREVIOUS: 1910s JOHN DEERE WAGON
Deere & Company began selling wagons that local manufacturers James First and Maurice Rosenfield produced at their business, The Moline Wagon Company. By 1910, they were part of the huge Deere family.

RIGHT: *John Deere Wagon Works marketed their wagons to freight haulers and other companies throughout the Midwest. It was one of Deere's first efforts at making and selling an industrial product.*

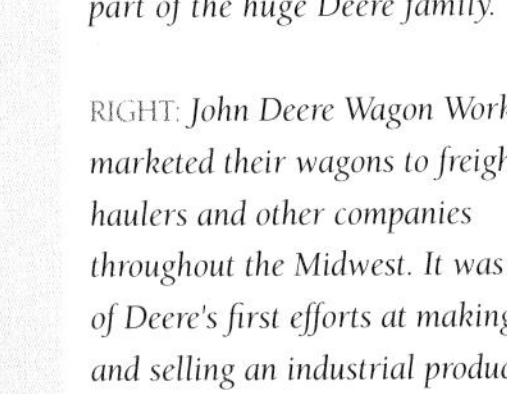

Historians and photo archivists argue over what this machine was. It strongly resembles Joe Dain's second prototype all-wheel drive model, using similar wheel hubs, spoke configuration, and front end. Yet the offset steering position is more akin to some of Max Sklovsky's attempts. Whoever designed it, it appears to have adequate power for pulling its double harvester load. Deere & Company Archives

He couldn't know. But daring moves, and taking risks, was something outside William Butterworth's repertory of acceptable actions.

Butterworth had to consider Charles Webber, of Deere & Webber. Webber had been Deere's Minneapolis branch manager. He had pressed Deere & Company to sell bicycles. Wayne G. Broehl, Jr. author of *John Deere's Company*, quoted a memo from Webber to the board:

"If there is anything in this bicycle business, any money to be made, we want to take hold of it."

There was money to be made. In 1895 the company listed $150,000 sales from bicycles alone (something close to $3.2 million in 2003 dollars). Promoters staged races. Manufacturers throughout America sold thousands of bicycles including, by 1896, John Deere's own private-label bike. Yet bicycles faded from public interest and from the sales summaries in 1897.

To Butterworth, questions concerning tractors must have triggered his worst imaginings. Bicycles were one thing; at first Deere only had marketed bikes manufactured by others. At its greatest commitment to bicycles, Deere simply relabeled outside products. But tractors were different; they required expensive machine tooling and possibly even building additional factory space.

Historians might speculate over Butterworth's concern: Was Dain operating his tractor experiment within Deere as an independent spirit? Or worse, was he an independent businessman who felt he was bankrolled now by the company's backers?

This was a new product line to Deere. It was one that had undone other formerly strong competitors, Rumely and Hart-Paar, to name just two. The conditions affecting agriculture were mercurial; fortunes had been lost in a single bad season. Bad weather followed by bad weather could doom a manufacturer who had sold products on credit.

Yet Webber and Dain both watched International Harvester and J. I. Case. They felt sure they could sense what might happen to Deere & Company if Butterworth did not accede and accept.

On May 9, Charles Webber reported to the executive committee that Joe Dain planned to revise his next tractor to make some improvements. Webber recommended keeping the tractor at work to determine its weaknesses. He suggested sending the new version to a different test site, to his branch at Minneapolis , where it could plow 300 or 400 acres and really get a thorough workout. Whereupon Ralph B. Lourie, manager of the John Deere Plow Company at Moline, suggested that it might be better still if there were at least five tractors out testing in a variety of conditions.

Butterworth prepared to speak again. But Lourie already had envisioned Butterworth's worries, and he had an idea. Would it be possible to start a new business outside Deere & Company to sell the tractors? Would that relieve Deere of any responsibilities? The board mused. What benefits would that arrangement offer? Was it even feasible?

Lourie explained that branch managers told him they were losing sales of plows because of tractors. Deere made plows with wheels, suitable for use only behind horse or mule teams. Neither farmers nor Deere engineers were able to adapt these to some of the machines available at the time, including their very own Melvin, where the plows mounted beneath the tractor. Lourie warned the board that it was vulnerable to competitors who sold tractors as well as plows. The twin spectres of J. I. Case and International Harvester loomed large.

Webber told Butterworth it was important that the bankers understood what this new tractor was. Theo Brown (who, in the early days answered directly to Ralph Lourie and knew this history intimately) quoted the minutes paraphrasing Webber's arguments.

"The bankers had very good reasons to be scared about gas tractors but they had in mind the Rumely, the Emerson and the Hart-Paar people. They have made a heavy, clumsy machine and have made a failure, and have not made any money. They [the bankers] think it is something we are going to sell on two or three years time [payments], while we are talking about something that is entirely different.

"The question to be decided in the end," Webber concluded, "was whether this machine or any little engine is going to be an economical thing for the farmer to buy. That we do not know as yet."

The board responded, dragging Butterworth forward. "Resolved: That without attempting to at this time define our final policy toward the tractor business further

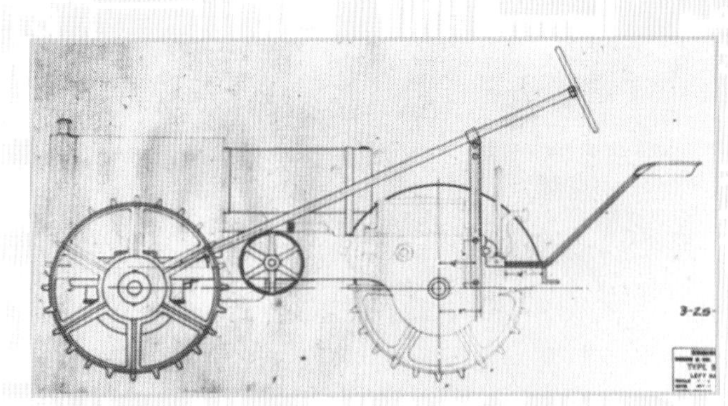

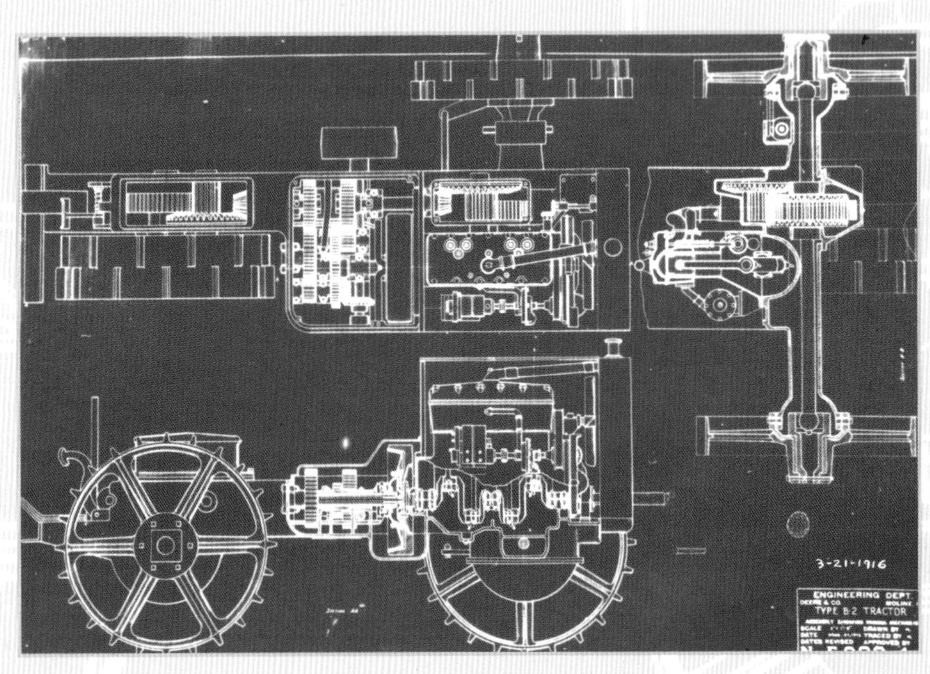
3-21-1916
ENGINEERING DEPT.
DEERE & CO.
MOLINE
TYPE B-2 TRACTOR
SCALE
DRAWN BY
DATE
TRACED BY
DATES REVISED
APPROVED BY

than the resolution passed at the Directors' meeting held February 13, 1915, but with a view of trying out more thoroughly the Dain tractor, Mr. Mixter be requested to cooperate with Mr. Dain in order to hasten the try-out of the present machine and to determine upon the improvements that should be made in it, with the authority to build from three to six of the revised experimental tractors to be thoroughly tried out this Summer and Fall."

Board member George W. Mixter was vice-president of manufacturing. He also was a great grandson of John Deere. He steadily had supported Butterworth throughout the year, but on this matter he counseled his older relative to reconsider. In a letter to Butterworth that historian Wayne Broehl unearthed, Mixter stated his case.

"The country is now flooded with attempts at practical small tractors," Mixter wrote, "and the extremely wide desire of the farmers to buy such a small tractor cannot be entirely overlooked. . . . If it be possible to build a small tractor that will really stand up for five or more years' work on the farm, I believe they will be a permanent requirement of the American farmer and," Mixter delivered his point directly, "especially in view of the plow trade they carry with them, this possibility cannot be overlooked by Deere & Company."

On July 19, according to his diary, Theo Brown got a visit from George Mixter. Brown kept detailed daily entries starting with his arrival at Deere & Company. Deere required it of every engineer and designer. For most of these men, their dairies represented daily records of the work they did, the ideas they had, and the inventions they conceived. The brainstorms that these inventors had after hours, or in their dreams, scrawled down or carefully drawn, they then had notarized the next morning. This certified the origin of concepts and products that often ended up patented, copyrighted, or otherwise protected from infringement or theft. These journals and documents sometimes ended up as evidence in court, deciding the birth and parentage of tools, machines, implements, and tractors. Before Brown died, he donated his diaries to his alma mater, Worchester Polytechnic Institute in Massachusetts. A copy remains with Deere & Company in the Company archives.

"Spent 2 1/2 hours in morning talking tractors with Geo Mixter," Brown wrote that night. Mixter reported that he had "both Dain and Sklovsky working on tractors but the results do not seem to be forthcoming." The next day Brown worked out his own idea for a transmission for a small tractor. Eleven days later, on July 31, Mixter proposed to Brown that Deere build its first small tractor at Marseilles, the plant Brown managed. Two months later, Mixter came to propose that Brown move over to Deere & Company to become manager of the experimental department at Ralph Lourie's Plow Works, starting January 1, 1916, at $6,500 per year (about $107,000 in 2003).

Throughout the summer and fall, Mixter worked with Dain testing and developing three all-wheel-drive prototypes. Brown began traveling to watch one version or another. He saw them in early and mid-November noting on November 8 that, "The tractor is pretty well along." On November 15, engineering had removed the engine to resolve steering problems. On December 19, Brown wrote that the "tractor did a good job of plowing today." Just before Christmas, Dain himself delivered his most recent results to the board.

OPPOSITE TOP: *By 1915, Deere engineer Max Sklovsky had designed his own version of an all-wheel drive tractor, the Model A-2. However, to save production costs, Sklovsky designed the tractor without a differential. This made steering a challenge. This drawing shows Sklovsky's second version, B-2, which operated better but still it used a costly engine produced outside Deere, by Northway. Its costs doomed this machine to history books.* Deere & Company Archives

OPPOSITE BOTTOM: *Engineering drawings of Max Sklovsky's B-2 prototype show why even this "improved" version had difficulty turning. While universal joints in the wheel hubs allowed the front wheels to pivot, the solid front axle (upper right) allowed no accommodation for differing speeds between the inside and outside wheel.* Deere & Company Archives

His first tractor weighed nearly 3,800 pounds and it used his innovative friction-drive transmission. This allowed shifting gears from low to high speed while moving. This transmission incorporated a double clutch with faces on both sides. Each clutch had an inner and an outer shaft. This kept both sets of gears in mesh constantly. Engaging one clutch disengaged the other. In a shop test on a kind of chassis dynamometer, Dain recorded a steady 5,000-pound drawbar pull in low gear. In the spring, this proved to be more than 3,000 pounds in actual field tests.

On Dain's tractors, chains drove the axles from the final drive. The development engineers earlier had reported the first chains were not strong enough and they broke under load. They replaced them with a heavier gauge chain and this cured the problem. Two front ratchets had broken and engineers replaced these with parts made from heavier metal. The rear-wheel-drive gears showed considerable wear. Yet this convinced Dain all the more of the wisdom of his all-wheel drive; splitting the traction had saved the rear end from likely destruction.

The second tractor weighed nearly 4,000 pounds and, at Charles Webber's direction, engineering sent it to Winnebago, in south-central Minnesota, for testing. It was there that Deere field testing staff developed the first economic figures.

"It plowed eighty acres," Dain revealed to the board, "at a cost of fifty-nine cents per acre, counting the man's time at thirty cents an hour. The soil here was of heavy black gumbo and was in poor condition owing to the almost continual rain—several days [that] we plowed; the neighboring farmers thought it too wet to plow with their horses. We pulled three fourteen inch bottoms six inches deep at two-and-a-half miles per hour." This was the same type of vexing soil that had made John Deere's reputation as a plow-maker almost 80 years earlier.

Engineering completed the third prototype just before the board meeting. They modified the transmission, replacing the worm-and-gear and internal gear drive with a chain drive to the rear wheel. Dain accompanied the new machine to Deere's Texas test farm for evaluation. He followed up his observations with a telegram to George Mixter, reproduced in Theo Brown's book:

> San Antonio, Tex. March 13, 1916
> Deere & Company
> Moline, Ill.
> Have followed tractor closely for two weeks.
> Conditions extremely hard and rough. Absolutely no
> weakness in construction. Gears, chains, universals,
> in fact all parts in good condition. Tractor has
> traveled near five hundred miles under extreme load.
> Change speed gear a wonder. I recommend to the Board
> that we build ten machines at once.
> Joseph Dain

While Mixter supported the tractor efforts, Theo Brown's diaries suggest that Mixter hedged his bets on just which tractor he might support. Brown's transfer to Moline slipped back to March 1 and Mixter came to call on him at Marseilles on January 5. When Brown showed him a sketch of a front wheel for a tractor, Mixter took Brown back to Moline and showed him drawings for a better one. Five weeks later, on February 10, Mixter threw Brown's future in doubt.

"May not go to the plow shop," Brown wrote in his diary that night. "George Mixter wants me to get behind the tractor and get it started." A week later, though, Mixter was back. "Going to be quite a proposition for George Mixter to get Dain and Sklovsky together on a tractor design. Max is extremely obstinate."

Still, it is not difficult to imagine the reaction inside the board room on that March day upon hearing Dain's own glowing reports of his tests. Mixter read the telegram and then added his own observations. He told his listeners that Dain had replaced his previous friction-type transmission. This new gear-type version still had a few bugs but Mixter and Dain believed they could work these out quickly in order to get the tractor to manufacture. Mixter believed Deere & Company could assemble the tractor in already-existing factory space while spending not more than $50,000 on patterns, jigs, new tools, and machinery ($827,000 in 2003).

If William Butterworth ever felt the carpet slipping from beneath his feet, it may have been at that moment. The minutes: "WHEREAS, Mr. Joseph Dain has developed several small tractors which have been experimentally tried out, the latest machine proving successful in Texas for a sufficient time to demonstrate its practicability from a general standpoint and

"WHEREAS, It is desirable that this machine should now be reconstructed to meet such minor questions as have developed in Texas, and to make it suitable for economical manufacturing and then turned over to a manufacturing organization;

"RESOLVED, That Mr. Dain be requested to reconstruct said tractor with such modifications as may be deemed wise by him and his associates, preparatory to economical manufacturing;

"FURTHER, That the Marseilles Plant [which became John Deere Spreader Works until 1994] be directed to take up this tractor work with the object of getting it on a manufacturing basis as a possible part of their regular line;

"FURTHER, That about ten machines be built by the Marseilles Company, at the earliest practical date;

"FURTHER, That both Mr. Dain and the Marseilles Company be directed to vigorously continue tractor development work."

On March 14, 1916, Deere & Company stepped resolutely into the farm tractor business, bringing Theo Brown along in its footsteps.

CHAPTER 3
1916–1918

IN THE BEGINNING

THERE WAS DAIN

By mid-June 1916, Theo Brown's experimental staff had begun work on the next five Dain development tractors as well as a "tractor cultivator," Brown noted in his diary on May 1. Engineering had begun assembling an additional Dain machine at Ralph Lourie's Moline Plow Works. Dain moved his gear-transmission prototype from San Antonio to Minot, North Dakota, where everyone seemed pleased with its performance.

A question of engines arose. Joe Dain had experienced difficulties in testing the various powerplants available on the market. These problems related to engine service and the inaccessibility of parts (meaning both the difficulty of their removal and the availability of spares). He also had doubts about their general reliability. Dain enlisted Walter McVicker's help.

McVicker had been a mechanical engineer with the Alma Manufacturing Company in Alma, Michigan, for four years. While he was there, McVicker also developed and introduced a novel new four-cycle gasoline engine, the McVicker Automatic. This used a separate chamber alongside the piston cylinder that took advantage of engine compression to push open the exhaust valve automatically. His engine did away with the exhaust valve pushrods.

In 1908, McVicker left Alma to open his own firm. A year later the McVicker Engineering Company of Minneapolis partnered with Mack Joy to develop and produce the Joy-McVicker tractor, which Alma Manufacturing then produced. It was, however, to McVicker's own engineering company that Joe Dain turned for help.

Based on specifications that Dain and Mixter provided him, McVicker quickly designed a new

PREVIOUS: 1918 DEERE ALL-WHEEL DRIVE
Board member Joe Dain designed and conceived this machine. Equipped with all-wheel-drive, it was the first tractor Deere marketed under its own name.

RIGHT: *Even a simple belt-pulley wheel was a complicated assembly. This 30-inch wheel offered an 8-inch face, common at the time, and drove a belt at the industry standard of 2,190 feet per minute.*

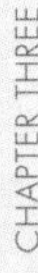

JOHN DEERE
MOLINE, ILL.
THE TRADEMARK OF QUALITY
MADE FAMOUS BY GOOD IMPLEMENTS

Walter Silver, who was Max Sklovsky's assistant, got the assignment to produce a two-row motor cultivator in June 1917. This early prototype, probably No. 1, required the operator to manage the cultivators with his feet. The steering wheel redirected two small tiller wheels that pivoted below his seat. Deere & Company Archives

engine specifically for Deere's tractor in mid-June 1916. Dain advised the executive committee that he expected to receive McVicker's first prototypes in the fall. Meanwhile Dain would fit Waukesha engines to the six new prototypes that would go out for testing in August.

Mixter sent a memo to the board on July 13 that fulfilled another requirement of its earlier resolution.

"Original cost figures," he wrote, "were $736 (for 1.25-inch steel) or $761 (2.25-inch steel). These figures are based on paying $200 for the motor. The writer...believes that the machine as today designed with the motor figured at $200 can be built for $600 (1.25-inch steel) as cost of manufacture." (The $600 is equal to $9,930 in 2003.)

"This means," Mixter added, "judged in light of other goods of our manufacture that the farmer should pay $1,200 for the machine [$19,860]. This is somewhat higher than had been considered admissible for a three-plow tractor. It is the writer's belief however, that an all-wheel drive will ultimately be the tractor the farmer will pay for."

Brown and a handful of Deere engineers and executives including Mixter, went to the Fremont, Nebraska, tractor demonstrations on August 9 and 10.

"There were thousands of automobiles there and the greatest crowd ever attending a demonstration," Brown wrote. "Henry Ford was there with his tractor. It was the first appearance." Ford and his tractor would enter Brown's life and Deere's company a short while later.

Meanwhile, Dain got three development models testing in Minnesota by mid-September. He left one in Minot, North Dakota, shipped another to Huron, South Dakota, and he had just sent the sixth to Fargo, North Dakota. Six weeks later, and just two weeks before Dain issued his next report to the board, Brown updated his diary with tractor information. On October 28 he was still working on the tractor cultivator. He had received a larger engine from New Way Motor Company in Lansing, Michigan. He spent much of the day working on designs for a new two-cylinder engine with McVicker.

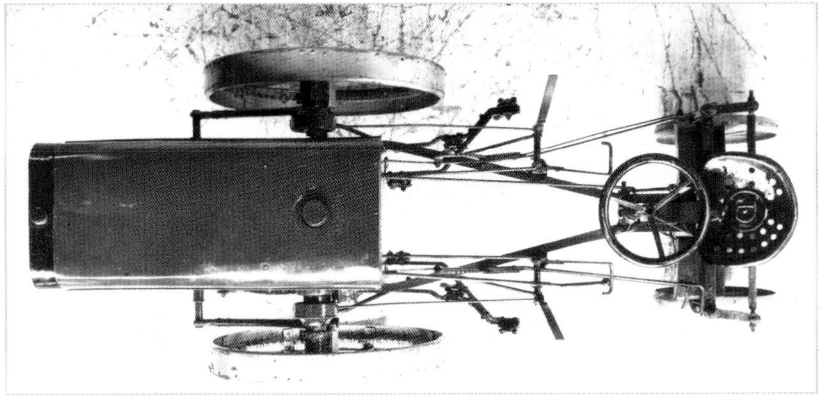

Walter Silver's No. 1 motor cultivator relied on the operator's arm strength and leg coordination. The steering wheel swung the rear wheels on a pivot. The two long diagonal levers just ahead of the steering wheel raised or lowered the cultivating shovels but it was the footholds, just below the wheel, that made the minute running adjustments. Deere & Company Archives

Two weeks after that, Dain reported progress to the board. Working out of the Deere & Webber Minneapolis branch, testers noted some trouble with the clutch collar and bevel pinion sleeve. They questioned various aspects of the engine itself and its belt power. But on the whole, their report read more like a paid product endorsement.

"The all-wheel drive makes its light weight possible," George Schutz, branch manager of Deere & Webber, wrote about the tractor, "and gives the maximum traction, the advantages of which are that the tractor will go through more difficult conditions without miring down than any other tractor, and in the event it does mire down, by uncoupling the plows it will always pull itself out, which other tractors cannot do." Schutz and a territory salesman John Molstad also noticed that the tractor's light weight did not compact the soil so much as their competition's tractors did.

The new Deere tractor's ostensibly complex drivetrain provided other benefits. "Four chains being used to drive the wheels," Schutz continued, "divides the strain on the sprockets and chains, making the chain drive, in our judgment, two or three times more durable than gears and much easier for the farmer to replace and adjust.

"Another big advantage of this feature," they concluded, "is that there is no noise. The noise made by the gears and the exhaust on many tractors, especially after they have been used for some little time, is almost unbearable."

Schutz's report also incorporated a kind of marketing survey that he and Molstad accomplished while visiting farmers throughout Minnesota and North and South Dakota. Schutz felt their comments were well worth considering as Deere got closer to authorizing regular production:

"A tractor, like a man or horse, cannot work to its limit continuously and last," one older farmer observed.

In Aberdeen, South Dakota, they found witness to that wisdom with a man who contentedly used a six-plow-rated tractor to pull only four plows. "He stated," Schutz recorded, "that he wore out one tractor in a short time by pulling all he could with it, and he made up his mind that the only way a tractor would stand up was for it to have enough power so it would 'play' with the plow, so to speak."

Meanwhile, a Fargo, North Dakota, implement dealer exposed a potential pitfall to Schutz and Molstad.

"If a customer has trouble—and they all seem to have an undue amount—he will blame the Fargo Implement Company just the same, and when the farmer is ready to buy a gang plow the probabilities are he will go to their competitor and get it."

Fargo Implement had sold 17 Waterloo tractors in the past two years. The owner suggested he could have sold 17 more but he was reluctant. His repair staff would have been overwhelmed, occupied full-time looking after the troublesome tractors. Yet, he also sold 17 of Deere's Pony Plows, one for each tractor. Without the tractor, he suspected he probably would have sold only four or five.

Schutz listened carefully and he thoroughly understood what he heard. His recommendations spoke with insight.

"This goes to show," he wrote, "that our dealers need a tractor badly but that they must have a good one. . . . Our tractor should be strong enough and have power enough to pull three bottoms in stubble, under almost any condition, as the majority of farmers, when purchasing a three-plow tractor, expect it to be able to do better and deeper plowing than they could with horses. In fact, a good many tractors are sold at times when plowing conditions are unusually hard for horses.

"We think," Schutz continued, "the matter of price should be forgotten for the present. Go ahead and build the tractor first class all the way through, using extra good magnetos, carburetors, etc., as well as making it extra good in other details. And when

that is done, if the price must of necessity be $1,500 to market them profitably, let's sell them for that."

He did question whether the new tractor really needed to be so costly when competitors' tractors of greater weight sold for less (tractor and implement costs in those days always related directly to the weight of steel or iron used). But his arguments offered unconvincing statistics, and he never took into account that Deere's new tractor was all-wheel drive. His most effective argument, however, was yet to come:

"In considering the matter of price we must remember the more tractors we sell the more tractor plows we will sell!"

George P. Schutz signed his name with a flourish reminiscent of John Hancock's signature on the Declaration of Independence. Yet William Butterworth still was mired in the gumbo of caution.

With its hood up to assist cooling on a hot summer afternoon, the All-Wheel Drive gleams in the sunlight. The tractor measures 6 feet 4 inches wide.

ABOVE: *After a false start or two, Dain settled on the large Perfex radiator. The forced cooling system used an engine-driven centrifugal water pump.*

RIGHT: *Heavy drive chains connected each front half-shaft to the transmission. The All-Wheel Drive offered two speeds in forward and reverse, and a top speed of 2.6 miles per hour.*

Joe Dain's four cylinder engine incorporated four cast en-bloc cylinders each of 4.5 inch bore and 5 inch stroke. The three main-bearing engine enjoyed forced oil lubrication.

More Tractor Ideas, Not Fewer

Conversations among board members urged Deere to investigate producing a tractor with more power. Could they produce a machine capable of pulling more than just three plows? Board members wondered if they should plan a motor cultivator as well. (This raises the question of just how much of George Mixter's experimental work with Theo Brown occurred far outside board scrutiny.)

Walter Silver, an engineer working for Brown, had begun developing a motor cultivator early in 1916. His concept mounted an existing Deere horse-drawn cultivator ahead of a powered unit. Operators steered the cultivator by turning a large horizontal wheel that in turn pivoted the front half. It was an early form of articulation. With the cultivators just below and ahead of them, operators could look down at the work they did and make subtle adjustments to the direction that the machine headed. By late fall, Brown joined in its field development, often going out to Deere's nearby test farm to watch it work. In its early configurations, it ran an air-cooled 7.5-horsepower New Way single-cylinder engine.

It was a time when motor cultivators were on every manufacturer's mind. International Harvester's Ed Johnston was developing one, as were B. F. Avery, J. I. Case, and several other makers. Joe Dain made a quick sketch in February proposing his all-wheel drive in a cultivator configuration. The operator sat ahead of an engine that Dain mounted cross-wise on the frame. Two rows of cultivators hung between the front wheels. Dain narrowed his large rear wheel so his tractor would fit between rows without crushing the crops.

While Silver had conceived his machine as a cultivator, it didn't take long before Brown and others began testing it under a wider variety of field chores. On November 20 Brown wrote, "In the field all day with tractor, where we tried disc harrow and grain drill. It looks as though they would work pretty well. Mr. C. E. White was out and thought if we could turn a little sharper that we would be in good shape." (Charles White was another board member on the side of tractor development.) On December 19 that year, Brown wrote in his dairy, "Got new tractor out today, put it in Dain's tractor room, testing with twin cylinder engine. Runs smoothly." Silver had mounted the new McVicker twin horizontally.

On January 17, 1917, Brown conducted two tours of "all the tractor and implement firms in the area. Ten firms. Saw nothing new." A month later, on February 11, he visited the Marseilles plant to check on assembly of the first tractor there because McVicker's latest two-cylinder engine had arrived the day before.

Rather than attempting to brake each of the three wheels, Dain's foot lever tightened down on this flywheel driven off the transmission. This applied braking force equally to all three wheels.

Grousers for improved traction bolted through the wheel rims. Dain designed the All-Wheel Drive on a 6-foot 2.75-inch wheel base. It weighed close to 4,600 pounds.

On February 22, Brown spent the day at Marseilles. An avid photographer, he made pictures of the tractor working with a single- and a two-row cultivator, a mower, a plow, and a disc harrow. But a week later, it all unraveled. March 1: "Clutch trouble, bearing burned out in flywheel, and broken frame. Carburetor and mag problems. Wiley of Kingston [magnetos] and Erickson of Dixie [carburetor] came to help. Unable to get tractor to idle."

Still, Deere's sales department had enough confidence to publicize the new machine. On the first day of spring, *Farm Implement News* published a story announcing, "Deere to Make Small Tractor:"

"Deere & Company, Moline, IL, are reported to have practically perfected a motor cultivator, unique in principle and design, and which, in addition to cultivating row crops, will do substantially all of the farm work ordinarily done by one team. It pulls as well as pushes, hauls a drag harrow, small grain drill, mower, or single plow; in short, anything that can be done with one team.

"The retail price will approximate the cost of a span of good horses. The trade name of the machine will be the 'John Deere One Team Tractor.'"

World War I Intrudes

Three weeks later, however, the outside world moved in on Deere & Company. Brown wrote in his diary on April 4 that the Senate voted for war against Germany and that on April 5, Good Friday, the United States declared war. These were two of three calamitous events within a single week that would affect Deere and Brown. The third, and closest to home, came on April 10: "L. R. Clausen put in charge of 'Tractivator,' I was considerably hurt." Until 1916, Leon Clausen had been manager of Dain's former hay works in Ottumwa, Iowa. With this promotion, Clausen moved to Moline.

Meanwhile, Charles Webber's protégé, George Peek, had gone on to manage the Omaha branch. The board named him to Deere's executive committee soon after his branch promotion in 1916. Peek wrote to Butterworth as a committee member. He advised, despite the war in Europe, that Deere continue development and even expand tractor manufacture. Butterworth knew that he had to miss the mid-September 1917 board meeting. He wrote back to Peek and asked him to handle the chairman's proxy at that meeting.

"I have acquiesced," Butterworth began, "in the experimental work which has been done, but I am beginning to feel that we are wasting the stockholders' money in going any further with it. . . . Ford's active interest in the tractor business means unlimited capital and resources for marketing. . . . I want it plainly understood that I am and will remain opposed to our taking up the manufacture of tractors and will take steps to stop it if an attempt is made to start. . . . If it comes up, I want you to stop it."

While Butterworth saw Ford as a considerable threat to be avoided, others, and especially George Peek, felt that Ford—and International Harvester—presented competition that no longer should be avoided. After the board secretary read George Schutz' encouraging letter out loud, Butterworth learned a painful lesson: Never miss a board meeting.

"September 12, 1917: RESOLVED, that Mr. Dain be authorized to continue his negotiations with the thought in mind of buying not over 100 of the Dain tractors outside with the view of continuing the development on the tractor line, the purchase to be made on a fixed price basis."

This "outside" supplier was to be none other than Deere & Company's Marseilles works in East Moline. It was here that the company's first binders had been built. It was at Marseilles that Theo Brown had assembled Dain's development tractors.

On October 24, Joe Dain traveled with George Schutz to Huron, South Dakota, to watch three of his prototypes. In 1916 Deere & Webber had loaned one of these prototypes to their agent, F. R. Brumwell, who owned three ranches. After a year of use, Deere engineers

In those days there was no danger of a printed decal with the warranty wearing off. Deere offered their serial number and their promise on brass. This is #191879. The tractor sold for about $1,650 in 1918, roughly $19,725 today.

OPPOSITE: *The business end of the tractor shows the levers that control (from far to near) the long drawbar height adjustment handle, the crank-shaped forward/reverse gear selector, speed gear selector lever, and foot brake.*

overhauled the tractor and replaced the original Waukesha powerplant with the new McVicker four-cylinder engine. Brumwell had been impressed enough with the tractor that he had bought three, each with the new McVicker engine. The agent kept one. He sold the other two to customers, these being possibly the first recorded sales of John Deere tractors.

In visiting other test sites, Schutz and Dain concluded, once and for all, that the early Waukesha engines developed inadequate power for the kind of work farmers expected from a three-plow-rated tractor. The 1917 versions with the new McVickers were more powerful. Heavier drive chains eliminated the breakage problems. The new gear-transmission ran submerged in oil, guaranteeing cooler running and better lubrication.

Servicing had been a significant factor in McVicker's design for the new engine. It permitted major engine overhaul, removal of the cylinder head, even pistons and connecting rods, without tearing the entire engine down. Farmers could service the transmission merely by removing a cover plate.

"Finally," Schutz wrote in concluding his report of the trip with Dain, "we firmly believe the machine is perfected to a point where it can be successfully manufactured commercially, and we strongly recommend you proceed with the construction of at least 100 as soon as possible."

Charles Webber and fellow board members Charles Velie and Floyd Todd quickly approved the report. Webber forwarded it to the executive committee.

Joseph Dain Sr. never lived to see even a seventh John Deere tractor built. Overworked and overtired before his trip began to South Dakota, he contracted pneumonia during his two-day visit. On October 31, 1917, Theo Brown noted in his diary that "Mr. Dain died this afternoon in Minneapolis on a business trip. A very able and kindly man."

Following Dain's Death, His Tractor Lives

Brown quoted the minutes from the executive committee meeting held two weeks after Dain's death, on November 19, 1917.

"RESOLVED, That Mr. Clausen be requested to proceed with the manufacture of 100 tractors of the Dain type using for that purpose such members of the organization as are available and such outside assistance as it is advisable to obtain . . . , and

"FURTHER, It is the opinion of those present that the services of Joseph Dain, Jr. who has had wide experience in the development of the tractor in connection with the work of his father, should be made use of to the fullest extent and in as important a capacity as his experience and abilities permit."

BELOW: *This simple braking mechanism did not appear on Dain's first and second prototypes. By the time Deere's board launched production of the model in October 1917, Dain had died of pneumonia.*

JOHN DEERE
MOLINE, ILL.

It stretched just 12 feet 6 inches long and stood 4 feet 9 inches tall. Its large single rear wheel measured 40 inches in diameter and 20 inches wide while the two fronts were 36x8. The engine developed 24 horsepower off that 30 inch belt pulley.

By this time, Lt. Col. George Mixter had taken a leave from Deere & Company, to fulfill his U.S. Army obligations. Clausen became acting head of manufacturing in Mixter's absence, removing him from day-to-day participation in the Tractivator development.

All-Wheel Drive in Production

The man next named responsible for the manufacture of the new John Deere all-wheel drive tractors was Elmer McCormick. He was superintendent at the Tenth Street factory, the former Root & Vander Voort engine shops that Deere leased for its binder works in East Moline. McCormick had worked closely with Dain almost from the start while he studied engineering at the University of Illinois. McCormick had contributed in minor ways to the design and engineering of the All-Wheel Drive.

In their commitment to produce the tractor, the board brought in other departments at this point. Advertising produced a duotone sales brochure. The cover showed the machine pulling a three-bottom plow, headed away from the camera, under the heading of "The John Deere All-Wheel Drive Tractor." The single sheet promotional piece, folded in half and in half again to standard letter size, opened up to reveal a full-side profile photograph and another six smaller engineering detail photos. Specifications covered the back page. Engineering produced an "Instruction Book and Repair List for the John Deere Tractor" dated July 1918. Deere's tractor business now was going public.

The late Frank Hansen owned this tractor and supervised its restoration. His attention to detail shows in this view of the 4.5x5 inch four-cylinder engine. That he enjoyed running it as well shows in the discolored exhaust and the slightly tarnished Stromberg M-2 carburetor.

On December 11, 1917, Leon Clausen reported back to the executive committee. Marseilles was ready to begin assembling the 100 tractors. Manufacturing had let contracts to McVicker for the engines. Clausen reported that he expected the first half of the planned production would be completed and ready for shipment by June 1, 1918.

While the war had raged on in Europe, Deere filled its production capacity by manufacturing "escort wagons," ammunition carts, machine gun carriages and a "combat wagon," for the U.S. Army. In August, the war department ordered 5,000 of these wagons from Deere, the first 166 to be shipped by November 6. For his work and success in meeting that deadline, Theo Brown noted that on December 14 he received a "$1,000 mark of appreciation bonus for work on [the] Combat Wagon."

Just after the new year, 1918, Brown reported to his diary that he and the experimental department had been assigned to develop a two-bottom plow suitable for the Fordson tractor. Henry Ford already had shipped the first several thousand units to England's Ministry of Munitions as the "official farm tractor" of war-time England. Now he began delivering back-ordered models to U.S. and Canadian farmers. He had assigned his engineers to look into implements, but soon afterward Ford announced that Ford & Sons, his tractor manu-

Walter Silver's second motor cultivator moved steering to the front wheels. By the time his third and fourth versions got out for testing, the farmers who operated it were wondering if Deere could make this lightweight, maneuverable machine do more than just cultivate. Deere & Company Archives

facture division, would not produce tools for the tractor. He had decided to leave that task to others. It was a decision that spawned scores of new businesses making implements and accessories for Fordson tractors.

Over the next six months, Brown got involved again with tractors. On March 27, board member Harold Dineen, a plow works vice president, met with Henry Ford to show him the plow that Brown and his crew had devised for the Fordson. On March 28, Brown received a new Fordson for the experimental department and they "shipped two small plows to Ford." Three days later, on March 31, 1918, in an effort to conserve war-time rationed fuel, materials, and labor, the government inaugurated Day Light Savings time. A week after that, a new Waterloo Boy tractor appeared unexpectedly at Brown's experimental shops. Brown learned it was intended for use on Deere's experimental farm.

On April 22 and 23, Brown and others met with Henry Ford and discussed with him ideas and improvements to Deere's two-bottom plow. A week later, on the 29th, an internal meeting examined other Fordson tractor implements. "It is considered one of the biggest things Deere & Company has been confronted with for years. Fordson Tractor might revolutionize the implement business," Brown wrote that night.

CHAPTER 4
1918

OELICH
RACTION
RACTOR
FROELICH, IA.

BUSINESS PROGRESS IS NOT ALWAYS TECHNOLOGICAL ADVANCE

Like any better-than-average industrial project, Deere conceived, developed, tested, and produced its revolutionary All-Wheel Drive tractor in utter secrecy. Not only did engineering not want the competition to know, William Butterworth did not want Deere's bankers to find out.

Butterworth agonized. Farm and machinery trade publications regularly published stories of the demise of another one or two of the 165 tractor companies still in business at the end of 1916. North American manufacturers had produced 62,742 tractors in 1917 (and shipped 14,854 to war-torn Europe). However, war-time needs for steel and other manufacturing materials threatened all domestic industry in 1918. The United States Government Priorities Board began to speak of rationing steel and of limiting first-generation development prototypes. It would allow just 10 of these, no more than 50-second generation test models, and it proposed limiting total production by all manufacturers to 315,000 tractors. The government hoped this still would be enough to continue to feed and clothe the world. When the combatants reached an Armistice on November 11, 1918, needs for Europe's restoration stoked manufacturers' optimism. At year's end there were nearly 250 firms claiming they made farm tractors.

What Butterworth had on his hands clearly was a superior product. It was full of technical innovation. It appeared to be very reliable and strong. It seemed to be a good value, even at the $1,650 asking price (about $19,725 today) quoted by F. R. Brumwell's Huron, South Dakota, branch agency.

PREVIOUS: 1892 FROELICH *George Erbe's replica first debuted in time for the Froelich centennial in 1992. Only one other replica exists, a full-size model at Deere & Company's world headquarters in Moline, IL.*

RIGHT: *George Erbe of Monona, IA, spent five years working on this one-half scale replica he completed in 1992. Working from drawings and period photographs, the replica now lives inside the restored Burlingame Store at Froelich, IA, home of the Froelich Foundation for the Preservation of Tractor History.*

The All-Wheel Drive would go head to head against the likes of Harry Wallis' Cub, a nose-heavy rear-wheel-drive machine that already had advanced the tractor technology benchmark by enclosing the engine and transmission in a single rolled-steel casting. At the other end of the spectrum came Henry Ford's diminuitive Fordson. It was lightweight and economical, but limited in its power and capabilities. International Harvester Corporation (IHC) mainly offered its massive and cumbersome Titans and Moguls, machines that were throwbacks to previous decades and the days of prairie sodbusting. However, IHC had just introduced its startlingly compact International 8-16. Deere's competitor intended this innovative machine, like Ford's Fordson, for small farms and more modest means.

Six weeks after an executive committee resolution to go ahead with production of Deere's All-Wheel Drive, Joe Dain was dead. Three weeks after his death, the board revived his tractor by approving a production run of 100 machines. This was probably a compromise figure. Likely, the board settled on it to keep Butterworth from going through the ceiling and to keep his bankers from going out the door.

All of this provoked young Willard Velie, the youngest son of Stephen H. Velie. When his father died, Willard assumed both Stephen's job as Deere's corporate secretary and his father's seat on the board. Even when Willard left Deere to operate Velie Carriage Company in 1900, he remained on the board. (Velie family relations were not only business; Stephen had married John and Demarius Deere's daughter Emma.) Velie Carriage evolved into Velie Engineering Company. That metamorphosed into Velie Motors Corporation which, by 1916, produced the Velie Biltwell 12-24, a four-cylinder farm tractor. The Biltwell weighed around 4,500 pounds and sold for about $1,750. It was not all-wheel drive. It was from his position as both outside-competitor and family insider that Velie appeared once again to haunt the board.

Wayne Broehl chronicled the written confrontation that Willard launched. Velie reminded the board of its unanimous resolution from March 5, 1912, "to produce a tractor plow . . . at once." He pointed out that after nearly six years having passed, 12 tractors had been built, $250,000 had been spent, and the company position had deteriorated against its competition because of its unwillingness to move ahead. Velie was outspoken and forceful in presenting his conclusions and he aimed directly at the status quo.

"We cannot profitably make as small a number as 100 tractors, [because] in the process [of doing so] we become competitors of the independent tractor manufacturers, who have been heretofore our 'allies'. . . . I cannot refrain," he stressed, "from remarking that we should build tractors largely and whole-heartedly, or dismiss the tractor matter as inconsequential and immaterial."

It was near the end of January 1918. On the 25th, during a board meeting, Velie recited his own letter to Butterworth into the minutes. It had almost immediate effect.

The manager of the company's Harvester Works, W. R. Morgan, recently had come from a similar job at International Harvester Corporation. In reaction to Velie's letter, Morgan expressed strong concern over the impact to Deere's potential sales that newcomer Henry Ford would have on any tractor market once his machines were widely available in

LEFT: *Benjamin C. Van Duzen earned his first gas engine patent in March, 1891, and soon after began marketing horizontal engines ranging from 2 horsepower up to 30. A year later, he brought out his vertical versions, which claimed easier starting because uprights "overcame the end motion caused by the piston in horizontal engines."*

John Froelich operated a custom threshing service that he ran from 1888 until 1892 using a J. I. Case straw-burning steam traction engine. He worked more than a year to produce his first gas tractor, then quickly gave it a 52 1/2-day shakedown, threshing for hire across South Dakota through the fall of 1892.

the marketplace. He feared Ford's name and his resources as one would a formidable bully. But having heard the evidence of continuing customer demand and growing frustration because Deere did not have a tractor, Morgan voiced support to Velie's recommendation: "If it is coming, and I believe we cannot stop it, we should get into it some way."

Frank Silloway was acting head of sales, filling in for George Peek who had followed George Mixter in the war effort. Silloway resurrected an idea from earlier board meetings. As Deere geared up production for Dain's tractor, its need for a major tractor manufacturing facility became very clear. Deere already had investigated other manufacturing facilities in the Midwest. The board knew of the Waterloo Gas Engine Company, some 110 miles northwest of Moline. It already had acquired one of their models and shipped it to Brown for evaluation and possible implement development.

One significant element that made this company appealing to Deere was an acquisition that the Gas Engine Company had made a few years earlier. In October 1912, it had purchased the Waterloo Foundry. Prior to that deal, the foundry company manufactured its own tractor, the 8-15 Big Chief Tractor, introduced in 1911. The Big Chief used an opposed two-cylinder, horizontally mounted engine. The Engine Company's first tractor, the Waterloo Boy Model 15 carried over the same configuration. Without doubt, these two machines were the distant predecessors to the Waterloo Boy Model L shipped to Brown.

Given Deere's limited tractor production capacity at that time, Silloway had considered the slow start-up that this insufficient capacity almost certainly guaranteed. Demand could soon outstrip supply, further frustrating his dealers. He wondered if Deere might be better served by acquiring an existing company with established products.

Silloway had heard that the Waterloo company was available and its president George Miller wanted to retire with cash in the bank. Knowing little more than that, but coupled with the fact that various branches had sold Waterloo Boy tractors with greater and lesser success, the board dispatched Silloway to gather information.

What he learned impressed him. Silloway found a company producing two models, a single-speed Model R introduced in 1914, and a newer two-speed Model N just introduced the previous year, in 1917. Both tractors used a horizontally mounted two-cylinder engine. Both ran on inexpensive kerosene. In 1918, the R sold for $985 (nearly $12,000 in 2003), and the N sold for $1,150 (nearly $14,000 today). These came much closer to the price of Ford's Fordson and IHC's International 8-16 than their own All-Wheel Drive could.

Waterloo rated both tractors at 12 horsepower from the drawbar, 25 horsepower from the belt pulley. However, the new N used roller bearings in the engine. What's more,

OPPOSITE: The gear-driven camshaft ran the exhaust valve. After his success in 1892, friends and backers convinced Froelich to begin larger scale manufacture in Waterloo. Between 1893 and 1896, the new Waterloo Gasoline Traction Engine Co. produced three more machines. Each weighed around 9,000 pounds.

Despite the fact that these machines worked in the dirt surrounded by flying dust, no one gave any thought to the risks of exposed running gear such as Froelich's sliding gear transmission. The Waterloo company sold only two of the four and the buyers returned both of them to Froelich as failures.

Waterloo had adopted automobile-type steering to replace the Model R's bolster-and-chain steering system. In addition, the Waterloo firm marketed a line of portable and stationary engines capable of running either on gasoline or kerosene. Sales of all its models had been good, 2,762 in 1916 and 4,007 in 1917.

Silloway found the factory itself was large and well equipped with many new machine and production tools. In addition to the buildings, the company had acquired an adjoining plot of 38 acres of vacant land to handle anticipated expansion. With its own foundry, Waterloo Gasoline Engine was "vertically integrated," that is, completely self-sufficient.

Waterloo's Beginnings

The Iowa manufacturer had evolved from one of America's earliest experiments with gasoline engines. An itinerant thresherman named John Froelich had achieved some success working with a J. I. Case straw-burning steam traction engine and a threshing machine. With a large crew, he traveled through Iowa and South Dakota over four harvest seasons beginning in 1888. Fascinated by gasoline power, he bought a very early Van Duzen engine and mounted it on a Robinson tractor chassis. After more than a year of effort, he had a working tractor completed in time for the harvest in 1892. He gave it a 52-day shakedown trial in South Dakota.

His machine generated outside interest. The positive results of his trials encouraged him to begin full-scale production. He enlisted financial backing from George Miller and several other Waterloo businessmen. Together they founded the Waterloo Gasoline Traction Engine Company. Between 1893 and 1896, Froelich produced only four of his tractors. He sold two of these, but they came back branded as failures by their buyers. His partners encouraged him to continue production of the portable and stationary engines at least. These had worked, had sold, and had generated some profit. But Froelich was single-minded in his devotion to tractors. Lacking the support from his partners, he left his firm.

After Froelich's departure, the partners reorganized the company as the Waterloo Gasoline Engine Company and remained faithful to their own inclinations. Louis W. Witry, an engineer with Santa Fe Railroad in New Mexico, joined the firm and he took over as engine designer and engineer. Within a few years, the company again became interested in tractors. Witry and his partners enlisted Harry Leavitt who had more successful experience in tractor design and engineering. Witry began to experiment with crawler track adaptations. By 1913 the Waterloo Gasoline Engine Company had introduced their Waterloo Boy One-Man Tractor, a relatively small machine for the time, weighing 9,000 pounds.

The word *Boy* first appeared as a model name on Waterloo tractors in 1896. The company recently had introduced stationary engines to power water pumps, among other uses. It's likely the makers of this nearly self-sufficient machine used the name to parody the "water boy" who was still needed to fetch and deliver cooling water to the older-style large tractors around the farm.

While Deere's own tractor had four cylinders and all-wheel drive, Silloway seemed quite taken with Waterloo's machine. Witry's sales spiel justified their two-cylinders and rear-wheel drive. Upon Silloway's return, he described the various "advantages" in a long memo quoted in Wayne Broehl's *John Deere's Company.*

"1: A two-cylinder tractor can be built cheaper than a four, and price is an important factor because the tractor is a business machine and must win by its economy.

"2: The tractor, unlike the automobile, must pull hard all the time. The bearing must be adjusted for wear. There are half as many bearings to adjust on a two-cylinder tractor and half as many valves to grind.

"3: There are less parts to get out of order and cause delay.

"4: The bearings are more accessible on a two-cylinder horizontal engine than a four-cylinder vertical engine.

"5: Two cylinders will burn kerosene better than four.

"6: Four cylinders are not necessary on tractors. The fact that a tractor is geared 50 to 1 instead of 4 to 1 eliminates all jerky motion. The engine of a tractor can be made heavy and have a heavy flywheel and can be mounted on a strong rigid frame. Therefore, a two-cylinder engine is satisfactory in a tractor and when it is, why go to the four-cylinder type?"

Silloway's conversion was complete.

"The Waterloo tractor is of a type which the average farmer can buy. . . . We should have a satisfactory tractor at a popular price, and not a high-priced tractor built for the few. Here we have an opportunity to, overnight, step into practically first place in the tractor business."

When George Miller telephoned on March 14, 1918, to advise the Deere board that its option expired that day, Silloway became the board's squeaking wheel. He initiated the motion to buy Waterloo so that Deere would not lose the opportunity to obtain the established tractor manufacturing facility.

The vote was unanimous. Charles Webber, Charles Velie, Floyd Todd, even Butterworth and Dain Jr. voted to buy. (Mixter and Peek were at war and Willard Velie was absent). Deere paid $2.35 million (about $28.6 million in 2003).

Floyd Todd came to Brown's home Saturday, March 16, 1918, to inform him "that Deere & Company had bought the Waterloo Gas Engine Company outright . . . the day before yesterday. This includes the Waterloo Boy Tractor." Over the years, Brown came to understand the significance of this move. In his 1953 book, he theorized about what the Waterloo purchase meant. There were options that this acquisition presented for Deere's own tractor plans. With Waterloo's tractors in their lineup, once Marseilles completed the first 100 All-Wheel Drives, they would not need to assemble any more. The board certainly would not authorize any further development. Brown's plant finished the last of them in 1919. Deere shipped them all to Brumwell's Huron, South Dakota, branch.

"In 1918," Brown began, "most of the full line implement companies were building tractors, particularly International Harvester Company and Case. It was felt that it was imperative to get into the tractor business at as early a moment as possible in order for Deere & Company to hold onto their plow business. A tractor and plow were usually sold by the same dealer.

Even in half-scale, maneuvering the Froelich was an exhausting and extremely imprecise task. Robinson's steam engines used a chain-and-roller system but Froelich innovated this vertical worm-and-sector-via driveshaft-to-gear-and-chain arrangement that whipped and wandered as the tractor moved.

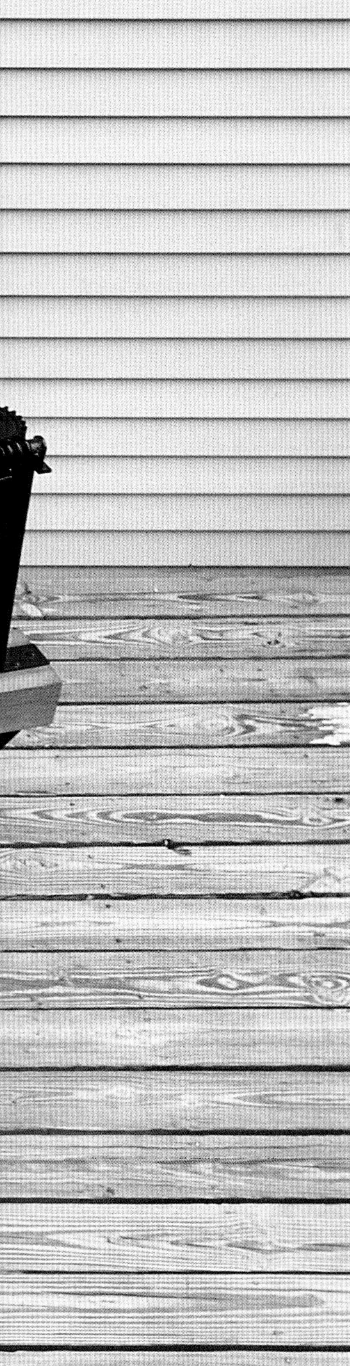

"The Dain tractor," he went on, "while a good tractor, was high-priced. . . . It would require considerable time to tool up for manufacture.

"Deere & Company had purchased the Waterloo Gasoline Engine Company and thus had a factory, a tractor, and an organization that was functioning, and so [Deere] was in the tractor business at one quick stroke.

"In concluding," Brown wrote, "it should be emphasized that in his thinking about tractors, Mr. Dain was ahead of his time, for he insisted that tractors must be made better in every way, and that price was not the main objective. Many features of the Dain tractor were better than those of most tractors of that period."

In his own conclusions two weeks after the purchase, Willard Velie wrote to William Butterworth to try to reassure the still-hesitant president.

"I am more than satisfied we have made the best move Deere & Company has ever made, and that it was an extremely fortunate thing we were able to buy this plant. I believe," Velie went on, "if we handle this proposition right, the Waterloo Boy will be to the tractor trade what the Ford car is to the automobile trade. Of course the Ford tractor will take first place, but if we can take second place that will be good enough for us."

Personalities, product development, and outside events would conspire to deprive Deere of that goal for decades to come.

John Froelich was not Rube Goldberg. In view of technology at the time, this machine is sophisticated in many ways. George Erbe went to exhausting lengths to research and recreate his homage to one of America's first farm tractors.

CHAPTER 5

1918–1920

GASOLINE

THE INDOMITABLE HENRY FORD

TAKES THE FIELD

On March 30, 1918, as Willard Velie sent his reassurances to William Butterworth in Moline, Henry Ford turned out 64 Fordsons that day and every day in Detroit. Throughout 1917 and into early 1918, he had shipped more than 4,000 tractors to the United Kingdom for its Ministry of Munitions. Selling them at cost-plus-$50, Ford had cut his profit to the bone to aid England's war-time agricultural crisis. But by March 30, he also had filled 5,000 of the 13,000 outstanding back orders on file for his Fordson in North America. Within another three months, Ford had doubled his production rate again. By July 1, he was building 131 a day.

It was not a perfect tractor. But it was small, light, strong, highly maneuverable, and extremely affordable. It weighed 2,710 pounds and it could pull 2,180 pounds. Years before Henry Ford would wage a price war on International Harvester, he sold the Fordson for $785 (about $9,400 today). By the end of 1918, he had manufactured 34,167 of them.

In 1918, International Harvester Corporation marketed two tractors, the Titan 10-20, the lightest weight evolution of its traditional heavy-weights, and the International 8-16. Sales of the two machines totaled 20,837. Deere & Company had a long way to go to finish second to Ford. Total sales of the Waterloo Boy reached only 5,634 for 1918. Yet while this figure was small compared to Ford's sales, it was well beyond what Deere could have done in second year's sales of its own All-Wheel Drive.

Frank Silloway was not disheartened. Each sale of a Waterloo Boy tractor also meant a potential sale of a Deere plow. Better than that, since Henry Ford had no plans to manufacture his own

PREVIOUS: 1914 WATERLOO BOY MODEL R
Travis Jorde's beautifully restored R is one of about 9,310 that Waterloo produced from 1914 through 1919. Jorde's tractor is possibly the oldest example.

RIGHT: *Waterloo Gasoline Engine Company introduced its first Standard 25-horsepower tractor in 1912, using a vertical, transversely mounted four cylinder engine. For 1914, Waterloo switched to horizontal two-cylinder engines for both its 25 horsepower Model R and the smaller 15 horsepower "Light" model.*

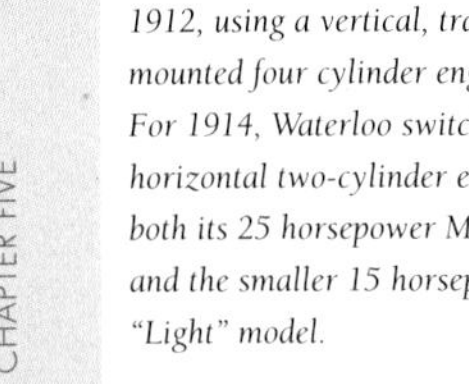

Despite the promise of its own all-wheel drive tractor, Deere purchased Waterloo Gasoline Engine Company. The complete tractor manufacturing facility and foundry came with Waterloo's tractor, the Waterloo Boy. For Deere, this proved a ready-made mass-production entrée into a business it previously had watched warily. Deere & Company Archives

implements, his 34,000 buyers had to use someone's plows. Theo Brown and others from Plow Works engineering and Deere's board had already visited Ford to discuss their plows for his Fordsons.

Deere's All-Wheel Drive and the Waterloo tractors were designed to use three-bottom plows. However, Harold Dineen, John Deere Plow Works manager, set his development engineers to work quickly to produce a new, lightweight, two-bottom plow. Dineen conceived it specifically for the smaller tractors, but most specifically for Henry Ford. Dineen's new plow weighed 410 pounds, which was 170 pounds less than the Oliver Ford had first examined. Silloway, Brown, and Dineen anxiously courted Ford.

Ford was impressed. On Monday, April 22, he told Brown, "You know, I am a good friend to Oliver, and when I see him, I'm going to tell him he has to go some to equal the Deere plow." Brown learned that Ford had invested $5 million (about $70.3 million in 2003) into getting his tractor plant up and running. Ford's Fairlane Farm comprised 7,000 acres of which Ford had 3,200 under cultivation.

But again, board reluctance intervened. This time it was Charles Webber who expressed scorn for Ford's small tractor and loathing for any Deere contribution to its success.

"I don't know, but this whole Ford proposition is a waste of material," he wrote to George Peek. "I imagine a lot of small farmers will buy Ford tractors and have no right to

OPPOSITE: *Waterloo and other early manufacturers used "blind head" designs, non-removable cylinder heads with external valves mounted in cages. Louis Witry and Harry Leavitt stuck with this design through 1915.*

KEROSENE
WATERLOO BOY

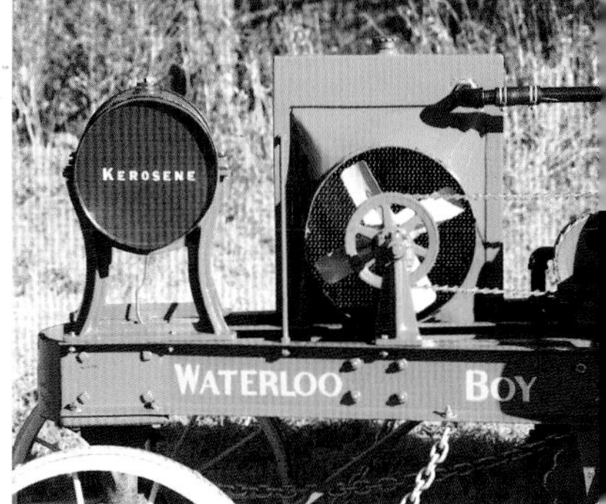

ABOVE: *Over its six year lifetime, Waterloo introduced more than a dozen variations, increasing engine size to as much as 465 cubic inches. Kerosene tanks grew larger, some stood on end, and others appeared mounted longitudinally. Soon they appeared in green.*

LEFT: *The Model R measured 142 inches long and 63 inches tall to the top of the radiator. It weighed about 6,200 pounds, and in 1917, this model sold for $850, about $11,000 today.*

INSET: *The introductory models used a 330-cubic-inch, 5.5-inch bore, 7-inch stroke engine that produced 25 horsepower on this belt pulley and measured 12 horsepower off the rear hitch. Operators started them using gasoline but ran them on less costly kerosene.*

RIGHT: 1916 WATERLOO BOY MODEL R
A vertical fuel tank and a larger radiator that engineers rotated to face the other side of the tractor are two differences from the earlier 1914 and 1915 models. This tractor, #1460, was the 60th manufactured in 1916.

own them; a lot of special machinery will be manufactured to go behind them, and I think the country would be just . . . a whole lot better off without the Ford tractor than with it."

Webber explained his feelings. "It is going to chew up a lot of material," he said, "and the implements that are designed to go behind it are going to chew up a lot of material, and that material might better be used for other purposes if there is going to be a shortage of material."

(The shortages of material did arrive in 1918. True to his character, Henry Ford offered to take over the responsibility for all U.S. farm tractor production and maintenance in exchange for all the other manufacturers' allocations of raw material.)

When the question of distributing Deere plows through Ford dealers came to a vote in mid-September 1918, the board protected its own dealers. If farmers wanted Deere & Company plows, they could come in and see all the other products their local agent had to offer. Including a better tractor! (By this time, Deere had promoted Brown to director of engineering for all plow and tractor development.)

In 1919, Deere sold 4,015 Waterloo tractors, down about 1,600 from 1918 sales figures, of both Model R and N. It discontinued the R at the end of 1919. Tractor contributions to the balance sheet recovered through 1920 when Deere's branches sold a total of 5,045 Model N tractors. The board set production at 30 a day in 1920 and it planned for 40 per day to start in 1921.

The tractor market boom continued though a shakeout of also-rans. This reduced the competition by more than a quarter in two years. Deere, Ford, IHC, Minneapolis-Moline, Allis-Chalmers, and Case competed against 181 other, lesser manufacturers at the beginning of 1920. With Deere solidly among the top five, Frank Silloway's assessment of Waterloo's value

WATERLOO BOY

to the company seemed prescient. Yet no one, not Silloway, Velie, or even Butterworth, Witry, and Leavitt, could have imagined the additional value that would accrue to Deere & Company in early April 1920.

1916 Overtime

This is a late 1916 model, fitted with the 1917 Waterloo 6.5x7.0 inch engine. The Model R tractors had a single speed transmission in forward or reverse. The subsequent Model N introduced a two-speed transmission coupled to the same larger engine.

Fighting the Farm Tractor—and Winning

World War I had depleted the United States and Western Europe of adult men and mature horses. Farmers in England and tens of thousands more in the United States had no choice but to adopt tractors. Deere's Waterloo Boy, the Fordson, the Wallis Cub, Case's 10-18, International's 8-16, and Moline's Universal all redefined "power farming." No longer did any farmer require the "water boy" as well as an engineer, fireman, and a plowman. The one-man tractor, at first a Waterloo model name, had become a universal reality. America went tractor crazy.

For each legitimate engineer and inventor, there was at least one con artist around to race them for the farmer's dollar. Some manufacturers sold stock in order to go into business while others sold only stock and not one tractor. In some cases, tractors were ill-conceived, inadequately tested, inaccurately advertised, and innately unusable. With so many companies in business, name duplication was an occupational hazard: There were three Generals, four Uniteds, five Universals, six Westerns, and 10 outfits calling themselves the American Tractor Company. Some of the craftiest schemers used some of the most legitimate names to dupe some of the nation's least sophisticated buyers. Henry Ford himself was a victim of a clever San Franciscan, William Baer Ewing, who hired a plant in Minnesota and an accountant named Paul Ford just to make use of Ford's name. The tractor from Minneapolis was a Ford while Henry's firm in Dearborn had been forced to incorporate as Ford & Son.

Unfortunately for Wilmot Crozier, he bought the wrong Ford. Crozier was a former educator whose neighbors elected him to the state legislature in Nebraska. He limped the wrong Ford back to his farm where it broke down, never to perform as advertised. Frustrated and wary, he bought a second-hand Rumely. To his pleasure, that machine exceeded its claims and his expectations. Its performance provoked him to wonder what else was out there, how well it worked and what he could do about it.

He was not the first to express these concerns, but he was the first in a position to do something. He got together with another Nebraska legislator/farmer named Charles Warner. They contacted University of Nebraska professor L. W. Chase, the former head of agricultural engineering. Coincidentally, Chase was the president of the American Society of Agricultural Engineers (ASAE). He had participated as engineer-in-charge at several international tractor demonstrations. The idea of standardized tests and evaluations had occurred to him nearly from the earliest days of gasoline tractor manufacture.

Crozier, Warner, and Chase each did their part in writing, introducing, lobbying for, and promoting passage of the Tractor Test Bill. Among other specifics, it called generally for "Every model of tractor offered for sale within the state [of Nebraska] to be favorably passed upon by a board of three competent engineers under control of state university management." Introduced in early spring 1919, the state legislature passed it into law July 15, 1919.

Tests would include endurance runs. Engineers would determine official horsepower ratings under continuous load as well as fuel consumption. They would make results available to the public. Companies with nothing to fear reacted with nearly as much enthusiasm as Nebraska's farmers felt for this new protection. The first tractor offered for test was John Deere's Waterloo Boy Model N.

The tests began March 31, 1920, and concluded on April 9. Several other manufacturers followed, and by the end of April another seven had begun testing. Before the end of April, Deere & Company learned that their tractor had passed the tests. Rated in advertising at 15-25 horsepower, the Nebraska engineers obtained actual results that were incrementally better: 15.98 horsepower on the drawbar, 25.51 off the pulley.

Deere's Waterloo Boy, the first tractor submitted, was the first one certified. Unfortunately, while the Waterloo Boy passed, the economy was failing. And the war over territory in Europe was about to see a strange turn. A war was coming home to the American Midwest.

Early Waterloo Boy tractors used an automobile type steering but Louis Witry and Harry Leavitt reverted to the chain-and-bolster (or aim-and-pray) system that nearly every other manufacturer favored at the time. It was simpler, more durable, cheaper to produce, and easier to clean.

ABOVE: 1920 WATERLOO TYPE T
Derived from the Waterloo Boy Model N tractor, this was the most sophisticated of Louis Witry and Harry Leavitt's developments. The oversize fan blew through an enlarged radiator, passing heated air over the combined gasoline and kerosene fuel tank, preheating it for better vaporization.

INSET: *Not all of Waterloo's machines were self-propelled. This portable power unit was most useful to horse farmers making the transition from steam power for their separate threshing machines.*

THE PRICE CUT HEARD 'ROUND THE COUNTRY

Henry Ford's goal, he said, in bringing out his tractor was to ease the "producer's" costs so that everyone could benefit. Not only food, but clothing should cost less, he said. The tractor, more efficient and less costly than a team of horses, could aid in achieving that goal. But money was tight.

Ford cut the price of his Fordson. His automobiles were successful and he used their profits to support losses he could accept to get his tractors onto every farm. On January 27, 1921, Ford cut the price of his basic Fordson from $785 to $620 ($6,234 in 2003).

Within a month, International Harvester Corporation felt the effects of the war declared in Dearborn. Cutting its own price from $1,150 to $1,000, IHC still left Henry's tractors selling for two-thirds the price of their own. Deere watched, waited, and then twice, in quick succession, dropped prices down to an eventual low of $890 in July ($9,250 in 2003).

Waiting six months, Ford then dropped the bomb. Increasing the stakes in his winner-take-all war, Ford cut his prices another $230. He telegraphed each of his dealers to confirm the new retail price: $395 ($3,971 today).

In a hard economy, even Ford suffered casualties. Sales fell by 32,000 from 1920. Ford dealers sold only 35,000 Fordsons in 1921. Fordson met the Waterloo in the branch office yards and on the account balance sheets of America. It was Armageddon.

Deere sold just 79 tractors.

If ever any event had made Deere's Waterloo Boy look dated, it was seeing Ford's compact little grey tractor on sale at less than half the price of the old-fashioned-looking

green-and-red Waterloo Boy. Waterloo had introduced the Model N in 1917 and had barely modified it from the R, and even from its 1912 predecessor. As the Deere tractors sat, unsold in the storage yard in Waterloo, they suddenly looked obsolete.

But Waterloo had not been sleeping, nor had it expected to sell the Waterloo Boy forever, even if Deere had not acquired it. Louis Witry had begun work in secrecy on a successor to the tractors that he and Harry Leavitt had created a decade before. In alphabetical sequence, they produced prototype designs that they assembled and tested. When they reached the fourth version, designated by the letter D, they stopped. They were satisfied.

1925 Waterloo Type T

The marketplace demanded it and even though Deere & Company owned Waterloo and already had introduced its revolutionary Model D, farmers still needed "portable power." For Deere it was a profitable, simple, reliable product they continued to market under its original name.

CHAPTER 6

1920–1925

JOHN DEERE
JOHN DEERE

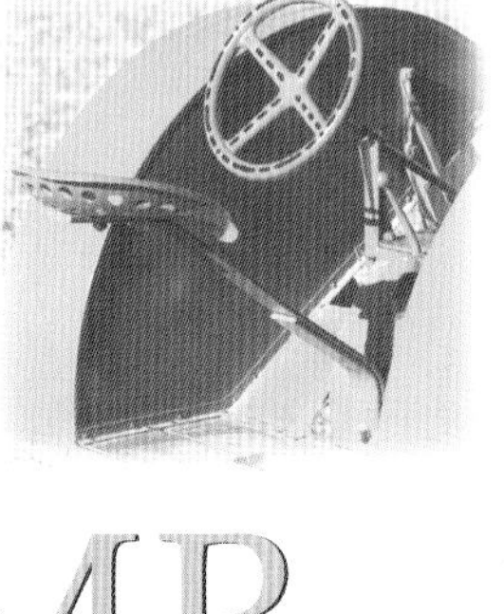

MR. SILLOWAY, THIS IS THE NEW TRACTOR YOU BOUGHT

PREVIOUS: 1924 MODEL D
When Frank Silloway urged Deere's board to acquire Waterloo Gas Engine Company, he knew Waterloo offered a marketable farm tractor. He didn't know that Louis Witry and Harry Leavitt already had begun developing this replacement. By reversing their two-cylinder engine, they shortened the wheelbase and created a unit-frame tractor.

RIGHT: *The 26-inch diameter spoked flywheel was a Witry and Leavitt innovation that allowed the farmer to use the heavy flywheel as a starting crank as well. To increase engine speed (and horsepower) Deere shrunk the flywheel to 24 inches beginning with 1925 production.*

Deere & Company found a compelling secret in Waterloo. The foundry had been a benefit to their acquisition. They knew about this before the board authorized the purchase, however. There was a bonus element as well, and it played a further role in eliminating the All-Wheel Drive tractor from Deere's plans. Yet it wasn't until shortly after March 14, 1918, the Waterloo purchase date, that Frank Silloway and Theo Brown learned anything about it.

When Silloway visited in 1917, he found an appealing physical plant. While doing his research, he learned about the company's past and present. Now, as a representative of its new owner, he was allowed to see its future. The evolution of designs from Harry Leavitt and Louis Witry had yielded their Model R in 1914. Over its five-year life, Waterloo sold that tractor in 13 styles, each given an alphabetical designation, RA through RM. The "RN" became simply known as the "N."

But until Deere had completed its acquisition, Waterloo's partners would not show Deere's board members everything they had done. Not until the check cleared, at any rate.

At that point, Witry probably would have taken Silloway into a room previously closed to him where they now would see Waterloo's new alphabet series. Witry would have told him what he had in mind and Silloway would have learned of plans to build a total of seven prototypes. He even would have found some of them already assembled.

In pre-Deere days, Witry and Leavitt referred to this new model as the "Style A." Externally, it was like nothing Silloway had seen before at Waterloo. This machine was smaller than their current

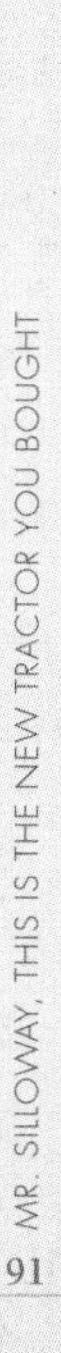

One of the most distinctive features of the first 50 Model D tractors was its composite, welded front axle. It simply wasn't strong enough and beginning with the 51st tractor, Deere switched to a hefty casting. This was the 10th D manufactured.

production models. The two design engineers had shortened the wheelbase, a feat they accomplished by reversing the horizontal two-cylinder engine on the frame. Now its crankshaft sat at the rear. They reduced ground clearance. In order for Witry to keep accurate testing records, he had serial numbered each of these prototypes. For the Style A tractors, he started with number 100.

Witry and Leavitt produced the next generation of prototypes. These incorporated corrections and improvements they derived from work on prototype numbers 101 through 106. Deere & Company, now the owners of the new project, chose to continue their alphabetical designations. The next generation "Style B" tractors began their numbering at 200. Waterloo's engineers assembled another seven prototypes and they tested those. The Style B version evolved into the "Style C" tractors and these numbers began with 300. Silloway then asked Witry and Leavitt to complete two of these by April 1922. Then Deere's board ordered another 10. By this time, the board felt it had the new model pretty close to where it should be.

From the Waterloo Boy Model N to the last Style C tractors, Witry, Leavitt, Silloway, and Brown had shortened overall length from 132 inches to 109. They shaved weight from 6,200 pounds to just about 4,000. Mean-while, Witry and Leavitt's improvements in carburetion, intake and exhaust valves, manifolds, and engine bearings increased drawbar horsepower from 16.0 to 22.5 from what basically was the same 6.5x7-inch engine.

When Deere's Experimental Department produced the first Style D tractor, it began its serial numbers at 400. Waterloo had numbered its production Model R beginning with #1026 and it reserved numbers up to 9,999. The N numbering started at 10,020 and by 1921 production had gone into the 20,000s. Deere set aside numbers up to 30,000 for its anticipated final production. The company believed demand for its Waterloo Boys would end before that point.

The left-side steering wheel sometimes interfered with the powerful flywheel. But Deere's engineers handled the new Model D as a "work in progress," and made steady improvements over its decades-long life.

Deere's board planned to introduce its new Style D tractor and to number this new model as the 30,000 series. Because their single evaluation Model D was so successful, tractor #30,400 was the only prototype Waterloo produced of the new Style D. Experimental department engineers, testers, and the board were all satisfied with what they had. Full production started with #30,401. (However, sales success being something that a manufacturer never questions or interrupts, production of Waterloo Model N tractors *did* reach 30,400. So Deere's registrars interrupted a block of serial numbers further on and they set aside an additional 92 numbers for the last of the Ns, beginning with 31,320 and concluding at 31,411.)

The evolution of the tractor from Model N to the Model D as it came to be known, was not without trials, tribulations, questions, and debates. Outside competition had heavily influenced Witry's concept.

Innovation from Beyond

J. I. Case Plow Works had absorbed a Case family member into its board. It moved his business into their conglomeration shortly after the turn of the century. By 1915, Case cousin and board member Henry M. Wallis had replaced his first gargantuan "Bear" tractor with the "Cub" that featured a unit-frame design incorporating the engine, transmission, and running gear into one seamless housing. It enclosed those moving parts completely, isolating them from weather and the destructive dust of the farm field.

USE HIGH-GRADE TRACTOR OIL
MEDIUM IN WINTER HEAVY IN SUMMER
DRAIN CRANK CASE OIL AT CENTER COCK
AND REFILL TO UPPER COCK AFTER EVERY
REMOVE STRAINER, DRAIN AND
WASH CRANK CASE WITH KEROSENE AFTER EVERY
RINSE OIL STRAINER CLEAN.
OIL INDICATOR MUST BE UP TO INSURE
LUBRICATION WHEN RUNNING.
JOHN DEERE
JOHN DEERE

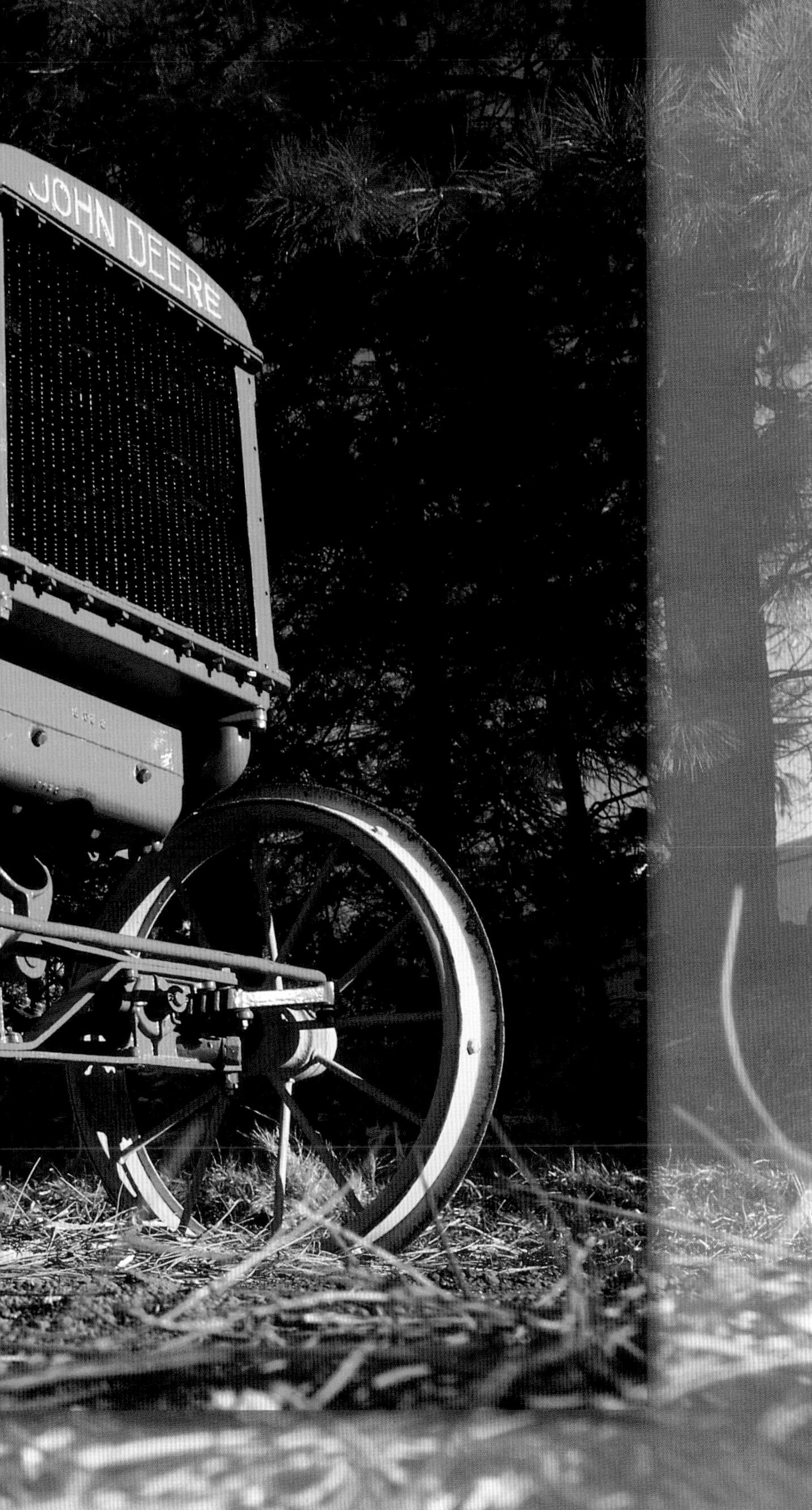

LEFT: *The composite front axle is clearly visible here and especially vulnerable. The 109-inch-long Model D was 33 inches shorter than the Waterloo Boy models it replaced. At 4,400 pounds, it also was nearly a ton lighter.*

INSET: *The Dixie aero-magneto provided spark ignition for the gas/kerosene engines. Waterloo's 6.5x7.0 inch engine now put out 22.5 horsepower on the drawbar and 30.4 off the belt pulley.*

1928 Model D Exhibit A

By 1928 Deere had substantially revised its workhorse tractor. Waterloo engineering relocated the steering to the right side so the steering column avoided the flywheel, and it switched to a solid flywheel to enhance safety. Its greater mass also smoothed out engine performance.

The 1916 Fordson followed suit, although Ford claimed and patented a version of the unit frame principle seven years earlier. IHC had introduced its unit-frame International 8-16 in 1917. Moline Plow Company, which had acquired the Universal Tractor Company in 1915, started selling Universal's splindly looking front-wheel-driven Model D beginning in 1918. Moline's Model D could be ordered with an electric starter, lights, and governor. Allis-Chalmers introduced its Model 6-12 in 1919, which was a tractor quite similar to Moline's Universal. Hart-Paar was poised to introduce its compact Model 10-20 in 1921.

Deere had not been stagnant. By late January 1920, Theo Brown had successfully adapted C. H. Melvin's power lift for use on a disc harrow. This used power from the tractor to raise the implement. Six weeks later, he signed a patent application for a power take off (PTO) for the Fordson tractor. Through the spring, he worked on tractor and horse plows. Regarding tractor plows, he noted in his diary the "consistent problems with depth due to various hitch heights on various makes of tractors. Attempting to get standardization in industry; [trying] various alterations to adjust plow depth. Also developing plows for different region demands and soil types of the country [including] New York, Texas, California."

Witry adopted the unit frame as well. Frank Silloway and others nicknamed some of his prototypes "bathtub tractors" because of the configuration. Other considerations arose. Deere's first production tractor, the All-Wheel Drive, had used McVicker's four-cylinder engines. The Fordson, the Universal, and the 8-16 also used fours. But Deere's Waterloo tractors stayed with two-cylinder power. In mid-1922, when board member Leon Clausen recommended that Witry, Leavitt, and Brown assemble 10 more "Style C" tractors for further testing, he also raised the question of two-cylinder engines versus fours. If everyone else used them, shouldn't Deere at least consider it? Charles Webber quickly responded. He based his answer on simple economics and ignored complex engineering and philosophical considerations: There was no money.

Simple Economics

The tractor war with Ford and International Harvester had cost the company many lost sales. The farm economy was in peril. Wartime needs for food and cotton had driven the value of farm land up 60 to 70 percent. But the end of World War I caught farmers unprepared. Farm exports that had reached $4.1 billion in 1919 fell to $1.8 billion in 1922. Worse, President Theodore Roosevelt's Country Life Commission in 1908 concluded that a primary cause for the struggles of modern farmers was "a lack of any adequate system of agricultural credit whereby the farmer may readily receive loans on fair terms." Eight years later in 1916, President Woodrow Wilson signed the Farm Loan Act.

Between 1916 and 1920, as produce prices held, farmers had little need for credit. But then prices fell when Europe no longer needed America's crops. Farmers who had acquired neighboring lands to capitalize on the wartime market, began to come up short. A poor spring crop further eroded whatever tractor and implement sales the company had anticipated while the previous year's surpluses tied over distributors and retailers. Deere laid off employees and cut the salaries of those who remained. Theo Brown became deeply depressed in mid-1920 as he saw vast numbers of friends losing their jobs at Deere. He took two summer months off without pay before returning to work September 1.

Through the first six months of 1921, it was Harold Dineen's Model 40 plow for the Fordson that kept the company afloat. Brown worked with Ford's manufacturing chief Charles Sorenson and tractor engineers Joe Galamb and Joe Farkas to improve it. Still, Deere remained barely above water. By June 1, the company reduced the pay by 10 percent for all employees making $3,000 or less (about $31,000 today), and by 20 percent for those who earned more than that. The company cut back to a three-day work week.

Deere & Company still had large cash reserves, but it would not authorize anything new. At Waterloo, by assembling few prototypes, Witry and Leavitt continued testing efficiently but frugally on their Waterloo Boy successors. Brown's experimental engineering department had little money for regular work let alone anything like the tens of thousands of dollars that it would cost to develop and test a new four-cylinder engine. What's more, Deere still had a large stock-pile of the Waterloo Model N engines on hand. These would fit the Witry/Leavitt prototypes and production versions. In the end, board member Charles Webber did not question engine technology but instead he followed the Deere family way of cautiously guarding their wealth. It was this consideration that dictated the decision to stick with the horizontal twins.

1927 Model W Stationary Engine

Michigan collector Mike Holder stumbled on an unusual stationary Model W. This was one of 75 that Deere manufactured for Pure Oil Company, with a double-weight 5-inch thick flywheel and six v-belt pulley on the back side to power its well pumps.

Stopping to pose for a photograph, J. D. Miller of Mechanicsburg, Ohio, shut down his very early production Model D, allowing the photographer a clear shot of its large 26-inch diameter flywheel and its straight-across steering rod. Deere & Company Archives

Price Wars Continue

In early 1922, Deere went to a two-day work week as Henry Ford cut the price of his Fordson. Oliver followed suit and dropped its No. 7 Fordson plow from $84 to $60, prompting Brown to note, "Necessary for us to get little Fordson plow perfected." A month later on February 18, when Ford announced that he did not need to approve the implements his dealers sold, Brown added, "Business seems to be on the upgrade." Then in November, Brown met with Irish inventor Harry Ferguson and British Army captain John Lloyd Williams "to see Ferguson plow and conduct field tests." Two weeks later on November 15, Brown met with Ferguson again. This time they toured the factory producing Deere's No. 40 plow for the Fordson. Ferguson asked about a license from Deere for the beam-grinding process.

Retiring the Waterloo

In mid-1923, it came time to retire the N and give birth to the new Model D. In 1921, while Deere had sold just 79 tractors, it had manufactured 786; in 1922, they only assembled 307. The board reviewed plans for 1923. Members saw already that it was shaping up to be another bad year. They revised projections further downward. Yet Leon Clausen pressed hard for first-year production of 1,000 of the new tractors. Wayne Broehl quoted the agonized board minutes and Clausen's summation:

"There is a national demand for tractors. We do not have to create it. And when a suitable tractor is built at a reasonable price to the consumer, it can be sold." By pointing out that Henry Ford's sales figures for "a suitable tractor at a reasonable price" were in the tens-of-thousands while Deere's sales of Waterloos had been only in the hundreds, Clausen won his battle.

And in that way, so did Deere.

Throughout the end of 1923 and through 1924, Deere manufactured 880 Model D's. Farmers responded nearly as enthusiastically as Clausen had predicted. While the tractor division showed losses in 1923 and 1924, it turned a profit in 1925 and sales figures grew from there.

Even after introducing the new tractor, Browns' experimental department continued to test it and advance its development. Deere's board knew it had cost the company next to nothing to continue loaning friendly farmers its prototypes for field testing in practical farming applications.

The first 50 Model D tractors appeared with a welded front axle and left-side steering. The flywheel, used for starting instead of a crank, as had been the case on the Waterloo

In a simpler time, fathers and sons worked the fields together. Back then, tractors simply pulled the tools behind them. It would take Theo Brown's imagination to begin poking holes through a frame to find places to mount implements and tools underneath, and in front of, as well as behind the tractor. Deere & Company Archives

Boys (and most other tractors) was an open 26-inch-diameter, six-spoked casting. It bolted onto the driveshaft. Witry and Leavitt not only had reversed the Waterloo Model N engine, but they also had improved the 6.5x7.0-inch horizontal twin, even though it remained coupled to a two-speed transmission.

Theo Brown's attention spread far beyond new tractor creation. He had dedicated several years to the concept of standardization. He had worked to reduce the number of tools needed to repair most implements, from 24 sizes and styles, to just four. He came into Model D development late in the process. It was not until late May and early June 1924 that Brown spent several days "in field with John Deere tractor and our various implements that will go with the tractor."

Witry, Leavitt, and Brown had observed numerous broken welds in the front axle from hitting rocks in the fields. They knew a solid casting would be stronger and also ensure better balance because of its greater weight. Beginning with the 51st model produced, the new front axle was a two-piece casting. Lightweight, short-wheelbase tractors such as the Fordson and the new Model D sometimes lifted their front wheels far off the ground if the plow caught. (Farm newspapers periodically reported that dozens of Fordson farmers had been injured or killed by the "rearing tractors," yet many other manufacturers experienced similar horrors.)

At the beginning of 1925, Deere replaced the original 26-inch-diameter flywheel with a 24-inch-diameter spoked version. Witry and Leavitt had concluded that the smaller, lighter-weight flywheel allowed slightly higher engine speed. Horsepower output increased with the smaller flywheels. Throughout the year, even as Brown directed plow, cultivator, and planter development, his involvement with tractors grew steadily.

CHAPTER 7
1925–1929

OHN DEERE

THEO BROWN'S MECHANICAL CULTIVATOR

For all the improvements in the farm tractor during the first 20 years of the twentieth century, it remained a machine for pulling. It started the crop-growing season by pulling a plow. It reappeared at harvest to run a thresher or pull a combine or binder. For decades, gasoline or kerosene tractors were best suited to the land and crops between the Mississippi River and the Rocky Mountains.

Theo Brown and others at Deere knew that farmers raising corn in the East and cotton in the South needed to cultivate their rows during the growing season. The tractors Deere and others produced in the early 1920s could not do that. J. S. Clapper, president of the Toro Motor Company of Minneapolis, was one of the most verbally aware of this shortcoming. Robert Williams quoted an interview with Clapper published in the *Automotive Industries* magazine issue of March 16, 1922, and reproduced in Williams' book *Fordson, Farmall and Poppin' Johnny: A History of the Farm Tractor and Its Impact on America*. Clapper appealed for "The All-Purpose Tractor on the Modern Farm."

"The most difficult operation in farming is the first and second cultivation of the tender plants and, unless the operator has an entirely unobstructed view of the rows and the machine has the necessary flexibility so that cultivating teeth or shovels will respond promptly to every move of the operator, good clean cultivation is not possible without injury to the plants. Unless we can give the farmer a machine capable of doing equally as good cultivation, easier and more economical to operate, and which will perform the work faster with less effort on his part than can be done with horses, we have little argument to persuade him that he should motorize his farm."

PREVIOUS: 1928 MODEL C
This machine came about because farmers wanted a tractor that could handle first and second cultivations. Deere's rival International Harvester had introduced its Farmall and so Theo Brown set out to develop an all-purpose model for Deere.

RIGHT: *Deere completed three prototypes in 1926, and 24 more in 1927 and it launched limited production of another 75 in 1928. By then, Deere's board called it the Model C, and engineering used it to help develop a new three-speed transmission as well as cultivation technology.*

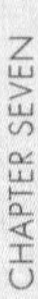

This was a great idea whose time never came. Here at Willard Velie's farm, an operator runs one of Theo Brown's prototype Model C general purpose tractors with a three-row cultivator. Misdirected by celebrated agricultural engineer, J. Brownlee Davidson into thinking three-rows was the sensible configuration, Brown and Deere spent months and months trying to make it work. Deere & Company Archives

Clapper preached to the choir, but he seemed to not suspect what his competition was doing. Things already were changing.

On July 17, 1923, the McCormick-Deering division of IHC registered the name "Farmall." International Harvester Corporation's engineers and board had used the term internally on prototype cultivators and tractors since November 1919. Soon after registering the name, implement designer Bert Benjamin and Tractor Works' chief engineer Ed Johnston completed assembly of 23 development tractors in various configurations and sizes, all called Farmall. Two of these eventually saw 15,000 hours of use, but tests on all 23 confirmed IHC's faith. Their board ordered production of 200 Farmalls for the 1924 introductory year, priced at $825 (nearly $8,700 today). This figure represented a substantial loss since these still were largely hand-made tractors. In the first four months, IHC sold 111 of them. At year's end, the price increased to $950 ($9,735 today) as production advanced from hand assembly to the regular production line. Profitability would soon follow.

The Farmall offered a narrow front wheel arrangement and wide rear tread width with high rear axle ground clearance. IHC, primarily an implement company just as Deere was, offered the new tractor with a complete line of implements. Deere board and family member Charles Wiman saw this new Farmall as a bold warning and a new challenge. While he believed Deere's Model D would succeed, he studied the Farmall and ordered Brown to design something similar.

Deere's board had offered Theo Brown board membership on April 24, 1923. Through the next year, board meetings often discussed the future of the tractor. Brown and the board saw their first Farmall on December 3, 1924, in IHC's Chicago showrooms on Michigan Avenue at the Chicago River. Five days later the directors in Moline "voted to increase tractor production from 3,000 to 3,800 next year."

In late January, Brown found an unexpected champion in Charles Deere Wiman, John Deere's great-grandson (and nephew of William Butterworth). Brown wrote about it in his diary on January 26:

"Charles Wiman wants me to take on gradually the general company job of being a sort of consulting engineer for the various factories in the line of experimental work . . . to give some real assistance to some of the factories that need it." His immediate assignment sent him to the Harvester Works to design a new corn picker to help in eradicating the devastating European Corn Borer infestation. However, company chairman William Butterworth added his own caveat to Wiman's assignment: "Don't take him away from the Plow Shop too much." It was from the plow shop that tractor ideas emerged.

In late June 1925, and again at the end of September, Brown traveled to the University of Iowa at Ames to meet with visiting engineering faculty member J. B. Davidson. With Davidson on Wednesday, September 30, Brown saw "new universal tractor drawings they have been working on."

"J. B. Davidson said:

1. Power furnished by gas tractor is cheaper than animal power.
2. Cultivation and harvesting of crops are obstacles to the use of the tractor.
3. Can a tractor be designed to plow and cultivate?
4. There is a demand for larger planting and cultivating units.

They rather favor 3 row outfits," Brown wrote at the end of the page.

On October 9, on another train to Ames from Moline, Brown synthesized everything that he'd seen so far into his own idea for an all-crop tractor. A week later, he completed a model of his idea, "to see how the cultivating units work. They look pretty good and seem to behave well in steering."

The solution to three-row planting, cultivating and harvesting was to develop a tricycle tractor with a narrow front end to slip between rows rather than to straddle them as the Model C had done. And then, create two or four row tools. By mid-1928, Deere had this GP Tricycle out testing. Deere & Company Archives

JOHN DEERE
JOHN DEERE

Brown's prototypes carried over the Model D wide front axle and wheel track width that straddled one row. As a result, he configured the new All Crop tractor as a three-row cultivator, following Davidson's hints. The machinery set one row outside each wheel and the third row below the center, beneath the tractor.

Within a few days, Brown mounted a three-row prototype cultivator on the front of a Fordson and took it into the fields for a demonstration to half a dozen engineers. H. B. McCray from Waterloo's tractor works told Brown he "was skeptical about the 3 row tractor . . . but after he had studied our model he said he was sold on the 3 row proposition." It was a sale that would come back to haunt them both.

One Era Ends, the Next Begins

On New Year's Eve, Deere finished 1925 on a positive note. Brown, as Deere's tireless engineer-at-large, had spent "100 days away from home, 47 nights on sleepers [trains], his employers closed a good year with $4,514,566 profits," (about $46.26 million today).

The first Model D production run of 1926 saw a new solid flywheel keyed onto the driveshaft of the tractors. Spinning spokes had injured some operators and the board deemed this change essential.

The board contemplated IHC's latest move. The Chicago firm announced on January 12, 1926, that it would accept No. 2 corn in payment for implements, exchanging one bushel for $1 (though Brown noted that No. 2 corn was going for .88 cents at that time). Within the next week, after reviewing Fordson sales for 1925 at 104,168 tractors, the board approved $25,000 in development money (nearly $255,000 today) for Brown's All Crop tractor. In the meanwhile, his next standardization challenge arose with an industry-wide effort to make power-take-off (PTO) shaft size and rotation speed uniform among all manufacturers.

OPPOSITE: 1928 Model GP with No. 1 Two-Way plow
By late 1928, the Model C had become the GP, terminology that was easier to understand over the scratchy phone lines of the day. The 5.75x6.0 inch horizontal two cylinder engine also has an uncommon flash-suppressor muffler on it.

BELOW: *For farmers working side hills, two way plows let them always fold the furrow uphill. Indiana collectors Paul and Mike Ostrander are dedicated and devoted students of Deere's general purpose models.*

1929 Model GP with Deere Model GP301 3-row cultivator

After many months of hard work developing and improving the three-row cultivators, Deere continued to produce 3-row systems into the early 1930s. By late 1929, Deere had moved the air cleaner above the engine into fresh, cooler air.

In short order, he added a mower to the All Crop, and by May 19 he had the first tractor ready for testing.

"All day with new tractor," he wrote that night, "first with cultivator. The power lift is fine, it works perfectly and is essential. It is possible to drive to the end of the corn, lift the rigs by power, turn around and come back in the adjoining row without stopping.

"We had some lost motion in the steering, which is bad with this arrangement. The Farmall has no lost motion and works much better than our outfit. One trouble is that the overhang of rigs on each side of center causes one side or the other to dig down and this tends to pull tractor to one side. Then one set of rigs is buried while [the] other is out of the ground. We decided to make a split frame, having carrying wheels on outside."

Still, it was not perfect.

The All Crop Takes on IHC's Farmall

"Started construction of cultivator," Brown wrote on Thursday, May 27. "We are convinced it is necessary to have flexibility. This is a real problem and we must soon get the answer as to whether or not the 3 row idea is workable."

Throughout June, he ran the All Crop and its three-row cultivator against the two-row Farmall. Deere's new flexible rig performed much better and steered more easily, especially after they "put on a Fordson steering wheel, which is larger." Yet Brown still found advantages to the Farmall, especially where its longer wheelbase and wider rear track made the ride over corn rows more comfortable while cross-cultivating.

Days later, Brown was in Omaha with J. B. Davidson comparing notes. On June 21, he wrote that Davidson "said he saw, on the Chapernan ranch near Corpus Christi, 4 Farmalls equipped with 4 row cultivators that farmers had made themselves by taking two 2-row Farmall cultivators and placing them side by side and then joining by flexible joints and gauge wheels. Davidson thinks this may have been done last year, although IHC built fifty 4-row cultivators in which extra rigs are placed at rear. These were condemned and not used. We should investigate this at once."

Barely a month later, July 23, 1926, Brown's assignment changed. "Charlie Wiman wants me to spend most of my time on All Crop problems and solutions. A Big Job," he wrote.

Charles Wiman, "Charlie" as Theo Brown now referred to him, had joined the firm a decade earlier in 1915 as a "line employee in the shop," earning 15 cents an hour according to Wayne Broehl. By 1919 Wiman had a seat on the board, and in 1924 it appointed him director of manufacturing just in time for the first wave of the Model D tractors. Both shop workers and board members liked and respected him. With the new tractor's increasing influence on company profit and policy, it was his efforts that had increased production to 3,800 tractors.

By October 21, Brown had a redesigned All Crop and cultivator ready for field tests. However, the three-row configuration still prompted head scratching. H. B. McKahin, Deere's Planter Works manager, watched it testing in Texas and pronounced it "unpopular." Yet Brown pressed ahead. Six weeks later, on December 7, he had a PTO gearbox ready for the machine.

Brown went through countless variations trying to make his cultivators perform flawlessly. The center plates guided the young plants safely past the sharp blades meant to sheer off weeds just below the soil surface.

1929 Model GP-WT with Deere Model GP201 2-row cultivator
The wide-tread configuration forced Brown and Waterloo's Elmer McCormick to devise a pedestal steering system and longer rear axles. Immediately, cultivating became easier as tractor operators could watch on both sides as plants slipped through the gates and weeds fell to the sharp shovels.

For the 1927 Model D, Deere splined the driveshaft to better secure the flywheel. It also enlarged the engine bore from 6.5 to 6.75 inches. In Brown's own small machine shop next to his office, a facility that Floyd Todd and Wiman arranged for him, tractor development continued as well. By early February, the board had such confidence in Brown's PTO experiments that they voted to include the device on each new tractor. Meanwhile Brown filled his time with All Crops and cultivators.

As spring lapsed into summer, Deere & Company regained solid financial footing. Brown, Todd, and, most influentially, Charlie Wiman worked to elevate the farm tractor's importance and influence within Deere's product lineup. Wiman continually promoted new developments that improved all of Deere's products. He looked carefully at his tractors' capabilities and limitations. He concluded that both the Model D and the new All-Crop machines had plenty of each.

Solving Problems by Building Experiments

To sort out the problems, the board authorized Brown on Monday, January 31, to "build 25 All Crop tractor outfits for this spring's use. It will mean training 12 men to look after these outfits in the field, to start them, etc. Agreed to build a 5 row cultivator to try out at Mercedes." (This was their winter test site in Mercedes, Texas, in the lower Rio Grande valley.)

In Texas, on March 2, 1927, "Today was a cultivator day. We had the Farmall and John Deere cultivating again." C. H. Hornburg, Deere's southern division sales manager, told Brown that he never thought corn could be cultivated with a tractor until watching Brown's demonstration. "However he is just not yet convinced that the 3 row idea is right. He says the blind middle row will not do," Brown wrote. "It seems of utmost importance that I stay here until the cultivator matter can be decided."

Hornburg questioned the blind row beneath the All Crop again three days later. As an experiment, Brown removed the middle row from their corn planter. "We succeed in planting with a good cross check. A trip across and back completes the cycle." Six days later, on March 16, Brown's diary read, "Busy on layout of revised 5 row cultivator. It is difficult designing."

Brown's sometimes cryptic diary next remarked that on April 12 and 13, 1927, "It looks now as though we had the basis of a real machine. We have started on a complete new layout, or rather a new machine. Many refinements."

Meanwhile progress continued on the All Crop tractor. Brown's April 26 entry referred to it as the Model C for the first time. The designation arose during the annual shareholder's meeting in conjunction with a quarterly directors meeting. In the afternoon, Brown brought them out "to the experimental farm to see the Model C tractor, planting, cultivating and harrowing. The cultivator did well. $875,000 was appropriated to put this tractor into production" (that would be nearly $9.05 million today).

By July, Deere was confident enough to announce the new machine. In a story published in the Chicago *Tribune* on Sunday, July 17, it claimed, "Company is putting out this season a few all work tractors, designed for row-crop cultivation and general farm purposes. The tractor, which apparently is still partly in the experimental stage, is said to straddle

JOHN DEERE

Theo Brown's contact, J. Brownlee Davidson from the University of California, led him to work vigorously on three row systems for Deere's GP. But IHC's Farmall pointed to an easier solution and Theo Brown and Waterloo's Elmer McCormick reconsidered their solution and devised the GP-Wide Tread, or GP Tricycle.

one row and cultivate three rows." More significantly, however, the story headlined the news that Deere & Company "now stands second in the farm implement manufacturing business of the world." Deere quoted a net income of $7.58 million, well behind IHC's $22.85 million. However, Deere had passed Case Threshing Machine Company to take the second spot.

On the next page of Brown's diary for Monday, July 18, he noted that Charles Webber "seems to feel we have gotten the cultivator in very good shape and thinks we should try selling some as two rows." Webber, at least, had decided the cultivator matter.

Deere's branch sales staff grew impatient. Farmall production in 1926 exceeded 4,000 units and output in 1927 topped 9,000 tractors. McCormick-Deering and IHC dealers had tractors to sell. For Wiman, even though the company's finances had improved, he still felt tense. Brown's three-row cultivators clearly were a question mark. The prototype Model C tractors also were coming up short on horsepower. Should Wiman order everything redesigned and launch new testing? That process would take two more years and it could set Deere back to third or even

1929 Model GP with Model GP201 2-row cotton and corn planter

Deere had become famous for its No. 9 and No. 999 horse-drawn planters that dropped seeds in precise increments that the operator could adjust. When Brown and his colleagues at Marseilles Planter Works adapted these machines to tractors, farming got easier and went much faster.

fourth place in the market. Or should Wiman go ahead with production and, as before, continue to develop and improve the product in the regular production series?

Another question still cried out: Was Deere to stick with its alphabetical heritage? The "Farmall" name had undeniable appeal and it quickly explained what IHC intended the tractor to do. Would the farmer distinguish between the Model D and the Model C? Around the board table, Wiman, Brown, Webber, and others heard names such as "Powerfarmer" and "Farmrite," and to everyone present these names had resonance. Still, Frank Silloway questioned how the Model C, less powerful and less capable than the D, could be called a "Powerfarmer." Yet he had heard objections from some of the branch salesmen. They worried, over the scratchy telephone lines of the day, that the letter C sounded like D. Branch or Waterloo plant staff might misunderstand. So it became *GP*, General Purpose, a name that would say it all with initials that would confuse no one.

Winter testing in California and Texas proved that the new Model C or GP compared favorably to IHC's McCormick-Deering 10-20. More encouraging yet, by leap year

ABOVE: *Test farm soil conditions in Texas and Arizona dictated development of unusual rear wheel styles. These slim bands wrapped with chunky grousers provided surprising traction in sandy conditions.*

RIGHT: *In his hurry to get the GP-WT models developed, Brown shipped tractors to Deere's test farm near Laredo, Texas and to Charlie Wiman's winter ranch in Arizona. The sandy soils they encountered there called for special wheels. The front cast "dish" style wheels sometimes were called "Texas wheels."*

OPPOSITE: *The shade inside the radiator brush guard regulated engine cooling depending on weather conditions. Mike and Paul Ostrander's early 1929 production GP featured the external steering mechanism and early off-set steering position.*

Wednesday, February 29, 1928, Brown had his first "tricycle" GP testing. (The term *tricycle* referred to its resemblance to a child's toy with a single or narrow-tread front end and wide-spread rear tires.) He fitted it with a two-row cultivator with steerable wheels for better maneuverability, or "dodge" around the tender young plants.

Wiman, Butterworth, and the board were impressed. In early 1928, after much discussion, on March 26 they authorized $3.9 million for construction of additional manufacturing facilities at Waterloo works. On April 24, Brown wrote that this would "increase D production to 100 per day and C's

JOHN DEERE

ABOVE: 1929 GP-EXPERIMENTAL
This is significant mechanical history and now a part of Walter Keller's exceptional collection in Wisconsin. Engineer Theo Brown experimented with a number of new developments on this tractor that included an over-the-top geared steering system and adjustable rear axles, developments that appeared in production years later.

INSET 1932 MODEL GP ORCHARD
Deere introduced the full-sheet metal covering for its GP models beginning in April 1931. Theo Brown and Elmer McCormick intended these tractors for orchard and grove applications where exposed rear wheels might damage or break tree branches.

OPPOSITE: *Brown shortened the air intake manifold and laid the filter on its side for better clearance. In all, Deere produced about 750 of these 4,250-pound sheet-metal clad tractors. They sold new for about $855, roughly $9,000 today.*

to 50 per day. [There was also] $250,000 for plow works expansion." Several board members objected, but Charles Webber argued that, "The tractor business is so definitely connected with our other tools. . . . We have suffered very much by not having sufficient tractors this year."

Three weeks later, in the *Farm Implement News* on June 28, 1928, Deere launched its General Purpose tractor: "Deere & Company have released their long anticipated general purpose tractor, to be known as the Model GP 10-20. The new model pulls two 14-inch bottoms, drives a 22-inch thresher, and plants and cultivates three rows of corn, cotton, or potatoes. In cultivating it straddles one row. . . .

"One man can cultivate as much ground in a day as four men with single-row cultivators and either horses or mules. The GP will handle from 25 to 40 acres a day depending on conditions. . . .

"The power take-off shaft is somewhat of an innovation, for it can be operated with either rear or front connections. The shaft turns clockwise at 520 rpm and has a separate gear shift. The inference is that some power take-off driven machine to be pushed in front of the tractor is in development." The magazine published four photos showing the GP with its three-row cultivator, a two-bottom plow, and a three-row planter.

By October, Waterloo manufactured 25 GPs each day. But an old concern reappeared. Deere and its customers expected the GP to produce 25 belt horsepower. Yet three weeks worth of production engines only had demonstrated 22.6 horsepower on test benches. The worry went beyond the new GP. For 1928, engineering enlarged the Model D cylinder bore by 0.25 inch, increasing output to 28 horsepower on the drawbar, 36 on the belt. But IHC had increased the bore of its 15-30 tractor by the same amount. That change reportedly added 5 and 12 horsepower to its drawbar and pulley ratings.

GP
JOHN DEERE

GP
OHN DEERE
JOHN DEER

LEFT: 1935 MODEL GP WITH DEERE 3-ROW CORN PLANTER
Deere's legendary planters, the No. 9 and No. 999, led Theo Brown to develop similar systems from his GP tractors. Gear driven turntables dropped seeds precisely in increments that Brown's innovative system controlled by a wire check-row apparatus.

OPPOSITE: *The wire drum ahead of the flywheel was an integral and crucial part of the success of Deere's tractor planters. As the wired played out, knobs on the wires triggered the planter to drop seeds precisely, ensuring the farmer's ease of cross cultivating fields.*

"With Charlie Wiman much of the day," Brown wrote in his diary Tuesday night, October 23, 1928. "He is very blue [underlining Brown's] because there has been complaint that the GP tractor is short of power. It did develop 25.6 HP and now only 22.6. It seems to me this should be rectified as soon as possible. He is discouraged (too easily) and thinks we should build a regular two plow tractor. All this is disturbing."

As Wayne Broehl reported, "Wiman even brought this issue to the board, telling them that he had 'given some thought to the proposition of making a straight two-plow tractor to be known as the Model B to either replace the GP or be an addition to the line.'" What's more, Wiman understood engineering. "No more horsepower," he stated, "could be built into our present Model D tractor without a pretty thorough redesign throughout. . . ."

Stories of overworked tractors breaking down and provoking finger-pointing, blame, and accusations of poor manufacturing and bad management came back to haunt Deere. Even after Brown's trials around Moline and on Texas test farms, GPs had troubles. They were failing. Some had required rebuilds in the fields. Worse, the three-row cultivator

JOHN DEERE

and other implements that Brown had conceived for the machine and that Deere had put into production were failures.

In addition, farmers found the steering difficult and inaccurate. Most GPs used a steering shaft that ran up the side of the engine. Road steering was a challenge. Brown and his design team returned to the drawing boards. In a one-year crash program, they produced a Farmall clone, the GP-Wide-Tread (GP-WT). Its narrowed front axle fit between two rows while its rear, widened like the Farmall's, straddled them. Brown and his engineers worked hard through the winter and spring on three-row and four-row cultivators and on a new tricycle tractor, completing the first 23 prototype GP-tricycles by mid-April 1929. Charlie Wiman was so confident about the wide-tread model that he authorized Waterloo production even before Brown ran his first field test.

Deere had its GP-WT available in time for spring planting. It met immediate acceptance in the South and Midwest. Wiman's bold gamble paid off. This ensured Deere would hold on to second place in the implement industry. Yet Wiman and Brown had luck too. Henry Ford, who had declared war on all tractor competitors, surrendered. The shortcomings of his little Fordson, and his refusal to improve or upgrade the simple machine, finally overcame price advantages. By the end of 1928, Ford conceded defeat. He moved tractor production to Cork, Ireland, and abandoned the business in the United States. Deere's tractor operation moved into second place as well, runner up to International Harvester.

Despite this encouragement, there were dark clouds on the horizon. After the director's meeting on May 21, 1929, Brown wrote in his diary, "A note of pessimism was sounded about 75-cent wheat and a depression in our business. Combines are moving very slowly."

They sensed but could not know. Real disaster was coming. When it gripped the country, 75-cent wheat would seem extravagant, and some of Deere's equipment would stop selling altogether.

LEFT: 1935 MODEL GP WITH SWEEP RAKE

This represents "mass production" woodwork from another era even while it is a recent restoration. While Deere produced approximately 30,750 GP models from 1927 through 1935, there is no good estimate of the number of sweep rakes that the company turned out.

OPPOSITE: *Once farmers cut and bound the grain shocks, they left them standing in the fields to dry out. Gathering the dried shocks was usually hand work until Brown and Deere's East Moline Harvester Works crews perfected mechanical (and later hydraulic) lifts. Then a shock sweep or sweep rake to effortlessly gather the dried shocks this became a near necessity.*

CHAPTER 8
1929–1935

JOHN DEERE

A SPECIAL TRACTOR

FOR EVERY CROP AND EVERY REGION

PREVIOUS: 1935 MODEL GP-O LINDEMAN CRAWLER
Jesse Lindeman in Yakima, WA, produced one of the most interesting Model GP variations with his crawler-version of the orchard model. Lindeman previously had done the first orchard version from a GP standard that Waterloo shipped out to him in 1929.

RIGHT: *Standard GP models stood 55 inches tall to the radiator cap but the Lindeman crawler version slunk down to about 45 inches, providing better clearance under low hanging tree branches. After using Best tracks for his prototype, Lindeman began casting his own tracks for his production run.*

It became a vicious circle. Just as tractors became more general in purpose and all-crop in execution, branch sales people and implement dealers devised special requirements and found new uses for the tractors.

Of the 23 original GP-Tricycles, Brown's engineers assembled about half-a-dozen with narrower rear wheel rims using 8-inch treads instead of 10s. They tapped square holes into the steel rims. They narrowed the rear track from 74 inches to meet the needs of potato growers in Maine.

Following the first six "prototypes," the factory issued an order in mid-November 1929 to assemble an estimated 150 "Series P" tractors per year. Known as "decision copy," the authorizing document circulated originally among those who needed to know. Decades later, it appeared in the Two-Cylinder Club's *Collector Series Volume I.*

"To meet the requirements for potato culture we will make a Series 'P' tractor which is similar to the General Purpose Wide-Tread tractor except change wheel tread to 68 inches by making shorter right and left quills, differential shaft, right and left brake cams and drawbar. Use standard front wheels 24 x 4 inches equipped with standard General Purpose guide bands. Use 44 x 8 inch rear wheels punched so that either 24 or 16 lugs per wheel may be used. . . . Power shaft and lift complete will be furnished standard with tractor, a new lift pendulum being required for the Series 'P' tractor. . . .

"A new serial number plate will be used, numbers beginning with P5000."

According to Two-Cylinder Club research, production reached 203 in 1930. But that was the only year Deere produced these models. During that time, Brown's staff designed a new rear wheel

OHN DEERE

RIGHT: INTEGRAL POWER LIFT IDEA
Theo Brown spent months working on an integral implement lift system. This version, from February 16, 1932, used the PTO and a geared shaft to operate a pivoting rock shaft. His note above, written near the depths of the Great Depression, reminded him and other engineers of their need to conserve Deere's funds wherever possible.

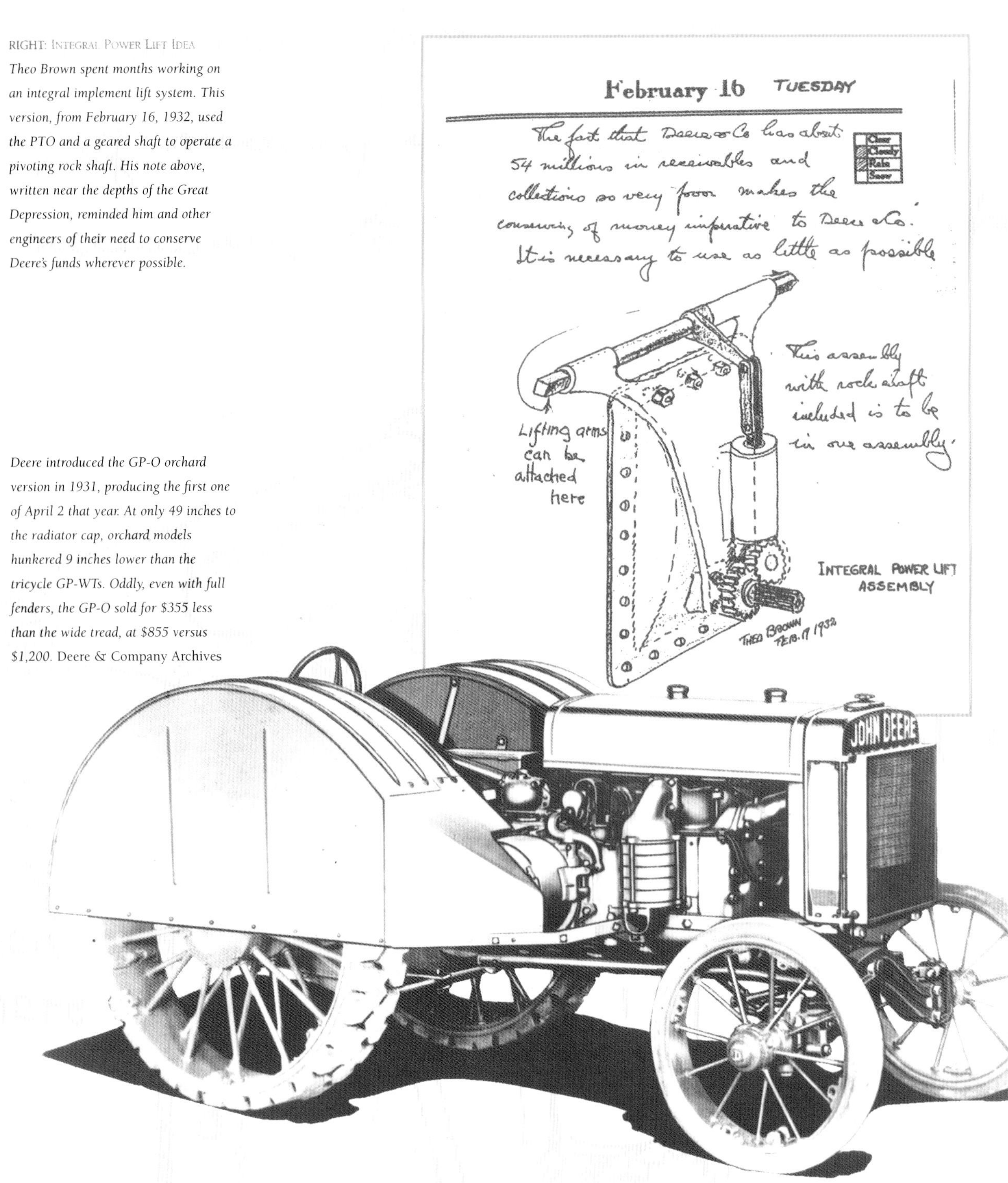

Deere introduced the GP-O orchard version in 1931, producing the first one of April 2 that year. At only 49 inches to the radiator cap, orchard models hunkered 9 inches lower than the tricycle GP-WTs. Oddly, even with full fenders, the GP-O sold for $355 less than the wide tread, at $855 versus $1,200. Deere & Company Archives

with a 3-inch offset that could be reversed on the shaft to accomplish the 68-inch tread width Maine farmers wanted. Deere retained the parallel front wheels, known as the "bedding" front end, standard on the P tractors, as an option after the factory discontinued P production. Shipping records indicated that the factory delivered all of the 203 Model Ps to branch houses or directly to farmers in the Northeast and in eastern Canada.

Another "decision copy," dated January 22, 1931, marked the end of the Series P, again quoted from Two-Cylinder Club research:

"To standardize equipment and to continue to furnish a tractor for potato cultivation we will discontinue production of the Series 'P' tractor and furnish instead a Wide-Tread tractor with special offset wheels to provide the same tread as now obtained with the Series 'P.'"

GP-O models worked as well beneath the trees as between them. Here an operator mows grass in an orchard in mid-July 1935, a few months after Deere ended production. The company assembled six experimentals and about 600 production models between 1930 and April 1935. Deere & Company Archives

1935 Model GP-O Lindeman Crawler
Throughout 1934 and 1935, Deere shipped 25 GP-O chassis out to Lindeman. He converted them to crawlers for his local customers growing apples on the sandy soils around Yakima, WA.

As specialized configurations took on wider applications, Deere's engineers responded.

In 1931 Brown and the others answered a longstanding criticism of the operator's position on the GP and the D. They relocated the steering wheel and gear to the tractor's right side. They also increased the D's engine governor speed from 800 to 900 rpm.

Meanwhile, farther west in Michigan, another crop-specific need arose. Historian and GP enthusiast Paul Ostrander, has investigated the curious and convoluted history of the "GP Special Equipment" models that Deere first conceived in 1930. In a story published in *Two Cylinder* magazine, Ostrander quoted "Decision 3148," dated April 21, 1930.

"To meet the demand from the field for a tractor to use on 28-inch rows we will provide 25 front axles and wheel assemblies to accomplish the following:

"1. Front wheel with detachable hub which can be used in two positions to give 50-inch tread.

"2. Due to increased loading we will use larger Timken bearings in front wheel, larger knuckles, spindles and a new front axle with increased section [ground clearance] directly under the center pivot.

"3. Rear wheels will be assembled in reverse position from present practice to change the tread from 29-1/2 to 55 inches.

"4. These 25 assemblies are to be made this year to go with the Cultivator made by the Plow Works, 20 of which are to be ready for shipment on or before April 15, and the engineering department will arrange to deliver the parts added by this decision to the sales department."

Then, on November 13, Brown sat in on a meeting with a number of other engineers and tractor planners at Waterloo to discuss improvements to the GP. In it, they decided:

"1. To make front axle for Michigan (adjustable).

"2. To make tractor strong enough so rear wheels can be reversed.

"3. To make front axle for California for 56-inch tread and then for 28-inch bean rows, there to use regular GP tractor with rear wheels reversed.

"4. To use this regular GP with Michigan equipment for Colorado and Wyoming.

"5. For 20-22-24-inch beet rows to use Wide Tread tractor and the Tractor Company [Waterloo] to work out proper wheel for these conditions.

"6. [Waterloo] has designed and will make heavier wheel to make Wide Tread suitable for 34-inch rows which means 68-inch tread."

And finally, "Swinging seat. [Waterloo] agrees to furnish swinging seat and to have ready January 1." Most, but not all, bean tractors appeared with the swing seat option.

Two months later, on January 21, 1931, Deere announced the bean front end, "GP Special Equipment AC773 Replacement Front Axle," in Decision #3682.

"To meet the demand from the field for a tractor for use on 28-inch rows as well as 42-inch rows, and give substantially equal clearance between front wheels and rows under

Converting these crawlers was a hand full of work. The two tall levers operated track clutches but with one side disengaged, the operation of the differential seemed to speed up the other side, making the tractor seem faster as it turned.

RIGHT: 1932 MODEL GP BEAN TRACTOR *To suit farming conditions that bean farmers in Michigan and northern Indiana faced, Theo Brown devised a new front axle. This provided 50-inch tread width in order to work on 28-inch bean rows. Brown and fellow engineers also replaced the front spindles, knuckles, and wheel bearings to handle the increased loading.*

OPPOSITE: *As time went on, Brown and his colleagues expanded their production to accommodate growers in California, Colorado, and Wyoming. By January 21, 1931, this modification had an official designation: "GP Special Equipment AC773 Replacement Front Axle."*

either condition of row spacing, we will adopt, as extra equipment to be furnished on special order only, a longer axle, which, fitted with standard "GP" wheels and knuckles, will give a 54-inch tread. Estimated annual requirement 350 complete assemblies.

"To provide better steering characteristics on this tractor, the steering arms have been re-designed to locate the tie rod behind axle and drag link to equalize the action of steering wheel each side of straight position."

The estimate of 350 assemblies proved wildly optimistic. Back on October 29, 1929, the New York Stock Exchange had crashed. The investment bubble fueled by the beginning of World War I finally had burst. Its immediate impact devastated the financial capitals of the United States and Europe. It took two years for its effects to move into America's farm land. In New York City, stock brokers jumped out of office windows to their deaths that day. In the Midwest, and across the rest of the country, farmers and others perished slowly, or else they barely subsisted. Ironically, many of them lived on beans for half a year or longer.

Perhaps because of this, by 1933 Deere had created a specific bean tractor, model AC890. A decision, #4337, dated March 2, 1933, at about the deepest point of the Depression, offered both GP orchard models and AC890 Bean Tractors on Firestone low-pressure rubber tires. It was a $60 option ($833 in 2003) that fitted 6.00x16 front and 11.25x24 rear tires to the machines.

JOHN DEERE
JOHN DEERE

RIGHT: 1932 MODEL GP BEAN TRACTOR WITH DEERE 4-ROW INTEGRAL CULTIVATOR
Neither Elmer McCormick nor Theo Brown had yet solved the visibility restrictions that upright exhaust pipes and air intakes caused. Deere introduced pneumatic rubber on bean tractors as a $60 option in March 1933.

OPPOSITE: *Almost the only way Deere's GP could accommodate four-row cultivation was with the wider tread width that GP Bean tractor model AC890s granted. For the operator, it was an act of faith that the two inboard panels were protecting the plants and not slicing them off.*

Deere's usually exemplary factory production records slacked during the early 1930s. The shortened work weeks and greatly reduced staffs make some history more difficult to reconstruct. Using a mix of intuition and factory records, Ostrander has theorized that Deere may have produced as many as 120 of these specialized machines. Factory records confirm the assembly of 66 of the AC890 models in 1934 and 1935 alone as the economy began its New Deal-driven recover. With the wider axles and special wheels, the bean models offer further evidence that Deere's General Purpose tractors often were special purpose machines.

About 2,000 miles west of Michigan's bean growers, and some 2,800 miles west of the potato farmers in Maine, another customer in Yakima, Washington, wanted his tractors without any wheels at all.

In 1920, Jesse Lindeman was barely 20 years old when he moved from western Iowa to central Washington. Two years later, when his brother Harry turned 20, they started Lindeman Power Equipment Company, selling Holt crawlers and harvesters in the Yakima River and Naches River valleys. In 1925, the C. L. Best Gas Traction Company and Holt Manufacturing consolidated assets and dealers under the name Caterpillar Tractor Company. The Lindeman brothers missed the cut. They quickly picked up a Cleveland Tractor Company "Cletrac" franchise. Crawlers were a near-necessity in the sandy, hilly terrain where the prevalent crop was tree-grown fruit. The Lindemans found few faults initially with the Cletracs and quickly became one of Washington's largest dealers.

In 1930, Jesse Lindeman became a full-line Deere dealer. He had lost his brother Harry due to a fatal auto accident, but now his youngest brother, Ross, joined him in Yakima. Rollin White, Cletrac's owner, had begun "tinkering" with his company and its machines. The crawlers slipped in quality. Deere's Model D impressed the Lindemans very much.

"What struck us," Jesse Lindeman recalled shortly before his death in 1992, "was that here was this wheel tractor, this Model D, and this engine burned what we called 'stove top,' this fuel that cost six-and-a-half cents a gallon, no tax. And all these farmers out here not only wanted that, but they had to have crawler tracks on it.

"So we just looked in our warehouse and found a used set of Best Thirty tracks and rollers," he explained. "It was a simple enough thing to do, but it was ugly!"

JOHN DEERE

Little brother Joe Lindeman did the tractor testing near Rim Rock at the north end of the valley. The D-crawler got the attention of other farmers in the region and the Lindemans assembled two more. Handling the tractor was a challenge. Like the Cletrac, it turned only with the use of track brakes that served as steering brakes. Farmers tugged hard on brake levers, fighting the power of the engine. This meant, Lindeman said, "It didn't turn very well. Track clutches had existed on some of the earlier Best and Holt crawlers, but we hadn't figured out that adaptation quite yet."

For a short while in late 1931 and early 1932, Deere's experimental department assembled eight or ten Model Ds as crawlers. But these "DCs" turned using wheel brakes, and while this worked, it was not satisfactory. Engineering shelved the project and then dismantled the prototypes and used the parts for other projects.

Ben Keator, Deere's Portland branch manager, and Pat Murphy, his sales manager, came to Jesse Lindeman with a new proposition. Deere was interested in producing an orchard and grove version of its new GP. Well aware of the work the Lindemans had accomplished with their D-O crawler, the engineering staff in Waterloo, begrudgingly, wondered if Lindeman would be interested in doing some development work.

"You better believe those engineers back in those wheel tractor plants were mad as the devil. As one fellow put it, 'Crawler tractors back here are a dirty word.' It was something you didn't speak about." Creativity is always viewed as the proprietary right of staff engineers and designers.

But a prejudice against crawlers was not hard to understand either. While both Best and Holt crawlers originated in central California, following their consolidation they relocated to Peoria, Illinois. Their goal was to be more centrally located to farming and construction needs throughout the Midwest and East. Caterpillar was an aggressive competitor.

Moline shipped a production GP to Yakima. Jesse examined the new tractor, modified its front end and reversed the rear axle gear clusters. This dropped its overall height nearly 7 inches. Now it fit more easily beneath the apple trees growing in central Washington. This tractor steered using track brakes, just as the Lindeman, the factory D experimental models and the Cletracs had done. This system was a handful. The differential speed made the outside track turn twice as fast as the braked inside track moved. The tractor actually seemed to go faster through turns.

Waterloo assembled five additional orchard versions based on the Lindeman modifications. Deere shipped one to southern California and the others went to the central California coast during the summer of 1933. Successful results produced the authorization to begin regular production.

Industry-wide, tractor makers were adding gears to their transmissions. For model year 1935, Deere introduced three-speed transmissions for the Model D. Demand for the new Ds surged.

"It was easier for a while for us to get the newer GP tractors," Lindeman said. Not only was it easier for them to obtain the GP, but also it was less challenging to adapt them to crawler tracks. "We didn't even have to change the drive! They had a chain drive on

the D-O and we had to change it to a smaller chain sprocket. And we put the fenders on it to get under the trees."

Lindeman and the factory included an elaborately plumbed intake manifold that relocated the air filter near the operator's right shoulder. However, Lindeman completed his work developing factory models, he turned his attentions again to the kind of machine his own customers needed.

He and his brothers converted 24 GPs into GP-O Lindeman crawlers. On some, they fitted long fenders for orchard applications. On others, without any fenders at all, they saved weight and costs. They configured the second generation of these tractors with steering clutches. These disengaged the drive from the inside track. When the farmer opeated the track brake as well, turning the crawler was easier and safer.

Deere's factory records indicate that Waterloo assembled 66 of these bean models during 1934 and 1935 though information is very vague for the earlier years. GP historian Paul Ostrander estimates total production nearer 120 bean models between 1931 and 1935. Michigan collector Mike Holder found and restored this example.

JOHN DEERE
JOHN DEERE

(Lindeman fitted, or refitted, all but one of the GP-O crawlers with steering clutches.) These improved machines earned new attention from Murphy's Portland branch office for Deere & Company Plow Works. Murphy and Keator both helped Jesse Lindeman get parts and they helped Deere engineers get a further look at Lindeman's modifications.

"When we got it finished," Lindeman recalled, "the John Deere people came out and they were impressed. And they looked it over carefully. What happened was they said, 'You must identify this as *not* a John Deere tractor. You used John Deere parts but it's a Lindeman.'

"I would have done the same thing. So we called it the Lindeman John Deere—of course we liked the John Deere name because it sold tractors." He hesitated for a moment. "Although now I hear that they refer to our tractors as John Deere Lindemans. Now they paint the Lindeman letters in the end plates yellow. I keep telling them we were too modest for that.

"The heck we were! We never thought of it!" Marketing was an unknown language to Lindeman. Sales took care of themselves—they sold all they could make.

"Keator and Murphy came out one time and talked about another new tractor, a smaller one. They asked if tracks could be fitted to a smaller tractor. Well, we were game." The Portland branchmen got sketches and drawings of the wheeled version to Lindeman.

"So they got us an early chassis," Lindeman continued. "It had no front or rear wheel assemblies. Just driveshafts and axle bolts. We drilled no more than ten holes in that whole tractor to attach our tracks. It was just lucky!"

As he thought back to that project, he laughed once more. With all the other work he had done for Deere & Company and on his own products as well, it was this one that would secure his place in agricultural history.

"Believe me," Lindeman, his eyes bright with the memory, "they didn't plan for any kind of crawler adaptation when they designed their Model B. It was really just lucky."

ABOVE: 1935 MODEL GP-O
The GP variation of the two-cylinder engine was 6.0 x 6.0 inches, or 339 cubic inches total displacement. At 950 rpm, the engine developed 18.9 horsepower on the drawbar and 25.4 on the belt pulley

OPPOSITE: *Deere manufactured its first GP Orchard model on April 2, 1931. Starting in October 1933, farmers could buy GP-O models on inflatable rubber tires for about $915, about $10,000 today. The cast Kay Brunner wheels were available through dealers.*

CHAPTER 9

1930–1937

JOHN DEERE
DEERE

DEPRESSION AND RENAISSANCE

American farmers put nearly 230,000 more tractors to work on their farms between 1925 and 1929. Their population in the United States surged upward from 549,000 to 782,000 during that time, thanks to machines such as Deere's Model D and the new GP. According to the United States Department of Agriculture (USDA), that count reached 1,000,000 by the end of 1931. Despite the Depression that devastated the nation by then, the USDA estimated that one farmer out of every six owned a tractor. To Deere's board, it signaled growing acceptance of the machine. To people like Charlie Wiman, it revealed a huge market left untapped once the economy improved: five out of every six farmers didn't yet own one.

Three landmark developments filled the decade from 1924 to 1934. Some historians suggest that IHC's Farmall launched "the Industrial Revolution in Agriculture." Its performance capabilities catalyzed Deere's engineering efforts. The second landmark, however, came from Deere, and its effect on other manufacturers was equally powerful. Once Theo Brown had perfected C. H. Melvin's power lift, Deere offered it on the GP starting in 1929. A Works Progress Administration (WPA) study concluded that this one invention saved each farmer 30 minutes every day because operators could pull a lever from their seat, rather than get off the tractor to raise or lower the implement by hand. The WPA suggested that the Power Lift might have saved a total of 1,000,000 man-hours a year! It was beyond the WPA's scope to estimate the muscle strain that Deere's power-lift alleviated.

PREVIOUS: 1935 MODEL A WITH DEERE MODEL 25 FRONT LOADER *Deere's new tractor presented a number of changes and improvements over the previous D, GP, and GP-WT models. Elmer McCormick added a frame to increase strength and he narrowed everything as much as possible to improve forward visibility.*

RIGHT: *Before hydraulics, cables raised and gravity lowered front lifts and other implements and tractor-mounted tools.*

JOHN

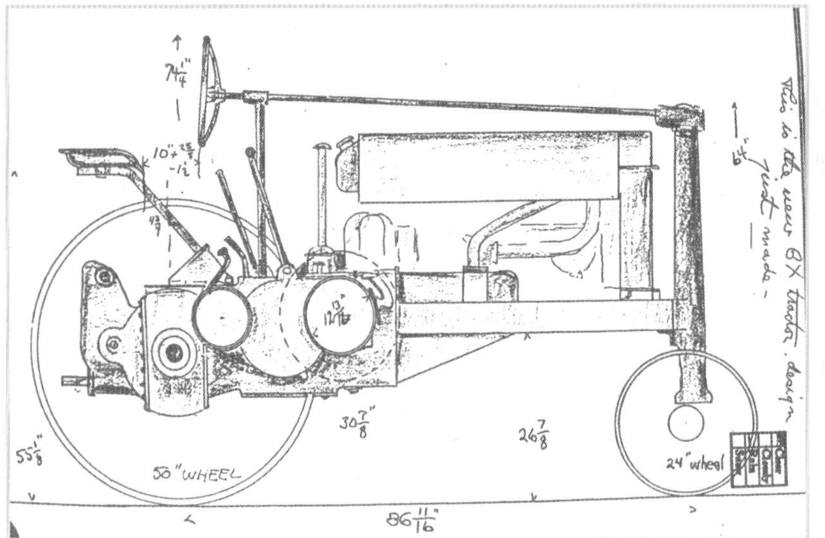

New G.X. Prototype Tractor

Brown's elevation drawing of the latest prototype tractor appeared in his diary on June 25, 1932. Its steering gear over the top of the small radiator shows the earliest thinking on how the Model B would come to production on steel wheels two years later.

Another Integral Power Lift Idea

Brown devised this implement lift version on April 22, 1933. His concept here used a "high grade worm and worm gear in oil inside cover." He employed a clutch to engage or disengage the worm and gear, connected by linkages to a rock shaft mounted on hangers separate from the mechanism casting.

The third development came from outside the farm tractor industry. Conflicting reports still add mystery to where the real credit belongs for the arrival of pneumatic rubber tires on farm tractors. Some say Allis-Chalmers' president, Harry C. Merritt, had to pilfer some aircraft tires from his friend Harvey Firestone to use as trials on the tractors and implements at his farm. Others insist that hobby-farmer and tire manufacturer/promoter Firestone did this first on his Allis-Chalmers-equipped farm. Then Firestone force-fed the concept to Merritt. (To further obscure the parentage of the idea, some historians report that Florida orange grove owners mounted truck tires on Farmall tractors in the mid-1920s since steel wheels damaged tree roots. Iowa corn farmers may have used them on their tractors as well when towing wagons to town.) The true origin matters only to historians set on granting a significant contribution its rightful ownership.

Rubber tires, or "air tires," as farmers called them, delivered a significant improvement in fuel economy, pulling power, road speed, farmer comfort, and safety. It's probable that the arrival of pneumatic rubber tires on the farm marked the beginning of the end of horse and mule farming. Farmers could see this turning point starting with the earliest tests in 1930 and 1931. Operator comfort was an important consideration in farmers and manufacturers accepting the new tire technology; Deere's latest overhead worm-and-sector steering system was much more precise, but it had taken all the road-impact-absorbing slack out of the previous linkages. The ride on steel wheels hammered the farmer's arms and shoulders on dirt or on gravel roads. Pneumatic tires cushioned every part of the operator's body. What's more, soft rubber tires allowed farmers to tow their produce wagons into towns with paved streets.

As early as September 1925, Deere had obtained horse-versus-tractor farming cost studies from Iowa State University's J. B. Davidson. Factoring in veterinary and blacksmith fees, Davidson calculated the value of time spent waiting while animals rested at the end of each row, and time spent hitching and unhitching the team morning, noon, and night. He showed figures to Brown proving that horse farming cost nearly twice as much per acre as gas tractor farming. The economics of owning and feeding a five-or-more horse team included the fact that farmers dedicated nearly one-quarter of their land to the animals' feed. Still, horse farming was the only option for operations smaller than 100 acres in those days. Charlie Wiman was not surprised when the 1930 Census revealed that four out of five American farms fit this category. He recognized that the small two-plow tractor signaled the beginning of a new way of life for some farmers. His goal was to reach the others who simply never trusted anything new.

New Products in Lean Times

Wiman pushed Brown and his staff to start on new products and new ideas in 1931. On the first work day of the year, Brown revised the GP tractor to include a live rear axle with reversible wheels and an extended splined axle. "Half the change in tread can be made by sliding the wheel and the other half by reversing," he wrote. Four days later, these reversible wheels had become part of the specification for the Model P potato tractor.

In 1932, International Harvester Corporation again led the way in tractors. It announced its new F-12 Farmall, a reduced-scale version of the second-generation Farmall, the F-20. Deere's limited tractor lineup put its competitive standing at risk. Three years after the stock market crash, the economy in 1932 hit bottom. Tractor manufacturer bankruptcies were nearly as common as bank foreclosures and farm auctions. Cotton that had sold for 10 cents a pound in 1930 returned 3 cents a pound in 1932. Wheat brought 12 cents per bushel and cattle were worth only $4.14 per hundredweight. A Midwestern drought made things worse. Thousands of families lost everything. Yet farmers have always been hard workers who refuse to surrender even in the face of indisputable odds. As a result, these same farmers harvested some 371 million acres in 1932, more than ever before in U.S. history. Those who could survive lived on beans for months and they had plentiful supply, for there was no market. Of 186 companies manufacturing or claiming to produce farm tractors in 1922, only 38 remained in 1930. Yet Deere, in business more than 90 years by then, had weathered similar economies.

In late May 1930, Deere shut down its tractor plant; "poor business," was how Brown described the cause in his diary. Yet business sometimes got surprised; in early August the board accepted an order for 4,000 tractors that Waterloo would manufacture and ship to Russia. This order kept the plant operating. Charlie Wiman and others on his board knew that things always turned around. Sometimes it took longer than other times, and sometimes elements of luck, such as the Russian order, were the cause. However, in order to profit when the money was widely available, Wiman knew his company had to develop new products even when financial support was tight. (In mid-December, as business slowed again, Deere's common stock settled at $29 1/8. It had reached $309 on March 26, 1928 (about $3,250 per share today). Having lost 90 percent of its value, Brown noted it was "the lowest for a long time. It might be time to buy. Business is not good. There is much unemployment."

Brown's adjustable rear axle worked by releasing a bolt and then driving the tractor forward or backward. The operator used the differential brake to hold the live axle from rotating. The wheel screwed itself in or out.

In early February, Brown led another meeting to consider "what a new general purpose tractor should be."

"It looks as though live axle and 48 inch wheels would be best for every place except the south where bedded rows are, and here we will need more clearance," he said, according to records of the meeting.

"30 horsepower with a layout of both 2 and 4 cylinder motors, integral power lift, etc.

"We are going to follow competitor's outfits carefully in the field this season."

On Friday, March 20, during a director's quarterly meeting, Brown outlined "the requirements for a General Purpose tractor." He tried to show the need for clearance under a tractor.

"There are two major requirements for a tractor:

"1. Stability

"2. Accessibility

And two for a cultivator:

"3. Clearance

"4. View

"It seems questionable whether a 2 cylinder motor can meet these requirements."

Elmer McCormick, an innovative engineer working at Waterloo, and others at the tractor plant, pushed for more cylinders. Wiman intervened and by late May, after enduring another push for four-cylinder engines from Waterloo, Brown got the go-ahead for a new two-cylinder prototype with his adjustable rear axles.

The economy guided the board's decision to stick with two-cylinder engines. Developing a new multicylinder powerplant would have cost Deere close to $250,000 (about $3 million in today's dollars). It was money Deere was unwilling to spend. Orders for tractors and implements had nearly stopped coming in. During Deere's June 17 director's meeting, the board discussed the effects of the Depression. It ordered all employees to take two weeks "vacation" on their own time.

By early July, Elmer McCormick had produced a workable prototype. He showed this new machine to Wiman, Brown, and others in Waterloo's test fields. But first, he demonstrated current Allis-Chalmers, IHC, and Graham-Bradley models.

"McCormick showed us a modified model of the Wide Tread GP in which the view was wonderfully improved. The fuel tank was tapered so as not to interfere with the eye from tractor seat. The seat was raised and brought forward to help see over pulley, the steering put on top of tractor, the air cleaner and muffler taken off the outside and

While it beat hand shoveling by a long shot, the front loader made it a greater challenge to get onto the A. The rope at left dumps the front loader.

1937 Model A with R. J. Piper posthole digger

R. J. Piper Manufacturing produced these front-mounted posthole diggers for Deere and other tractor makers. The digger ran off the belt pulley and used a little human muscle power.

out of the line of vision. His idea is not to make any more wide tread tractors unless new design."

During another demonstration in mid-September, the engineers devised the idea of making the seat adjustable, both up and down and forward and back. They also proposed raising the steering wheel three inches up and extending it 3 inches back.

Other Costs of the Depression

Their work, paychecks, and the isolation of thinking far into the future insulated Deere's engineers from the economy to some extent. For those outside the test farms and engineering labs, living was rough. It got to Brown. On October 13, he wrote, "With everything so quiet, it is very hard to get any enthusiasm in work. It is depressing to learn so much about hard times, cutting expenses, etc. An experimental man needs enthusiasm to do good work and I can see how this depression affects original thinking." Yet within days, Brown had conceived an expanded metal floor mat/boot scraper that one of Deere's plants easily could produce from cheap materials. It was a way to keep the company's workers employed. Wiman loved the idea. He assigned 200 men to make the scrapers, working three days a week for $3 a day. The workers could produce three during their shift. Deere's cost of materials was just 10 cents per mat. After 12 weeks of work, the board decided that it would give away the 21,000 metal mats to its farmer customers as a thank you for their business. By November 16, Deere had 250 men working on mats at the Plow Works. This reopened a plant that the board had shut down for six months when new orders almost stopped.

Guarded Optimism and a New Tractor

On a cold Tuesday, November 24, 1931, Brown again went to Waterloo. He drove out to see what Elmer McCormick and his staff had been working on. As snow flurries blew around them, they glimpsed the next generation tractor.

"The new FX tractor was assembled and we saw it for the first time. We were much impressed with its looks. It ran as quietly as a 4 cylinder and without vibration. Weight 4,600 pounds. 29 horsepower. . . .

"We considered making FX 36 horsepower and then making another tractor of 24 horsepower on same lines." On December 30, the board approved both of McCormick's new machines, the FX, as a likely Model D replacement, and its smaller companion, the GX. However, development proceeded slowly. At year end, Brown noted that Deere had nearly $54 million dollars in receivables, yet "collections are so poor that we must conserve everywhere." In late April 1932, matters had not improved. The board ordered all management to take a month off without pay sometime before October 1, the end of their fiscal year.

Elmer McCormick had completed large-scale drawings of the companion GX tractor and he offered them for inspection in late May 1932. Brown liked what he saw and he brought blue prints back to Moline for his engineers to use developing plows and cultivators.

On a hot day in mid-July, Max Sklovsky introduced his new small tractor to Deere's Power Farming Committee. This was a machine that he had devised quietly starting in late

R.J.PIPER
MF'G. CO.
PRINCETON. ILL
JOHN DEERE

ABOVE: 1937 Model A with R. J. Piper posthole digger

Piper's posthole digger worked best with an operator on the front platform to direct the tractor operator. The combination, however, put a huge load on the front wheels and made steering and maneuvering quite difficult.

RIGHT: *Deere used a number of magneto manufacturers for ignition for the A. This Wico was popular but Deere also specified Fairbanks Morse models as well.*

winter 1931 and that he continued developing through spring 1932. He had configured the machine as strictly a cultivator on a reversed tricycle frame using two front 24-inch diameter steerable wheels that he positioned 68 inches apart. Sklovsky propelled his machine through a single 34-inch diameter rear wheel. He told Brown and Wiman it would easily pull a single 16-inch plow. While Wiman was very enthusiastic, Brown worried about its steering. A decade earlier, Joe Dain had developed cultivator prototypes that had failed because they were unmanageable at the ends of the rows even though they maneuvered well among the crops. The front mounted cultivators placed too much weight on the steering wheels. After hearing Brown's opinions, Wiman tempered his interest.

Elmer McCormick moved ahead with his GX. On September 14, Brown, Harold White, Ben Kougle, and Ted Johnson, all Moline engineers and members of the Power Farming Committee, went to Waterloo to see McCormick's prototype run.

"It is a fine looking job, very clean, simple, and attractive," Brown wrote at home that night. "I drove it in the field and it handled very well. Steering was very easy and

JOHN DEERE
GENERAL PURPOSE
REG. U.S. PAT. OFF.

1937 Model AOS

The Orchard models dropped the operator's seat and shrouded much of the tractor's mechanical workings behind branch-saving sheet metal coverings. Walter Keller's tractor here is one of two AO-S experimentals that fitted an oil dipstick behind the flywheel.

Intended for apple orchards such as this, the streamlined orchard models moved air intakes and mufflers inside the sheet metal. As the tractor moved through the groves of trees, nothing on the machine caught onto branches.

JOHN DEERE
JOHN DEERE

positive. View was excellent." McCormick told them that the GX weighed 3,702 pounds, compared to the 1932 Model GP at 4,558. Waterloo tested the engine and recorded 24.75 horsepower.

Barely two weeks later, Brown got to operate McCormick's GX using Brown's four-row cultivator. "The view and handling are wonderful. The 1932 tractor and cultivator [were] in field too. The GX is so far ahead of 1932 Wide Tread that there is no comparison."

Two weeks after that, on October 13, Brown's Power Farming Committee "went to Clyde Ford's farm in Geneseo to see balloon rubber tires on a GP with 2 row mounted corn picker. With regular tires and lugs there was not power enough while with the rubber tires conditions as to power were considerably improved. Also the dirt falls off the tires as the tire is distorted." Soon after, Brown got a chance to plow with a tractor mounted on inflatable rubber. "It is surprising," he wrote on October 21, "how much more power is delivered to the drawbar. The tractor wheels don't slip."

Steel Tracks Join Pneumatic Rubber

As if pneumatic rubber weren't enough of an improvement, on October 27, Brown spent a day in the field with "Caterpillar attachment for D tractor made by Lindeman of Yakima, Washington. It performed well." Brown had assembled quite an audience on the farm outside Moline. Charlie Wiman, Frank Silloway, Elmer McCormick, and another dozen board members watched Jesse Lindeman perform his first demonstration. It was the first of many occasions when Brown witnessed the results of other individuals' labors.

Brown had spent much of the 1920s working on his own projects. He got the General Purpose tractor designed and built. He and his staff developed and produced planting, cultivating, and harvesting tools for it. Now, Brown observed to himself that the early 1930s were the years in which he watched colleagues and strangers alike introduce new ideas. From McCormick's FX and GX tractors to pneumatic rubber tires to Max Sklovsky's compact tractor concept, several new developments took their first steps during these years. Each of these tantalized or challenged Brown and the other Deere engineers.

On a rainy, snowy, November 7, George Nystrom spent the day with Brown. Nystrom worked for Allis-Chalmers. He had experimented with "low-pressure tires" for nine months.

Nystrom told Brown that 20 pounds per square inch (psi) was too much pressure for farming applications; it would allow the tire to slip on the rim. Nystrom concluded that between 8 and 15 pounds was the right range. He explained that rubber tires slipped less on side hills than steel wheels did. On lister ridges, the tire flexed to accommodate the ridge. Most significantly, Nystrom let Brown know that Allis-Chalmers had begun to offer pneumatic rubber on its big three-plow rated tractors as optional equipment at no extra cost.

ABOVE: *Elmer McCormick even conceived of the ship's bow-like nose treatment. This parted branches and tree limbs, slipping through them rather than tearing them or snapping them off as the tractor approached.*

OPPOSITE: *Waterloo's Elmer McCormick first conceived the "streamlined" Model A Orchard tractors soon after Deere introduced the A series. The 1930s steamlined era strongly influenced car, locomotive, and aircraft design but the smooth lines here greatly benefited fruit trees that no longer snagged on sharp edges and corners.*

ABOVE: 1937 MODEL AWH (KELLER) *Adjustable wide-front tread A high clearance tractors first appeared in 1937. Front and rear tread could stretch from 56 inches to 80 inches to accommodate a variety of row crops.*

RIGHT: *The first series A models used Deere's 5.5 inch bore and 6.5 inch stroke horizontal twin. These models used a three-forward gear transmission that provided speeds from slower than 2 miles per hour up to about 4.5 miles per hour.*

Brown understood what this decision meant to Deere; the Moline engineers began immediately to modify implements for these more compliant tires.

Meanwhile, by year end, Wiman gave Sklovsky approval "to draw up his idea and then the tractor works [will] make a detailed cost analysis." Cost appraisal began to rule Deere's experimental staff. Concept tractors and implements had to meet a price as well as fulfill a function. Engineers looked into arc welding and spot welding as ways they, and the manufacturing plants, might reduce costs.

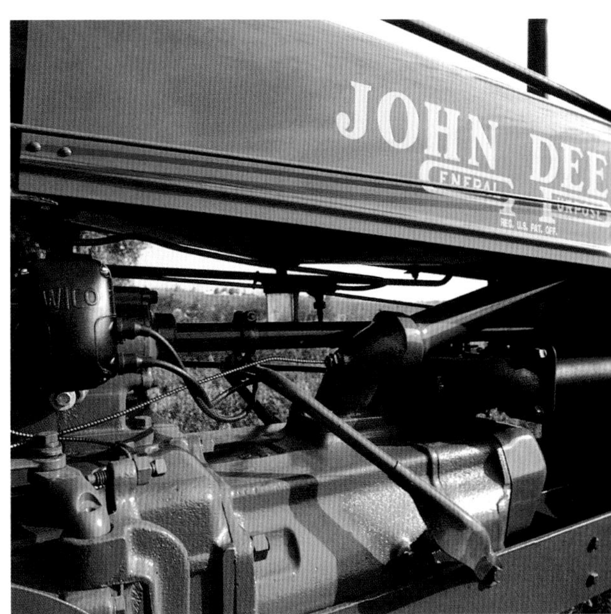

Pneumatic rubber improved the traction, ride, and usefulness of tractors. This AWH runs on 6.00-16 front and 9.00-36 rears.

Hardest Times for New Machinery

In early January 1933, McCormick showed Brown Waterloo's next proposal, the HX tractor. "This is a small size job for one 16-inch bottom," Brown wrote on January 6, "and is to be as near 65 percent of cost and weight of GX as possible. It is hoped to get 3 or 4 of these tractors built by the middle of April. . . . It may be thought wiser to have this small HX proceed the GX into production. The 7 GX tractors at Phoenix and Tucson started work in the field last Tuesday." With its single 16-inch plow rating, this was McCormick's assault on Sklovsky's tractor.

The economic news through January and February was the most discouraging yet. Banks in Moline closed for a week, or for good. Deere & Company helped bail out one institution by partially underwriting the foundation of its successor, the Moline National Bank. But others failed, and on February 16, Brown noted that people around Moline were "sore at Deere & Company because the bank was not saved. It is much more important to save Deere."

JOHN DEERE
JOHN DEERE

LEFT: MODEL AWH
Over the years, Deere has moved its tractor serial number plates from one part of the tractor to another. Company records are excellent and knowing the serial number can reveal the tractor's build date and its initial shipping destination.

In mid-March, Brown saw Max Sklovsky's revised prototype tractor in the field. Smaller than Max's initial designs had indicated, this one ran on 20-inch diameter fronts and a 24-inch rear-drive wheel. It still operated in the reversed tricycle configuration. Brown hated it.

"It will not work for potatoes.

"It will not work in 20-inch rows.

"It will not work on listed rows either in trench or on ridge."

From Brown's perspective, it still required too much room at the end of cultivated rows to turn the tractor around. What's more, Sklovsky had mounted the front cultivator shovels behind the front wheels. The tractor's short wheelbase made maneuverability around young plants very difficult. Within days, Brown had created a comparison study between McCormick's new HX model and Sklovsky's, damning Max's small machine to oblivion.

With the fields finally cleared of flawed intruders, Brown promoted McCormick's GX throughout its field evaluations during spring 1933. Operators ran the GX alongside IHC's Farmalls, and they tested the HX with Farmall F12s, near Wiman's Tucson, Arizona, farm. Deere introduced the GX as its Model A one year later. (Brown noted that he expected that

OPPOSITE: *The experiments Theo Brown made to improve tractor steering resulted in Deere's over-the-top linkage. It forced Waterloo works to refashion the radiator to allow an off-center fill cap.*

Engineering Challenges

Brown and his Moline Plow Works engineering staff constantly struggled to resolve problems they had not created but that plagued farmers widely. If the implement's hitching point was off the centerline of the tractor, the implement followed behind the tractor at an angle. This was a condition called "side draft," and it plagued many tractors and vexed farmers at the time. Brown designed a new one-piece transmission housing for Deere's tractors that McCormick used for the A and B models. This allowed them to relocate both the hitch and the PTO to the tractor's center line. The new housing replaced the larger original two-piece castings and it also provided greater ground clearance. Brown designed the casting with a top-mounted access plate through which to replace parts, and a bottom-mounted drain plug to facilitate transmission fluid changes.

Tractor designers originally based rear track width on what horse farming had established. This differed for various crops: A two-horse harness placed horse hooves 42 inches apart. So farmers planted and cultivated most row-crops in rows at that width. With the Model A tractor, Brown's adjustable rear axle offered farmers a track width anywhere between 56 inches and 84 inches. In addition to the greater track width variability, he and McCormick also improved the tractor's maneuverability through new foot pedal-operated right- and left-differential brakes.

Last but not least, implement engineer Emil Jirsa had improved the mechanical-lift feature of the GP. He and Brown developed and introduced on board self-contained hydraulics. Brown's long mechanical lift lever evolved into Jirsa's short switch. This system raised and lowered the tractor's integral implements using hydraulic pull-or-push cylinders. Lift arms attached the tractor to the implement and the farmer adjusted these to set the working depth of front cultivators. Once set, however, the system did not yet offer any automatic adjustment for draft as the tractor rose or fell over hillocks or swales. Deere named Jirsa's system Powr-Trol.

1938 Model ANH

The "N" in the letter combination refers to the single front tire, or "narrow" front configuration of this model. Deere introduced both the AN and AW (adjustable wide front tread) in 1935.

the first three Model A tractors would be built by February 10, with regular production beginning February 15, 1934.) Franklin Roosevelt's New Deal economy, recharged and jumpstarted, moved toward recovery. The board, catching its breath at last, allowed Brown's power farming group the luxury of additional prototypes. Soon, seven new HX prototypes supplemented ongoing field tests that the seven original evaluation units had completed. Deere needed accurate operations records on each of its prototypes. In January 1934, the company began paying farmers 25 cents a day to write, as well as plow or cultivate.

On January 30, during the quarterly director's meeting, the board approved manufacture of the HX for 1935, authorizing $250,000 for final preproduction modifications on what it now called the Model B. Deere had tested the A with 3-bottom 14-inch plows and the B with two 14-inch plows. However, understanding the human nature of farmers who often overworked the machines, the company labeled each tractor for use with one less plow. The new Model A was Deere's two-plow tractor and the company designated the B for a single. But each of these was much more than just a tractor model scaled down from the D and the GP.

(The prototype FX models disappeared from Brown's diaries without any further explanation at about the time the HX appeared. Current Deere & Company archivist Neil Dahlstrom theorizes that Deere would have required McCormick to keep a diary just as Brown and other engineers did. However, no record of the journal exists. Regrettably, the

JOHN DEERE

LEFT: *The Model A also introduced on-board hydraulics to farmers. The gearbox drove the pump, offering operators the capability to use much heavier integral tools.*

ABOVE: *Starting in 1938, Deere delivered Model A tractors with its new four-forward gear transmission, offering a "road speed" or "transport speed" specially for pneumatic tires. This top gear would allow 6.25 mph for towing loaded wagons into town for threshing or sales.*

JOHN
ENER

FX and other details from McCormick's creative career can be derived and deduced only from the records of others.)

Model A in Production Brings Variations

Brown, McCormick, and their engineers produced eight or so of the GX/Model A development prototypes. They had fitted two with the three-speed transmission on production D and GP tractors. On later prototypes, they tested and perfected Deere's new four-speed gearbox.

Brown's diary noted that the first Model A rolled off the line on March 19, about five weeks later than he had estimated. Full production for a standard two-front-wheel tricycle began in April 1934. For 1935, Deere introduced the single front tire and narrow front, designated the AN. This accompanied an AW, the adjustable wide-front-axle model. The AR, or A Regular, appeared in 1936 as a standard-front-axle. This was a nonrow-crop configuration.

In 1937, Deere added another letter that specified 40-inch rear wheels instead of the normal size 36-inch equipment. These were the first high-clearance models that Deere offered. The company designated them ANH (or Model A Narrow, High Clearance, for single fronts with a 16-inch tall front tire) or AWH (for the standard or wide front fitted with longer front spindles). Deere offered these high-clearance H tractors only on pneumatic rubber.

While Deere introduced the orchard Model AO in 1935, the "streamlined" version AOS appeared in 1937. According to Brown's diary, Elmer McCormick, having already narrowed the fuel tank at the rear to improve function, created these next steps at improving appearance along with function. This variation vented the exhaust below the engine, removed the tall air intake extension pipe and fitted modified body panels to better protect the trees from the tractor's mechanical works.

The range of Model A tractors grew more diverse. Waterloo's engineers could narrow their focus even while expanding their vision to include broader disciplines. A decade earlier, Deere already had produced a specialized Model D tractor, fitted with modifications for industrial use, conceived for yards never intended to raise crops. Waterloo updated it with the AI. However, this new tractor, introduced along with the AR and AO, adopted features of both models that included faired-in fenders and undermounted exhaust pipes from the AO and a modified standard front end from the AR. The AI represented a concerted effort to appeal to the industrial market. It would lead to a new product line and another tractor philosophy at Deere & Company: nonagricultural tractors for industry.

LEFT: *The arrival of pneumatic rubber tires, or "balloon" or "air" tires revolutionized farming. Their flexible sidewalls actually increased traction by working clotted dirt and mud out of the tire treads.*

OPPOSITE: *Manufactured in February 1938, this model featured the new enclosed fan-shaft driven by gears off the crankshaft. The flap valve beside the sparkplug opened to release engine compression to ease starting.*

CHAPTER 10
1925–1937

JOHN DEERE
OHN DEERE

A NEW DIRECTION AND NEW COLOR:

JOHN DEERE INDUSTRIALS

PREVIOUS: 1928 MODEL DI
Besides the yellow paint and a swiveling seat, the biggest differences were inside the final drive housing. Instead of the typical 38-tooth gear, Waterloo inserted 28 or even 22-tooth gears to provide a higher speed while still guaranteeing enough torque to pull or push any load.

RIGHT: *Deere first developed industrial tractors for its own needs around its plants and warehouses, pushing and tugging pallets and trailers of equipment from one place to another. By 1925, Waterloo had modified Model D tractors to fit its needs.*

Deere first found a need for industrial models in its own factories. Its agricultural tractors tugged raw materials and towed supplies around the Waterloo plant. With all the heavy equipment that assembly personnel needed to relocate and shift around the Harvester Works, Plow Works, Spreader Works, and its other operations, Deere's engineers quickly improvised a solution to a problem. Steel wheels slipped on concrete factory floors or tore them up, yet solid rubber tires mounted on their steel rims pulled loads easily and quietly.

Ag tractors moved too slowly. To reach useful speeds around the shop and yard pushing or pulling loads of raw materials or implements, engineers replaced the Model D's standard 38-tooth final drive with 28-tooth gears or even 22-tooth sprockets. These still offered plenty of low-end tugging power, but they moved the tractors along at 4 or 5 miles per hour around plants and nearby roads. Within in a year of introducing its agricultural Model D to farmers, Deere had "industrial" Ds moving around its plants in 1925.

(Nonagricultural use was nothing new. In 1920, the city of Waterloo had purchased a Waterloo Boy Model N. It towed a road scraper/grader and kept the city streets groomed after winter snows and spring rains.)

As branch salesmen visited Moline, Waterloo, or other plants for meetings, they saw these Model D-based industrial tugs working in the plants. They described these variations to their customers. By 1926, Deere had introduced advertising materials for "John Deere Industrial Tractors."

This 1937 BI runs a Parsons Landscoop front loader, dumping a bucket full into the bed of the waiting truck. The quarry owners apparently found solid front tires and pneumatic rears gave them traction and steering control they needed. Deere & Company Archives

These offered 40-inch and even 50-inch-diameter rear wheels, extension wheels, and wheel weight sets that ranged from 400 pounds a pair to 1,900 pounds in order to improve traction on smooth surfaces. Waterloo made its 28-tooth final drives standard equipment and offered the 22-tooth versions as an option.

Waterloo's chief engineer Elmer McCormick was as much an opportunist as he was innovative. He approached neighboring Hawkeye Maintainer Company who liked his proposal. He and Theo Brown supervised efforts to fit Hawkeye's Motor Patrol road grader to modified Model D tractors. According to Deere Industrials historian Brian Rukes, these models left Waterloo's tractor works fitted with oversize fuel tanks, modified brakes and a "revised" operator's platform that Hawkeye could order with or without fenders. Rukes learned that the Tractor Works and Waterloo's Hawkeye produced Motor Patrols only from 1929 through 1931. It's very likely the ailing economy had much to do with drooping sales. In fact, it seems that industrial output went

1936 MODEL AI

The late Lester Layher owned this industrial, the first Model AI produced. The cab's flip-up front window and removable rear doors allowed more comfortable operation during summer months.

Model AI tractors weighed 4,680 pounds without the cab or engine shields. Deere manufactured this first AI on April 27, 1936, and it produced the last one on June 18, 1941.

Looking for Business Down the Road

Early in 1935, Brown, Frank Silloway, and Charlie Wiman made the short journey over to Peoria to meet with Caterpillar executives. A decade earlier, Caterpillar's two competing parents, C. L. Best Gas Traction Company and Holt Manufacturing, the world's two largest crawler tractor producers, had consolidated operations under Holt's trade name, Caterpillar. This nearly indomitable manufacturer still found itself lacking when customers needed wheel tractors for smaller operations. Rather than spend hundreds of thousands of dollars developing a new line, Cat approached Deere. Wiman and Silloway met with Caterpillar's Harry Fair and Raymond Force on January 9. Their conversation yielded an agreement. "Caterpillar tractors for agricultural purposes would be available to Deere dealers, and that our own tractors, as industrial tractors, would be available to Caterpillar distributors." A month later, Caterpillar proposed taking Deere engineers through all their factories and their southeastern distributorships. Cat wanted Deere's staff to meet customers and state officials "to get as good a picture of what is wanted as possible . . . in the industrial adaptation of our tractor," as Brown wrote on February 6.

The resulting arrangement helped Caterpillar and it greatly benefited Deere. Caterpillar allowed its dealers to sell Deere products. Deere dealers did the same. What's more, in areas of the country where either brand was missing, the agreement encouraged one or the other to form a joint Deere/Caterpillar distributorship. Caterpillar virtually gave Deere its combine business. (It was the only crop-harvesting equipment Cat still produced. It was nearly legendary for its ability to work along side hills. Deere wanted this kind of harvester in its line up but, as with Cat, it was unwilling to expend the development costs to create its own.) Within a short time of signing this agreement, Deere introduced the industrial Model DI in early spring, for a base price of $1,556.50 (about $20,450.00 in 2003) and equipped with solid rubber tires. Within a year, buyers could order the DI with dual inflatable rears.

the way of all sales through the disastrous early 1930s. (Waterloo production of 35,677 tractors in 1929 fell precipitously. Deere sold just 765 tractors in all of 1933.)

Other factors influenced Deere's decision to enter the industrial tractor market. As writer/historian J. R. Hobbs pointed out in the April 1999, issue of *Green Magazine*, Deere did have industrial experience. Through its partnership with Moline Wagon Company and the Fort Smith Wagon Company, Deere had begun selling wagons in the 1880s. Over time it produced wagons for commercial, logging, oil field, and even U.S. Army wartime use. It also may be that Waterloo's Model D Industrial fit a need that Deere's competitors already had identified. Both Ford and IHC aggressively pursued industrial sales. IHC considered it a major market for its products as early as 1929. With Deere, it wasn't until 1935, under a much healthier economic climate, that industrial tractors reappeared, following the arrival of Deere's Model A.

With the A and B Came the AI and BI

Theo Brown and his experimental department colleagues had continued development work on the GP. Elmer McCormick and the other Waterloo Tractor Company engineers and operators put the finishing touches onto the first production Model FX/A tractors. Waterloo and Moline staff invested another year in testing before introducing the smaller

1936 Model AI with crane
Deere manufactured this one around Christmas 1938 and it was the first that Waterloo shipped in 1939. It went straight to Cedar Rapids Steel where they mounted the LaPlante-Choate crane.

IN DEERE
JO

companion Model GX. Brought into production as the Model B, Deere characterized it as being "two-thirds" of a Model A both in power and scale. Moline's improvements to the GP eventually gave it power output approaching the D. The original performance gap between the two was something that management and the sales staff had found valuable as a sales tool. Now the new B fit the same framework. Deere discontinued the GP soon after it brought out the Model B in 1935.

Farmers first saw Deere's AI and BI at the National Road Show. This was an annual multicompany, national dealer's new product introduction event. For 1936, it took place in Cleveland, Ohio, between January 20 and 24. Deere and Caterpillar, partners in marketing and promotion, occupied exhibit space next to each other. At the same time, Ralph B. Lourie, Deere's Moline branch manager, recommended to the board that Deere "completely segregate the industrial side of our business from the agricultural side." Whether this was something that Caterpillar suggested or Lourie innovated is unclear. In a company so decentralized as Deere was, Lourie's idea was an easy sell.

(On the agricultural side, the same evolution of variations occurred with the B as had happened with Model A tractors. Soon there were BN models with a single front tire, a BW with its wide front end, the BNH and BWH high-clearance models, BR regulars, BO orchards, and BI industrial tractors. In addition, Deere offered limited-run special versions for beet and other vegetable crop farmers based on their 20-inch wide rows. These were the BW-40 or BN-40, also available as higher clearance BWH-40 or BNH-40 models. Designations and variations became as numerous as there were crops to grow in the ground, or roads to pave.)

Each of the Deere's industrial models appeared in vibrant "Hi-Way Yellow" paint. Caterpillar created this color in 1931. Cat took on the safety challenge posed by so many companies painting agricultural equipment dark green or gray. A number of automobile and truck drivers had been seriously hurt at night when they hit darkly painted tractors and other road building equipment parked on the road edge. Cat's manufacturing department said it could not paint the tractors in the orange or silver that product planners first selected. But they could do yellow, they said. Cat's management then pushed it hard as a marketing tool. The vibrant "safety colors" brightened up the crawlers and sparked sales.

By the summer of 1937, however, Deere yielded to its own marketing pressures. It began offering its industrial tractors painted however the customer requested. Waterloo already painted its own shop tractors bright red. Other customers ordered colors ranging across the rainbow from yellows to blues, but in very limited numbers.

Sales of Deere's industrial (and agricultural) tractors went well despite an economy only just recovering from the Depression. Deere & Company had turned the tide on IHC and it steadily closed the gap between the two companies in sales figures. In early 1935, Theo Brown noted in his diary that Waterloo GP tractor production had reached 116 a day and its output of As and Bs was heading toward 150. Allis-Chalmers, which had introduced its Model U in 1929, had come on strong with rubber-tired versions in 1933 and

OPPOSITE: *Once Cedar Rapids Steel mounted the crane, it delivered the tractor to Deere's Cedar Rapids foundry for yard and foundry work hauling large castings around. LaPlante-Choate used a second power take-off shaft mounted off the belt pulley gears to operate the crane winch mounted on the tractor cowl.*

JOHN DEERE

1934. In late 1934, A-C introduced the WC, the first U.S. farm tractor designed specifically to operate on pneumatic rubber tires or "air tires," as farmers called them. At this point, however, all the tractors from all the makers looked pretty similar.

The resemblance was confusing. If it had not been for the beginnings of "logo colors," corporate color schemes, the task of identifying one make of tractor from another across a field might have been nearly impossible. Deere engineers knew this benefited testing and development work; competitors had trouble identifying new development models from afar. While this helped the engineers keep curious competitors away, it frustrated sales staffs that always looked for something new and exciting to sell.

Theo Brown and Elmer McCormick knew they made a good product. However, McCormick, more than anyone else, understood that in order to make the tractors sell better against the competition, they needed something more.

Brown and his staff had provided farmers with hydraulics and adjustable front- and rear-wheel tread width. McCormick's colleagues in Waterloo had introduced high-clearance models to serve cotton and corn growers. Deere & Company had developed and brought out extremely narrow-tread models to satisfy the beet, asparagus, and celery growers. The company had given their tractors every technological advance they could manage. Deere's board was thinking hard about its customers and the future. In early 1935, Charlie Wiman, Frank Silloway, and tractor-and-combine production vice president Charlie Stone made that clear to Brown.

ABOVE: 1937 MODEL BI *Engines were standard issue 4.25-inch bore, 5.25-inch stroke 149-cubic-inch twin-cylinder models. The Keller family's red BI, like all standard BI tractors, weighed 3,620 pounds.*

OPPOSITE: *Seeing a Deere tractor in something so close to McCormick-Deering red is almost scandalous. However, Waterloo's industrial production line manufactured and released BIs in orange, white, and blue as well as its own green and yellow.*

OPPOSITE TOP: *When is a Deere not green, or even yellow? When it's a custom order and this nearly traitorous color selection is what Elmer McCormick's Waterloo Tractor Works specified for its own shop mule.*

RIGHT: 1937 MODEL BI
The B Industrial models measured just 53.75 inches wide, 115 inches long, and 51.75 inches to the top of the radiator. Electric lights and starting were optional.

OPPOSITE: *Shop and industrial tractors vented the exhaust to the floor unlike the agricultural models that directed it upward. Deere offered a variety of front and rear tire tread options in addition to this one.*

OPPOSITE INSET: *Recognizing that industrial tractor operators spend much more time seated than farmers while they worked, Waterloo offered padded vinyl seats as an option from the earliest of the industrials. Jared Schultz' tractor is beautifully restored and runs smoothly.*

JOHN DEERE
JOHN DEE

RIGHT: 1937 MODEL BI WITH PARSONS BLADE
With short exceptions, once Deere began producing industrial tractors, it did not stop. It is a market that has expanded to include construction and road building equipment in the past 40 years.

"I am informed," Brown wrote on February 6, 1935, "that we should immediately begin thinking about the tractor we will build in 5 years from now. Rubber tires are changing the picture and it may be the tractor should be so designed to do truck service as well as plowing—this might mean spring suspension, and this in turn might mean a device to throw out the spring action when plowing." His next day's notes went further. They listed synchromesh transmissions and overdrive higher speeds for times when the tractor served as a truck.

A year later, in March 1936, the same group met again,

In a meeting on March 9 with Silloway, McCormick, Stone, Wiman, and others, Brown devised a list of "suggestions for tractor design." These included seeking yet another "easier way to adjust rear wheels." But other ideas emerged:

"Consider use of differential brakes to disengage and steer and let front wheels caster around turns.

"Easier attachment of implements.

"More clearance under tractor and lengthen wheelbase of 'B.'

"Better seat—rubber pad or suspension.

"Streamline the tractor."

Wiman and Silloway continued their forward thinking. Brown and McCormick could meet them idea for idea, concept for concept, on the engineering needs. But for a couple of years now, McCormick had believed that Deere's tractors needed further improvement. It was not an update either he or Brown could provide. It was something called "style."

OPPOSITE: *As many options as Deere offered for its agricultural and industrial tractors, there were an equal number from outside suppliers quick to market their own variations. Don Merrihew's BI works with a front blade from Parsons Plow Company of Newton, IA. The Parsons rig required remounting the front axle about 5 inches behind its normal position.*

JOHN DEERE
JOHN DEERE

CHAPTER 11

1937–1938

JOHN DEERE
A

HENRY DREYFUSS, MEET ELMER McCORMICK

PREVIOUS: 1938 MODEL A WITH 1949 MODEL A
Along nearly every inch of the unstyled tractor on the left and the styled model on the right, observers can spot differences, improvements, and redesigned elements to make tractor farming easier, more efficient, more comfortable, and safer.

RIGHT: *The "unstyled" tractor that Waterloo produced from April 1934 through as late as 1949, left, looked dated and even antique next to the "styled" Model A that Deere began producing on August 1, 1938. Henry Dreyfuss' bold design, right, encased the radiator and steering tower behind the "streamlined" sheetmetal.*

Elmer McCormick wasn't the only one in the tractor business who was aware of the need for better looking machines. This awareness had been a long time coming. Competition drove it, mostly. However, McCormick had annoyed Charley Stone incessantly with the idea. Stone had headed the Harvester Works since 1923. In 1934, Deere's board promoted him to vice president of all tractor and harvester production. He was a conservative like many on Deere's board. He told McCormick that he was not wild about the idea. Nor was he even convinced of the need to do anything like this. However, he decided, if McCormick still wanted to go ahead with it, Stone wouldn't stop him.

In mid-August 1937, McCormick arrived without an appointment at the fifth floor offices of Henry Dreyfuss Associates at 501 Madison Avenue, at 52nd Street in New York City. The secretary and receptionist, Rita Hart, listened to him in polite amazement. Then she rushed into Henry's office and blurted out, "There's a man in a straw hat and shirt garters out there who says he is from Waterloo, Iowa, and. . . ."

"Where?" Dreyfuss said. "Never heard of Waterloo, Iowa."

"He says he is from John Deere and he wants to see you about doing some work."

"Who," Henry Dreyfuss said with growing interest, "is John Deere?"

While Elmer McCormick waited, Dreyfuss and Hart paged through the Standard & Poor's *Directory of American Corporations*. Dreyfuss, then just 33, had recently landed a choice assignment from New York Central Railroad (NYCRR). NYCRR had selected his company to redesign

DEERE

JOHN DEERE
A

Waterloo's Elmer McCormick understood better than anyone else at Deere the potential that better looking (and better functioning) tractors and equipment could offer for sales. With his boss's blessing he went to New York, met Henry Dreyfuss, and dramatically changed Deere's history.

When Henry Dreyfuss took on the assignment to improve the appearance of Deere's tractors, his staff designer Jim Conner created these and other concepts. The final design, shown on the facing opposite page, shows how Conner, Dreyfuss, Elmer McCormick, and Deere's board cleverly blended the most powerful of the design elements.

their premier cross-country train, *The Twentieth Century Limited*, to make it look "more like transportation for the Twentieth Century." This assignment had been one of Dreyfuss' longest-standing goals. Dreyfuss and Hart read more of the description of Deere's company. They recognized that they would be the first industrial designers to work with a big name in this huge industry. (Oliver-Hart Parr introduced an industrial designed Model 70 Row Crop in 1935.) They opened the door and invited McCormick in to have a seat and tell them what they could do for him.

McCormick had traveled 1,100 miles by rail to get to New York. For a portion of his journey, he'd been a passenger on *The Twentieth Century Limited* that the railroad had carried over from the Ninetieth Century. As one of Deere's more progressive thinkers, he already had recognized the positive effects of industrial design on other products. For more than two years, he had wanted this opportunity. The long ride from Waterloo had given him more time to polish what he would say. He got right to the point.

"We'd like your help in making our tractors more salable," he said simply.

Henry Dreyfuss was born in 1904 in New York City. He had graduated from the Ethical Culture School in 1922. Then he apprenticed for one year with Norman Bel Geddes, designing theater costumes, scenery, and sets. Just 19 and out on his own in 1923, he wrote a bold letter to the Strand Theaters, criticizing their set design. Startled by his bravado, they hired him at $50 a week. For the next five years Dreyfuss oversaw production of 250 weekly shows running on all the Strand's stages. Burnt out after a brutal work pace even for a 23-year-old, he moved to France at the end of 1927. But he returned to New York a year later and began to solicit work as a designer. In 1929, he moved to 580 Fifth Avenue and relabeled himself as an industrial designer. His first job was to convince manufacturers that they needed his services. His first clients needed door hinges, nursery furniture, and medicine bottles.

OPPOSITE: 1946 MODEL AWH
The first styled Model A wide front high clearance models appeared in September 1940. Farmers could adjust front track from 56 to 80 inches all with 24 inches of ground clearance. The rear sat 3 inches higher and would extend 12 inches further on each side.

JOHN DEERE
JOHN DEERE

RIGHT: 1948 MODEL B ROW CROP *Electric starting meant farmers no longer needed an exposed flywheel to spin the tractor engine to life. But the engine needed the flywheel to run smoothly so Dreyfuss and his staff encased it inside a smart looking shield.*

OPPOSITE: *In June 1937, Deere extended the length of the Model B tractor by 5 inches to 125.5 overall so integral equipment mounting points would match on A and B tractors. A year later, on June 14, 1938, Waterloo produced the first styled B and replaced the previous frame with a new, stronger, lighter one of pressed steel.*

JOHN DEERE

ABOVE: 1950 MODEL AR
The final versions of Deere's powerhouse AR, beginning in 1940, used the same engine block as the company's long-lived Model D. It developed 26.2 horsepower on the drawbar and 36.1 on the belt pulley.

INSET: *Deere produced these styled models, called the New Improved AR, from June 1949 through May 1953.*

OPPOSITE: *The 6-gear transmission provided speeds ranging from a creeper 1.25 miles per hour up to ll miles per hour. The 5,597 pound tractor could pull 4,372 pounds in low gear.*

During the next several years, his philosophy coalesced. He codified it as his Five-Point Formula. Dreyfuss based it primarily on emphasizing an object's function: The form of an object should follow *from* its intended use. He urged his clients to pay attention to the:

1. Utility and safety of the object
2. Ease of maintenance
3. Cost of production
4. Sales appeal
5. Appearance

He mounted his motto in his office lobby. It would be called a mission statement today, and it explained the practical application of his philosophy:

"We bear in mind," he had written, "that the object being worked on is going to be ridden in, sat upon, looked at, talked to, activated, operated or in some other way used by the people individually or en masse. When the point of contact between the product and the people becomes a point of friction, then the industrial designer has failed. On the other hand, if people are made safer, more comfortable, more eager to purchase, more efficient—or just plain happier—by contact with the product, then the designer has succeeded."

After reading that sign in Dreyfuss' office, Elmer McCormick knew he had come to the right place. The potential of working with Deere & Company enticed Dreyfuss. While Dreyfuss went home, McCormick stayed the night in the nearby Waldorf Astoria Hotel. The two men caught the New York Central and headed west the next day.

BE CAREFUL
JOHN DEERE
AR

ABOVE: 1950 MODEL B WITH DEERE COTTON PLANTER

Precise seed positioning became a hallmark of Deere's planters for virtually any crop. Theo Brown and his implement engineers constantly experimented and improved their products.

OPPOSITE: *Chain-driven gears delivered cotton seeds in precise intervals. Farmers from the deep south to the far west came to rely on Deere's planter quality.*

What Dreyfuss accomplished is what retired senior partner Bill Purcell described years later as "a clean up really, it wasn't a great change." This was the view from Purcell's broadly experienced perspective. He went on to participate in all the "great changes" that would come to Deere & Company over the next three decades. But to the farmer, the appearance and the function was so dramatically improved that somewhere someone coined a word to refer to the effect. Henceforth, those tractors "cleaned up" slightly or changed greatly by Henry Dreyfuss, or his colleagues Raymond Loewy who redesigned IHC's tractors, or Brooks Stevens who worked on Allis-Chalmers' machines, were forever known as "styled" tractors. Those not bearing the industrial designers' improvements still were "unstyled."

JOHN DEERE
JOHN DEERE

RIGHT: 1951 MODEL AH

Henry Dreyfuss Associates not only redesigned the front of the tractor, they cleaned up the rear of both the A (foreground) and B (at rear). By organizing where hydraulic fittings attached to the tractor and by providing a shield for the spinning power take-off (PTO) shaft, they made Deere's tractors safer to operate and easier to use.

OPPOSITE: 1951 MODEL BH STEWART CONVERSION

Because farmers irrigate most vegetable crops in California, Deere devised the narrow-front (or single front tire) high crop models for that market. Bedded crops leave deep irrigation troughs just wide enough for tractor tires.

It is a curious word choice. The tractors received much more than mere "styling" or appearance improvements. Even from the start, the machine underwent fundamental design changes. Subsequent tractors received engineering changes as part of the Dreyfuss industrial design process. But Deere & Company already had engineers and designers on the payroll so some method had to be designated to explain to the board, the branch sales staffs, and to farmers which of Deere's machines were new and which were not.

Before the end of August 1937, Henry Dreyfuss & Associates had prepared more than a half dozen design studies for new sheet-metal for the Model A and B tractor. A combination of elements taken from the sixth and eighth proposals coalesced to become the landmark "styled" John Deere tractor. These new lines enclosed the steering column and radiator behind a strong-looking grille. But the improvements also affected function because narrowing the radiator cowling and the gas tank covering significantly improved visibility forward and down. This went beyond what McCormick had done himself on these models.

Dreyfuss always did the initial concept sketches himself. From there, his designers reorganized the instrument panel to make it easier for the farmer to read while bouncing through the fields. The back end of the tractor received some attention as well. They "cleaned up" its appearance with the goal of making it easier to recognize the different functions of various fittings.

JOHN DEERE
JOHN DEERE

Stewart replaced standard clearance axle housings and drive quills with its own variations. With 9.5-42 inch rear Firestone tires, farmers had nearly 36 inches of clearance under the axles to protect plants during cultivation.

The tractor seat seriously concerned Dreyfuss and his staff.

"The farmer was still sitting down while the wheel was [positioned] well up there and very vertical," Bill Purcell explained. "This was because the rear wheels were still very small really, and every bump over a plowed field was so uncomfortable that the farmer really *had* to stand. So the steering wheel was still, very logically, set up high.

"When you stood up," he continued, "you could lean against it, put your hand right on top of it. In that way, it was very good. Much better than standing away from a sloping thing which would hit you in the stomach."

What's more, even with the tractor at rest, the seat didn't exactly fit.

"Henry asked them once how they designed it." Purcell smiled when he recalled their explanation. Dreyfuss had carefully developed his Human Forms. These constituted a thorough collection of measurements and dimensions for a fictional Joe and Josephine. Joe and Josephine allowed Dreyfuss to design virtually any action or apparatus to fit nearly any size person. The Deere tractor seat did not fit *any* Joe or Josephine.

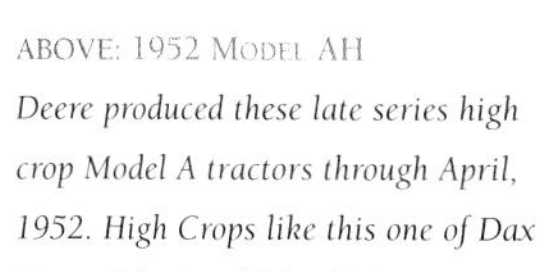

ABOVE: 1952 MODEL AH
Deere produced these late series high crop Model A tractors through April, 1952. High Crops like this one of Dax Kimmelshue's sold for $3,056 in 1952.

LEFT: *Six-gear transmissions allowed the late Model A tractors a range from less than 2.5 miles per hour up to 12.3 miles per hour in 6th or road gear. That speed felt much faster sitting on top of a narrow front high clearance tractor.*

The Model 5A John Deere combine and its operator towered over the 1938 styled Model B working its way through the wheat. Deere introduced the 5A in 1934 and it remained in production into 1941, available with either a 10 or 12 foot header. Deere & Company Archives

"Elmer McCormick told Dreyfuss that they used Pete," Purcell continued with a laugh. "They looked around the factory to find the fellow with the biggest behind. They had him sit in plaster. And that became the seat size."

Deere introduced the newly styled Model A and B tractors to the public for the 1938 season. While farmers viewed these smart-looking machines with caution, the branch sales staffs quickly embraced them. At last they had something dramatically "new and improved" to sell. When Deere's advertising brochures and service manuals appeared for the new-looking Model A and B tractors, the copywriters described them as "Tomorrow's tractor today."

Sales of the Model A remained steady at about 11,000 per year from late 1938 through 1942, suggesting that "styling" had little effect on Deere's larger tractor sales. (The D, still Deere's largest, got Dreyfuss styling in 1939; for the next few years, it sold 3,000 or so units annually.) Yet production of the improved Model B (with 20 percent more drawbar horsepower) jumped between 15,000 and 20,000 through the same time. Other improvements sparked sales as well, but Theo Brown's assistant, Wayne Worthington, described the per-tractor costs of improved operator efficiency and modernized appearance as "the best $100 we ever put into a tractor."

OPPOSITE: 1952 MODEL AO
Deere's 5.5-inch bore, 6.75-inch stroke twin cylinder developed 34.1 horsepower on the drawbar and 38 horsepower on the belt pulley at 975 rpm. These 4,900 pound tractors could pull 4,045 pounds in low gear.

JOHN DEERE

CHAPTER 12
1938–1947

JOHN DEERE

MAKING TRACKS

FOR SANDY SOIL

"It was a really good looking tractor," Jesse Lindeman said. "It just looked to us as though Deere had deliberately built a chassis to take crawler tracks. No other tractor I've ever seen was that close from the start." He recalled his first impressions of Waterloo's Model B that Seattle branch salesmen Ben Keator and Pat Murphy arranged for Deere to ship to him.

"We had our own steel foundry and we cast our own idlers, track rollers, and sprockets," he recalled. "We made our own tracks, too, but they weren't as nice looking as they should have been. So I drew up a plan for samples and sent them back to a foundry in Coraopolis, just up the river from Pittsburgh, Pennsylvania.

Lindeman had developed a system for Deere's GP that he perfected on the BO for mounting tracks. His technique "automatically" positioned them so that each time the assembler put a pin in a pair of links it lined up the next ones as well.

He learned about hydraulics from Deere & Company, copying what he viewed as another good idea and adapting it to raise his bulldozer blade. He previously had used the belt pulley. He had assembled three crawlers to demonstrate to the U.S. Army. His operators raised or lowered the blades on these prototypes by reversing the pulley direction.

Lindeman developed a three-way blade for the Army tests. Pulling and resetting a single pin reshaped the blade as a V-plow, a diagonal blade or a flat bulldozer. With its PTO-operated winch, its capabilities exceeded the tractor's compact dimensions.

PREVIOUS: 1944 MODEL BO LINDEMAN
Lindeman's blade would pivot left or right and with the addition of the screw-thread hand-crank adjustment, operators could control angle and pitch of the blade.

RIGHT: *Jesse Lindeman and Theo Brown worked closely developing live hydraulics, the continuously running hydraulic systems, for Deere's tractors. In some instances, Lindeman worked ahead of Brown and Deere.*

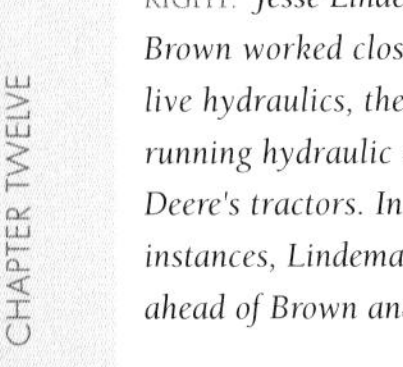

LINDEMAN
E 200
WICO

ABOVE: 1944 MODEL BO LINDEMAN
Jesse Lindeman had loved the Model B Orchard tractor. "It just looked to us as though Deere had deliberately built a chassis to take crawler tracks."

OPPOSITE: *Lindeman began producing crawlers on Model BO chassis in 1939. He stopped only when Deere introduced the Model M and then bought his company to manufacture crawler model MCs.*

However, Lindeman did manufacture a dozen crawlers on rubber pads during the war. The U.S. Navy ordered them to run on the paved docks alongside their ships during reprovisioning. But the pads suggested other uses to dock crews and ship hands. Soon they were chugging around in the holds of ships to clean out iron ore scrap and slag. The rubber pads avoided cutting up the ship's steel floors or striking sparks from the standard steel track pads.

This adaptation, and Wiman's pressure on the Army to test Lindeman's BO, kept Deere & Company supplied with steel throughout World War II. The War Production Board found itself "convinced" that Deere's crawlers were "essential materiel." Lindeman got priority treatment especially since the Waterloo plant was shipping chassis to Lindeman without rubber tires.

In 1946 Deere & Company advised Lindeman and his brothers that it would discontinue the Model BO in another year. But engineers from Waterloo and from the new plant

JOHN DEERE
JOHN DEERE

OPPOSITE: The late Harold Schultz tracked down this rare machine and he, his son, and his grandson all worked to restore it. Without the blade and hydraulics, BO Lindeman crawlers weighed 4,420 pounds.

at Dubuque, Iowa, that Deere scheduled to open that fall, wondered if Lindeman would be interested in working on the development of a crawler for a new model they still were developing.

When Lindeman accepted the offer, Deere made the family another one, hoping to buy their company. Terms were generous enough that Jesse and his brothers could not refuse. On January 1, 1947, Lindeman sold the company to Deere for $1,245,000 (approximately $10.5 million in 2003). Deere stopped production of the BO crawlers after just 1,600 units in 1947 when it introduced the Model M. The MC crawler version began regular manufacture in time for the 1949 season. In an effort to consolidate far-flung subsidiaries, Deere moved all its Yakima operations back to Dubuque in 1954.

Manufacturing the $1,360 BO Lindeman crawlers had kept the 422 employees at Lindeman Power Equipment Company very busy. At peak production the staff assembled an average of 2.5 tractors every day in their 10-acre factory and grounds at 1011 South Third Street. Just as Deere had done with its A and B, Lindeman had built other adaptations of his crawlers for customers. He manufactured a wide-tread model for row-crop adaptations.

ABOVE: While Deere and Lindeman produced 1,675 of the BO crawlers, Lindeman's plant in Yakima, Washington, only manufactured a dozen with rubber pads for the U.S. Navy.

"We sold a few of the adjustable track Lindemans. They were built on square tubes that we used for the framework between the track and the tractor. The track was clamped on. The sprockets were on sliding shafts so we could move everything out exactly to the row crop width.

"We just put a short shaft in for the average person. You could put in any length square shaft in there and any length sprocket shaft, within reason, and get any track width you needed."

Jesse and his brothers and Waterloo's engineers made the BO-Lindeman crawlers adjustable for crop row width and comfortable for operators. The seats would go up or down, in or out. But in the end, it was another technology altogether that offered a flexibility the crawlers couldn't match.

"In the earliest days of these crawlers," Lindeman reminisced, "they were the best way to get around the hills in the orchards. But then rubber tires came more and more into use and they got better and better. That's what did in our small steel tracked crawlers for orchard use."

JOHN DEERE

CHAPTER 13
1937–1938

JOHN DEERE

LETTERS PROLIFERATE,

LINES EXPAND

PREVIOUS: 1937 MODEL BWH (LONG WHEELBASE) AND 1938 STYLED BW.
Starting with serial number 42,200 in mid-1937 with its unstyled Model B tractors (and on all styled Bs), Deere extended the frame length 5 inches. This allowed farmers to use Model A tractor integral implements and tools on the B series tractors.

RIGHT: 1937 MODEL BNH (SHORT WHEELBASE)
As Theo Brown and Elmer McCormick looked at the future of their tractors and implements, they saw a problem looming that would cost Deere and its customers money. Mounted tools would not fit both tractors.

Max Sklovsky, as Deere's chief engineer, continued to work on his compact tractor prototype. Theo Brown and Charlie Wiman remained wary, though in early 1936 Wiman suggested Sklovsky shift the engine location from ahead of the operator to the rear, mounted over the rear wheels. This, Wiman observed, would open up the view ahead to the crops to be cultivated. As Brown had noted in his diary, dealing with Sklovsky, a very willful man, challenged him. Juggling a number of projects in the air, and trying to work around Sklovsky was wearing him down. It got worse in mid-May, however, when Brown saw yet another approach to the question of small, single-plow tractors.

On May 13, Brown got to see Ira Maxon's prototype Model Y. Where Sklovsky's invention still plagued him, Maxon's logic impressed him. Maxon was Max Sklovsky's son-in-law, a relationship that further complicated Brown's reaction to their two prototypes. The stress of working with so many projects with so many personalities at once was exhausting Brown. This got worse still when retired chairman William Butterworth died following several days of business meetings in New Jersey on May 31, 1936. The legacy he left behind set the 99-year-old company on the course that enabled it to survive and thrive when others failed. His cautious management still allowed the development of both tractors and combines. Alliances he had formed benefited the company well. Butterworth had been the company's slightly remote if benevolent father figure. Since the early 1930s, his nephew, Charlie Wiman, had run the corporation. Wiman, who had started in the

JOHN DEERE
GENERAL PURPOSE

ABOVE: *McCormick's staff had designed the Model B on a 44.5 inch frame, giving the tractor an overall length of 120.5 inches. Brown's implement staff already had begun designing integrated tools to fit frame holes.*

RIGHT: *The special 40-inch row width high clearance models first appeared briefly in 1937 in unstyled models (Deere produced something like just six of them), but they were slightly more prevalent as styled models beginning in 1938. On the longer frames, these California vegetable specials would accept any of the Model A integral mounted tools.*

shops and learned the business literally from the floor up, operated Deere's business in a style derived from his uncle's. Yet Charlie improved upon methods and ideas in ways that struck his employees as sound and his investors as shrewd. As Wayne Broehl pointed out, Wiman "looked upon the company as a producer of a critically needed physical good - agricultural machinery."

Theo Brown and Charlie Wiman watched Maxon's Model Y in the field on June 12. Brown liked the machine he saw. This created a dilemma that further unraveled him. He took his work seriously and had come to believe that each prototype needed a full set of implements and tools before its development could advance. But Wiman gave him a direct order and Brown left Moline on June 14 for a two-month vacation.

By the time Brown returned to work on September 8, his colleagues had accomplished quite a bit. On October 16, his 25th anniversary with Deere & Company, he saw a Model B with a 5-inch longer wheelbase, an experimental quick-detachable mounting apparatus for integral implements, and the latest variation of the larger three-plow rated prototype tractor known internally as the K.X. Barely two weeks later, the board approved production of the K.X. as Deere's Model G and authorized $250,000 for tooling.

McCormick's engineers at Waterloo already had begun work to develop its companion, code named the O.X.

Throughout 1937, final development work continued on the K.X./Model G. Charlie Stone's factory at Waterloo geared up to start manufacturing the new tractor. Farmer acceptance of rubber tires forced Deere to offer them more extensively; however, Deere's decentralized management meant that one factory did not always communicate with

1938 Model G-Experimental

Deere introduced its new Model G in late spring 1937 just before an unusually hot summer throughout parts of the country. Elmer McCormick's engineers had calculated the size radiator necessary to cool the engine but it wasn't adequate.

another. By mid-May, the company needed 76 different sizes to fit the tractors, combines, and other implements it manufactured. Brown and McCormick co-organized a wheel committee to simplify and standardize the sizes and numbers of tires and wheels that Deere inventoried. At the same time, Lou Paradise, now the Harvester Works plant manager, joined Harold White, McCormick, and Brown to begin establishing design parameters for "a 12-horsepower general-purpose type tractor with plenty of clearance under the front end." By July 23, McCormick's designers had completed design work and a prototype for this "small tractor to weigh 1,700 pounds."

Competition outside Deere was fierce. The company held on firmly to its number two position behind International Harvester in tractor, combine, and implement sales. Yet industry observers knew a part of the credit for this was due to Deere's marketing arrangement with Caterpillar. Business Week magazine, in an overview of the farm implement industry that it published on March 7, 1937, explained the relationship and put it in context with the competition.

"Under the arrangement, which is based on the fact that Caterpillar has a short [limited] line and Deere a long [full] line of agricultural implements, and that these lines are non-competitive except at a few minor points, the two companies use each other's sales outlets wherever it is to their mutual advantage. . . .

"Harvester and Allis-Chalmers, No. 1 and No. 3 respectively, of the Big Seven, bump into this arrangement in all parts of the country. It worries them no little. But Harvester's research, its good reputation among farmers of the wheat and corn belts, and its far flung sales organization worry Caterpillar and Deere. And Allis-Chalmer's willingness to poke its nose into any field that seems to offer profits, such as tractors, and to pioneer new products such as the small, low-priced combine, worry them, too. It is all part of the merry fight that has long characterized the industry. . . ." However, there was another important and even more dynamic element to "the merry fight." This one provided nearly 50 percent sales gains to many of the companies. It came from farmers who previously had bought other brands.

"The year was a 'take-away year,'" the magazine continued, "[meaning] that an unprecedented number of farmers who wanted a plow, a harrow, a combine or some other implement or piece of machinery, and wanted it right then, went to dealers representing the companies whose products they were accustomed to buying, found that the dealers didn't have what they wanted, and wound up by buying from another company altogether." It forced manufacturers to accelerate production. If they did, the rewards were huge. International Harvester's tractor and implement sales increased 57 percent from 1934 to 1935. Deere jumped nearly as much, from $50.9 million in 1935 to $71.5 million in 1936, almost 45 percent.

"This year," Business Week concluded, "the farm implement companies, big and little, are determined not to be caught napping." After dozens of them attended the Western Tractor and Power Farm Equipment Show at Wichita, Kansas, industry executives returned and sped up production even further than their already heightened pace.

Work accelerated in experimental departments as well. In some cases, engineers competed not only against other manufacturers but also against plants and divisions within the same corporation. Decentralized management characterized Deere & Company beginning in the 1880s and 1890s. William Butterworth had codified this concept into company modus operandi in 1915 when he made each factory and every division autonomous. This independence sometimes duplicated efforts. Occasionally, however, this resulted in remarkable innovation. At Deere, it had led to the GP tractors from Theo Brown's Plow Works, and to the A, B, G, and H models from McCormick's Waterloo Works. But it also led to the proliferation of tire sizes that forced Brown and McCormick to reconfigure 76 varieties down to a somewhat more manageable 48. By late 1937, it finally led Charlie Wiman back to Brown.

"He feels Allis-Chalmers is getting ahead too fast in tractors and small combines," Brown wrote on Tuesday, November 2. "He is worried about experimental work, in that we have not enough men with vision. I am to try to get more talent if I can find it. I told him with our system of decentralized control, I was up against it to butt in." Brown's reluctance was justifiable and it proved to be prescient as well. Forced to "butt in" anyway, his intervention would come back to haunt him. It would frustrate him, then hurt his feelings and finally break his spirit a dozen years later.

The huge Midwest wheat crop of 1931 had depressed prices. Throughout the next year in the central plains, drought made planting anything a challenge since farmers had little money for seed let alone soil-conserving practices. Exposed dirt blew away in strong winds. The drought continued through summers and winters. The USDA estimated that one several-days-long dust storm in May 1934 peeled off nearly 300 million tons of top soil from western Kansas, northeastern New Mexico, southeastern Colorado, and the panhandles of Texas and Oklahoma. This gave rise that year to the region's nickname, the Dust Bowl.

Rumors of jobs and better farming conditions forced thousands of impoverished families out of Oklahoma, Kansas, and Texas. These "Okies," migrated to California in the middle and late 1930s. There big ranch owners irrigated their fields, raised huge crops, needed hundreds of temporary hands for harvests, and relied on the railroads to get their produce to distributors around the country. When rains returned to the Great Plains in the late 1930s, farmers who had remained began a halting comeback. Their outlook improved as crop prices increased with the hints of a new European conflict.

Development continued with the O.X. tractor prototype. Charley Stone and Elmer McCormick hosted a successful field demonstration for Brown and others, and two days later, on November 11, the group began modifying the rear end to accommodate the "Q.D." quick-disconnect integral implement mounting system.

At year's end at Waterloo, Brown watched as the "First small O.X. general purpose tractor was run today. 2000 pounds, 200 more than planned. Pleasant tractor to handle. 4 will be sent to El Centro [test farm in southern California] first part of January." A week later, Brown shipped to McCormick his concept drawings for a swinging seat support for the O.X. (later known as the Model H).

For the tractor staff, 1938 started well. Deere's internal calculations suggested that, despite the drought, nearly 20 percent of America's farmers now owned tractors. Charlie Wiman's efforts were making a dent. For farmers the attraction was obvious. In 1900, according to USDA statistics, plowing with a horse team took more than two hours to turn over an acre. With a tractor on rubber, an acre required barely 30 minutes. Brown, McCormick, and the others attended the Harrisburg, New York, Farm Show on January 18 and 19, 1938. He recorded that night the show had "100,000 in attendance each day; all tractors shown were on rubber. Much interest in our L tractor and A and Model B."

To solve the overheating problem, McCormick's engineers ultimately enlarged the radiator. In order to avoid redesigning the steering pedestal, the engineers cut a notch into the new radiator.

CHAPTER 14

1937–1946

RETIRING THE HORSE ON THE SMALL FARM

PREVIOUS: 1937 MODEL 62
This compact tractor (and its predecessor known as the Model Y) were the first tractors from Deere's Moline Tractor works. This was the former Velie Motors Corporation plant that became Deere's wagon works. Ira Maxon, Deere's chief engineer, hired Willard Nordenson to supervise the new small tractor project.

RIGHT: *Nordenson knew the tractor needed to be short but also to provide great forward visibility for cultivation. He tucked the front wheels under the engine and offset the driver seat slightly to the right and the steering wheel slightly left to fit the operator onto the tractor.*

The "Alphabet according to John Deere" nearly always has sparked curiosity about what might have been *between* the letters. What were those tractors and letters that never reached production? When Ira Maxon's engineering group first conceived the Model L, they still referred to it in its earliest prototype designations as the Model Y. It is a gap and a leap that has not yet been explained. It is probable that Deere management required the individual who conceived the lettering systems to enter an explanation in his own diary. Regrettably, no code book exists to decipher why the K.X. became the G or how it happened that the Y became the Model *number* 62, and why this designation reverted to the alphabetical L.

Still, the need for the tractor was clear. Deere management conceived this as the model for the smallest family-run operations, a category that still represented a great percentage of the total number of U.S. farms. These farmers used a two-horse or two-mule team for plowing and harvesting. Maxon designed the Y and developed it as a one-plow tractor. Recognizing that this machine necessarily would be smaller than any other in Deere's line, the board chose to veer away slightly from previous procedure. Instead of assigning the new project to Theo Brown's overworked Plow Works experimental department (it was developing a full set of implements for the G [K.X.] and H [O.X.] models at this time), or to Elmer McCormick's engineers at Waterloo (who still were perfecting the G and H), this request stayed in Moline.

Deere & Company used one of the plants of the former Velie Motors Corporation as the Wagon Works in Moline. Willard Velie Sr. had died in late October 1928, and his son, Willard Jr.,

DEL 62

ABOVE: *Willard Nordenson broke new ground with this compact machine, which used a parallel tube frame and mounted the engine longitudinally and upright. Nordensen went outside Deere for an engine, choosing an 8-horsepower Novo for some of the 26 prototype Y models but Hercules NXAs for the production models after that.*

INSET: 1938 MODEL L
With the new Model L, Deere replaced the lower chin casting with the company initials. From 1936 through 1938, Moline Tractor Works manufactured something like 1,502 of these tractors.

OPPOSITE: *These Hercules engines displaced 66 cubic inches using 3.0-inch bore and 4.0-inch stroke. They developed 9.0 horsepower on the drawbar and nearly 10.5 on the belt pulley.*

died the following March. When their survivors finally settled the family estate, Deere bought the plants outright in April 1937. Then, 20 months later, Deere renamed the factory. Five months after that, in May 1941, it established the Moline Tractor Division. Ira Maxon, its chief engineer and manager, inherited the outline for this new project.

The challenge for Maxon was that most of Deere's tractor research and development funds went to Waterloo. These resources still were tied up in developing McCormick's G and H models. As successors to the Model A and B, the board felt it was critical to bring them to production on time. Maxon felt his hands were tied. He contacted an old friend, Willard Nordenson. "Nordy," as Maxon and others called him, was a former engineer with Deere who had gone off freelancing during the early 1930s. While he was known more as a specialist in engines, Nordenson explained in an interview with Gary Olsen, editor of *Tracks* magazine, that he quickly became involved in the "whole product."

"An engineer didn't specialize back then as they have to do today," Nordenson explained. "Of course, the project is more complex today than it was back in the thirties. Today we have all the electronics. Yesterday's machines were a lot simpler involving basic mechanical principles.

"It was very easy to get the product from drawing board to actual build. We worked directly with customers and dealers. There were no big meetings—just small groups of us working on the product, doing our own research and testing." However, Maxon had confronted his "engine man" with the real challenge: the board gave Maxon virtually no budget to develop this new machine. Nordenson understood that his power requirements would be much less than the current multiplow production tractors. With no money available to design a new Deere engine, he went outside to find one.

He selected a two-cylinder 8-horsepower Novo. Nordenson's first few prototype Model Y tractors used the gasoline-only Model C-66 engine. He knew that farmers would work his tractor not only for plowing but also for cultivating. Forward visibility was critical. He mounted the small Novo longitudinally and upright. Its crankshaft ran parallel to the direction of travel unlike the transverse and horizontal arrangements of engines on other Deere tractors. He slid in a Ford Model A automobile transmission along the drivetrain ahead of the differential. This combination, born of economic necessity, later provided an advertising advantage. The gearshift followed the standard H pattern familiar to any car or truck driver. Deere promoted the tractor for use on estates, golf courses, and even cemeteries to operate lawn mowing equipment. Nordenson gave it a familiar foot clutch as well. Mike Mack, the former director of Waterloo's Product Engineering Center, worked with Nordenson on a number of projects. When he spoke to Rod Beemer for Beemer's book *John Deere Small Tractors*, Mack explained that Nordenson used to say, "I don't think an operator has enough hands to use a hand clutch." Deere's marketing and advertising always emphasized these facts in promoting the ease of operating the new Model L.

JOHN DEERE
JOHN DEERE

1938 Model L with optional Mud Lugs

Deere intended the Model L tractors to suit the few farmers still using a two-horse or two-mule team on their small farms. Deere charged $477 for the 1,570 pound tractors in 1940. The yellow accessory wheels literally paddled the tractor through mud.

Nordenson mounted the engine on a stubby frame consisting of two nearly parallel round tubes. He joined these together by using a flat piece beneath the radiator. He cast this iron banjo housing with steel rings in two openings to provide a better weld for the tubular pipes. A banjo is a relatively common engineering or structural element so named because its appearance resembled the instrument.

The design never stopped delivering challenges. Elmer McCormick, Louis Witry, Joe Dain, and nearly every other designer of larger tractors before Nordenson had located the front steering wheels ahead of the radiator. They aligned the chassis so it ran nearly parallel to the ground. On the Y, Nordenson placed the front wheels under the engine's rear cylinder, just ahead of the flywheel. This severely shortened the already diminutive wheelbase, which greatly enhanced maneuverability for cultivating.

The chassis sloped down noticeably from front to rear, as though meant to allow for some kind of drainage. In fact, this rearward rake came by virtue of front spindle heights versus rear axle placement and tire diameter. In addition, because the tractor's overall length was so short (91 inches compared to the 120.5 inches of the earliest unstyled Model Bs), Nordenson had to offset the driver's seating position slightly to the right to accommodate all the mechanical components. He also shifted the engine and steering positions slightly off-center to the left as seen when looking at the tractor from the rear. For the first time on a Deere tractor, users operated both rear brakes using the right foot to press two pedals linked together. Nordenson kept the foot-operated clutch pedal on the left, just as in cars and trucks.

Jack Kreeger, a collector and historian in Omaha, Nebraska, has made a very thorough study of the Model Y, the subsequent 62, and the regular production L and LA versions. His

ABOVE: 1941 MODEL LA
The LA differed in many ways beyond its Henry Dreyfuss-directed appearance. The tractor grew two inches in length and gained nearly 700 pounds in weight.

INSET: *The new model used Deere's own vertical two-cylinder engine with 3.5-inch bore and 4.0-inch stroke. Output increased to 13.1 horsepower at the drawbar and 14.3 at the belt pulley.*

OPPOSITE: 1947 MODEL LI
Don Merrihew's industrial is one of the last 20, manufactured in early 1947. Industrial serial numbers ranged outside regular L and LA production, stretching from 50001 in 1942 through 52019 in early 1947.

research suggested that Nordenson's group assembled something like 26 Model Y prototypes but only a few of these used the Novo. Its single-quart oil capacity was insufficient to keep the bottom end lubricated when the little tractor worked hard. Crankshaft and main bearing failures quickly doomed the Novo. Early into the development of the Y prototypes, Nordenson and his colleagues selected a Hercules two-cylinder 3x4-inch engine. That version, basically produced to a John Deere design, remained in use through the 1937 production life of the Model 62, the second-generation development tractor. It carried on through the 1938 production of the unstyled Ls as well. This amounted to slightly more than 1,580 tractors.

Tractor Works designated another short-lived experimental row-crop version as the LW, or "L Wide." Nordenson configured this single front-wheel tricycle with an adjustable rear track. Jack Kreeger's research indicated that Nordenson's staff built only one. While Tractor Works operators tested it extensively, Nordenson and Maxon eventually dismissed it as a product for which too limited a market existed.

ABOVE: 1942 MODEL LI
Deere produced Industrial Model LA tractors from 1942 through 1946 (though it assembled very few during the war years.) This pre-war model had electric lights and starter with the battery covered alongside the engine.

While Henry Dreyfuss had performed only a "cleanup" on the Model A and B tractors, the Model L was his virtually from the start. For Deere's larger tractor markets, the company continued to manufacture and sell unstyled versions alongside the styled machines. Tractor Works introduced the "styled" version of the L on the model's first anniversary in August 1938. Beginning with the 1939 model year, Deere no longer offered original unstyled Model Ls.

As early as November 1937, Dreyfuss got involved with the Model L project. Correspondence and drawings, sequentially numbered from the start as each topic arose, went back and forth between Maxon and Dreyfuss. As each new element came under scrutiny, an assortment of paper went by airmail to and from designers and engineers. Seat shape and gear change lever configuration and the shape of the perforations in hood and grille sheet metal provoked suggestions and alternatives. Dreyfuss's staff and Nordenson's engineers drew and redrew. Just after New Years in 1938, Dreyfuss flew to Moline and met with Maxon, Nordenson, and H. S. Barnhart to discuss details on the new Model 67 tractor, which was Deere's internal designation for the "styled" Model L.

Their conversations dealt with such minutiae as matching the finish of the steering wheel-nut to the finish on the fuel tank cap. They wanted to make rear fender edges similar to those on the Model 62. The foot pedals received attention, but both sides marked those for future examination:

"For the present," Barnhart's minutes reported, "the design is to stay as is, but in the future they will be made of forged steel and some design work must be done on this by the office of Henry Dreyfuss."

The group scrutinized the front and rear name plates. Following the meeting, a letter from Dreyfuss' office referred to Model 67 name plate samples #37 and #38. "You will note

JOHN DEERE
JOHN DEERE

that in (drawing) #37 we have adhered to your standard form of lettering, whereas in (drawing) #38 we have taken considerably more liberty."

Maxon selected #38 for the styled L replacement, the Model LA.

Beginning in 1941, Deere produced its own engine for the LA. It still was a version of the Hercules that Nordenson had used in the prototypes. Deere redesigned it to accommodate a generator and self-starter. By this time, electric lights and self-starting were a common option package.

Immediately before Deere introduced the LA, it ceased production of both the L and the early styled L Industrial. Deere then introduced an LI to replace the earlier model. It fitted these with the Deere engine and the LA's larger rear wheels.

"Our goal," Willard Nordenson recalled, "was to build a very *economical* product that was simple to operate and service. We were trying to convert farmers from animal power to tractor power."

ABOVE: *While these little machines weighed just 2,285 pounds, they could pull 1,936 pounds in low gear. Their 3-speed H-pattern gearshift was just like a Ford truck and made it easy for novice tractor operators to climb on and go to work.*

RIGHT: *Willard Nordenson planned these tractors for a new generation of operators. He placed both brake pedals together on the right and the foot clutch on the left, in familiar positions for drivers coming from trucks at the time.*

Sales brochures addressed that conversion. Beneath an appealing photo of the Model L at work, the brochure asked, "A Good Question—What are farmers doing with their work animals when they purchase a Model 'L' Tractor?

"Answer—They are trading them for cattle, hogs, or other income-producing live stock."

"We came up with a machine, the Model L," Nordenson said, "that could be delivered from Moline for $465. The Model LA, which had 50 percent more power, could be delivered for $545.

"The thinking in those days," he concluded, "was to make an affordable product for the largest number of people." The Model L and LA summed up Deere & Company's answers to the question of small farm power.

Deere's Model 62 cultivates a family garden along side the larger corn crop. Deere manufactured the 62 only in 1937. As the predecessor to the compact Model L, these tractors are easily recognized because of the bold JD initials cast beneath the radiator. Deere & Company Archives

CHAPTER 15

1938–1943

JOHN DEERE
JOHN DEERE

NEXT GENERATION GPs

ARE SPELLED G AND H

PREVIOUS: 1939 Model H
Deere introduced the Model H for 1939, selling it at $595. By February 6, 1947 when Waterloo stopped production, it had manufactured more than 58,000 of these H models in all their variations.

RIGHT: 1939 Model H
Waterloo's Elmer McCormick first attempted to narrow the hood of Deere's row crop tractors with the Model A and B. Henry Dreyfuss' designers found ways to tighten the dimensions even more to improve operator visibility forward and down.

It was an era of optimism and growth. While city folks bought new homes and cars, corporations enlarged their work forces, sales staffs, and product inventories. Farmers felt some sense of the expansion of the economy as well. Land that had belonged to their neighbors, less fortunate during the early 1930s, now was theirs. Farmers today tell stories of older farmers whose parents leased their farms in the 1920s. When the hard times hit, they lost the farms and their possessions as well. Ten years later, the same banks that had foreclosed on loans for $200-an-acre land, resold the land at $200 per acre to farmers who paid it off in five years. Then those farmers went after more land.

Deere & Company's Model D remained in production, along with the A and B. However, technology had advanced enough that Deere knew it should cater to the successful farmer who was considering replacing his old Chevrolet with a new Pontiac. The Pontiac not only offered more features, it provided more power. In Detroit, carmakers sensed the first tremors of a horsepower race. (Theo Brown, a true economic expansionist, owned both a Pontiac and a Buick.)

A similar upgrading was stirring among farm tractor manufacturers. As many options as there were for General Motors' Pontiacs, Chrysler's DeSotos and Ford's soon-to-be-introduced Mercury, there was equal variety for farmers. Massey-Harris offered a four-wheel-drive row crop tractor, the GP, and then followed it with a more-conventionally configured Challenger. Oliver introduced the stylish Model 70, and the Graham-Paige automobile company introduced its even-more stylish Graham-Bradley tractor, a machine that it sold exclusively through Sears Roebuck & Company catalog and retail outlets.

140 170 200 230
WATER TEMPERATURE
OIL PRESSURE
JOHN DEERE

OPPOSITE: 1941 Model HNH
Electric starting and lighting were options on all H models. This HNH sold new for nearly $650 with its options.

OPPOSITE INSET: *The power-take-off (PTO) and the hydraulic Powr-Lift were standard features on H model tractors. California Hi-Crops ran on 6.00-12 front tires and 8.00-38 rears to slip into the troughs between crop beds.*

BELOW: *Deere's 99.7-cubic-inch engine measured 3.56-inch bore and 5.0-inch stroke. At 1,400 rpm, the engine developed 12.5 horsepower at the drawbar and 14.8 off the belt pulley.*

The economy that brought growth to American industry also began the upturn in agriculture. This same economic boom also induced growing disaffection and dissatisfaction among farm children and hired hands. City jobs paid better wages for labor that demanded only 50 to 60 hours a week. Farm chores never ended. City workers got vacations. Commercial offices and industrial plants closed at midday Saturday and remained shuttered Sunday. There was no 4 a.m. milking at a steel plant or in an insurance office on a cold Christmas morning. But it was a seduction based on appearances.

The Second Depression - 1937-38

The reality of the late 1930s was framed by experiences from the first half of the decade. While prosperity had returned, few trusted it. Farmers who had gotten by with aging or failing equipment during the early 1930s replaced it in 1935 and 1936. But they bought larger tractors, harvesters, implements, and other tools.

JOHN DEERE
WATER TEMPERATURE
OIL PRESSURE

JOHN DEERE
JOHN DEERE

OPPOSITE: 1941 Model HWH
Dreyfuss' designer Jim Conner was responsible for the classic, powerful "face" of Deere's styled tractors. He drew nearly a dozen variations but Deere's chairman Charlie Wiman and the board felt this version best blended function with appealing appearance.

LEFT: *The Keller family's tractor is the first HWH assembled. Its adjustable front and rear axles gave California farmers great flexibility in matching tire tread width to crop rows.*

In many cases, this eliminated the need for a hired hand. The U.S. Census concluded that unemployment or underemployment in the cities had kept farmers, their families and their farmhands on rural lands because they couldn't afford to leave. When rains returned to the Midwest in the late 1930s and farm crop output increased, prices dropped again, creating another depressed cycle that lasted through 1938 and finally abated in 1940 with the onset of the next world war. Then, too, there were millions of jobs in the cities.

Now farmers found themselves with less help and more work to do. The tractor assumed a greater obligation to help its operator meet larger demands. Manufacturers listened to their branch managers who reported what the farmers wanted: more power, more capacity, more versatility, more, more, more. While the early Deere GPs had been two-plow rated, that was no longer enough.

Deere, IHC, Allis-Chalmers, Minneapolis-Moline, and the rest of the manufacturers had responded by making each successive change an increase in strength and an improvement in features and appearance. By mid-February 1937, all the executives within Deere had seen the first styled Model B tractors. They urged the project forward. That May, Deere & Company began production of its new Model G as a three-plow tractor

1946 Model HN with Deere integral 2-row cultivator

Just as Waterloo's engineers had done with the larger Model G tractors, they achieved higher horsepower output by increasing engine speed. Model H engines ran at a rated 1,400 rpm compared with the B engines they replaced which ran at 1,150 rpm.

with the same four-speed transmission recently introduced on A and B models. It offered the new G either on steel wheels or pneumatic rubber. With its three-plow capability, Deere promoted it as the tractor to replace both of the farmer's five-or-six horse teams. By the time the first production Gs appeared at their branches, the company had recorded its best year ever. In 1937, Deere reached $100.4 million in sales, and enjoyed its second most profitable year ever, with $14.9 million in net income.

Good but not Great

The Model G was a big step forward, but it was not flawless. Henry Dreyfuss and Associates helped in the design of the early Model G tractors. Unstyled at introduction, these models featured a small engine cowl and an exposed, sloping steering column that lead to an outside vertical steering post. This enhanced the visibility forward and downward, however, this slim configuration took advantage of an ill-conceived engineering decision based on the fact that petroleum distillates and some of the other lower grade fuels burned cooler than kerosene or gasoline. McCormick's engineering staff had concluded that a small 11-gallon cooling system would keep the engine within the proper temperature range for its maximum operating efficiency. However the size of radiator that Deere fitted couldn't meet the challenges of summer work in warmer climates. Many of the first year's Model Gs, something like 2,750 of the 4,500 produced, suffered chronic cooling problems. Later versions replaced the small radiator with a larger one on which engineers creased the top to accommodate the steering wheel shaft. Adding the extra rows in the new radiator increased capacity by two gallons and this solved the problem very effectively.

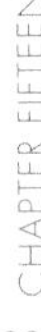

Dax Kimmelshue's narrow front H was one of about 1,100 that Deere manufactured over the lifetime of the model. Deere's integral two-row cultivator took good advantage of the tractor's onboard hydraulic system.

ABOVE: 1947 Model G

Deere's G replaced the powerful Model A tractors and first appeared in 1941. Styled models with Henry Dreyfuss' and Jim Conner's fine sheet metal began in January 1947.

RIGHT: *The G was a business-like machine that weighed 5,624 pounds and sold in 1947 for $1,879. It sat 68 inches to the operator's seat.*

Deere & Company issued a product recall. Dealers replaced the smaller radiators and also modified the shutters by removing the outside lever linkage and replacing it with a crank mechanism and lever hidden under the cowl, all under warranty.

Farmers with a critical ear heard something different with the Model G. In fact, the sound of each of the Deere's tractors, widely known as "Poppin' Johnnies" by this time, had varied slightly. This was due to engine specifications: The big D produced the fullest voice of the lineup. The B's "pop" had a higher pitch due to its engine's higher operating speed. Both the A and G ran at the same engine speed but their bore and stroke differed and this affected the tone of their sound.

By the time the public saw the Model G, Elmer McCormick's engineers at Waterloo were well along with development of their other project, the O.X. companion to the G. Even as they acknowledged the market for larger tractors, they conceived this one basically as a single-plow machine. They intended the O.X. to supplement the agricultural market not quite fully served by the Model L. This was a true row-crop GP. Frank Silloway's marketing and sales people even proposed that this tractor, renamed the Model H before production began in late 1938, was the perfect second tractor for farms needing something suitable for large vegetable gardens.

McCormick and Brown continued to develop the adjustable rear track. The farmer could adjust the span between the rear wheels of the Model H through a broad range, from 44 inches to 80 inches. Deere retained the two-cylinder engine coupled to a three-speed transmission. The "Decision Copy," dated September 30, 1938, even went so far as to describe its appearance. *Two Cylinder* magazine reproduced the memo:

"Section IV. Desirable Mechanical Features

"G. Appearance - "The tractor follows in appearance that of our styled model 'A' and 'B' tractors, with simple external lines carefully laid out to bring out the impression of ruggedness and strength."

Curiously, while Waterloo Engineering referred to prototypes for the Model H as the O.X. series, according to the Two-Cylinder Club's research, this O.X.-designation reappeared on other post-H model experimentals decades later. To further confuse things, O.X. prototypes of the Model H appeared in both styled and unstyled versions. One unstyled prototype sported an inclined steering shaft ahead of the radiator and a matching parallel-angled steering wheel pedestal. It looked very rakish, as though it were swept back by the wind or high speed. After a series of development models, production of the tractor began in mid-January 1939, built only as a dual-front-wheeled tricycle. On March 21, Brown and others saw the styled Model H and production changed over shortly afterward.

Henry Ford Returns

Henry Ford may have withdrawn from the tractor business, but he certainly had not forgotten the machine or the industry. In all of Theo Brown's encounters with Henry while Deere devised plows for the Fordson, Brown came to understand the passion Ford had for "his hobby," the farm tractor. Of course, the Fordson had been, for much of its life, a fairly

OPPOSITE: 1953 Model GH

Iowa collector Bob Pollock has made a habit of finding and restoring Deere's tallest, highest giants. Waterloo manufactured just 235 of these high crops. In the United States, most went into cotton or sugar cane farming in the south.

BELOW: *G owners had their choice of front ends, from this adjustable wide front, to single narrow versions, to row-crop variations with or without Deere's revolutionary Roll-O-Matic that accommodated sidehills. These front tires are 7.50-20.00 and add to the tractor's remarkable crop clearance.*

profitable hobby. So, soon after his automotive engineers had proven his new V-8 engine reliable, and gotten the next generation of cars off the drawing boards and onto test roads, Henry put some of his engineering staff to work devising his next tractor.

After his creative engineers had come up with a number of spectacular missteps, Irish inventor/salesman Harry Ferguson showed up at Ford's doors with a very workable concept that he had introduced in 1935. Ford threw his entire tractor engineering staff at the machine. On April 27, 1939, Henry Ford presented it to the public. The Model 9N "Ford Tractor with Ferguson System" provided the farmer with yet another compact tractor. However, due to Ferguson's clever engineering (his innovative three-point hitch and the integral two-bottom plow), this lightweight machine had the effectiveness of something bigger and heavier. This time, too, with Harry Ferguson's help, Ford offered a full line of implements.

Just like Deere's early Model G, Ford's 9N was not without shortcomings. Ferguson's hydraulics, while used in a new configuration to control plow draft, worked perfectly only in ideal conditions. Ford engineers worked on the problems of taming Ferguson's hydraulics. Brown got to operate one during the Waterloo Cattle Congress Tractor Show on September 26, and he was not terribly impressed.

"Hard to maintain uniform depth," he wrote, "much wheel slippage, can't control width of cut. All in all, not satisfactory. All the Fords (this was No. 322) have aluminum cast panels, sides, cowls, etc., as dies could not be made quickly enough, so this tractor must have been very, very expensive to make." The same day, he also saw and ran IHC's Model A, B, H, and M tractors.

"Got on Model A IHC but their 'cultivision' is interfered with by steering wheels, etc., so it is hard on the eyes. Their B is an attempt to make a wide tread out of A."

Throughout 1939, Brown had been working on cabs for the Model A and B tractors. "There is considerable interest in a cab for tractors. Steel cabs are noisy and hot." Brown's initial creation functioned just like a convertible top on an automobile. A later version flipped over the windshield when the operator wanted or needed to stand. By late October, Brown had sent a prototype flip top to Waterloo for McCormick's engineers to test further. (As with many ideas in Brown's diaries, there is no follow-up, suggesting either the idea failed in the field or its potential manufacturing costs killed it.)

G
JOHN DEERE

1953 Model GH

The 412.5-cubic-inch engine on the Gs measured 6.125-inch bore and 7.00-inch stroke. At 975 rpm, it developed 34.5 horsepower on the drawbar and 38.1 off the belt pulley.

All throughout 1939 and into early 1940, Elmer McCormick's engineers also worked on a single-front-wheel variation on the Model H, designated the HN, that was "better adapted to the cultivation of vegetables, which are planted in rows of 28 inches or less," as Brown noted. McCormick's staff completed the first successful experiment in late 1939. Waterloo's previous level of development success was so high that McCormick's staff fabricated only a single HN prototype. The second HN tractor Waterloo assembled was the first production model, introduced as 1940 models.

By late April 1940, Brown's perspective on Ford's 9N tractor had changed, as it had throughout the industry. After Deere's Annual Meeting on April 30, 1940, Brown wrote, "Ford competition is beginning to worry us. The hydraulic control particularly. I sensed this last year and have two patent applications pretty well advanced with claims allowed which should be a better way of doing what Ford tries to." Just two days later Brown went out to Waterloo to discuss his new power-lift concept with Charley Stone and Elmer McCormick. During this visit, Waterloo's "new R.X. tractor was shown and explained. We also saw one at work in the field. This tractor is to be in place of the Model A tractor starting July 1, 1941." With no power lift or tools designed for it yet, Brown knew his next assignment. "We will want to work on implements to be controlled hydraulically for depth. Need a device so tool will return to same depth when lowered." Yet, the risks of decentralization struck again in mid-June when Brown sat in on a three-hour meeting to discuss the plans and concept for a new 18-horsepower tractor. It followed nearly the same specifications as Waterloo's R.X. prototypes.

As early as December 1938, Brown's diaries began to report on events in Europe. On December 5, he wrote, "Hitler's persecution of the Jews in Germany is a terrible thing and is a reincarnation of the dark ages." Almost a year later, in the margins of Thanksgiving Day, November 30, 1939, he observed, "Russian invasion of Finland is horrible." On March 1, 1940, he noted that "Sumner Welles of the State Department is in Germany to see Hitler and find out if any peace is possible. He is making the rounds of Europe, but it is feared without much chance of success." Two months later he updated, writing, "War news most disheartening. Germany getting the best of it in Norway." Then, two days later, on May 2, he noted, "Allies withdrew from Norway," and four days after that, "The Question is 'Will Italy join Germany in war on the allies?" On May 10, he copied most of the front page headlines from the *Moline Daily Dispatch*, reporting Hitler's invasion of Belgium, Netherlands, and Luxembourg, and noting, "This appears to be one of the momentous days of history." Reflecting that observation, he began with that date to devote nearly as much space in his diaries to war news as to Deere's internal engineering developments. Often, Deere's notes barely had room in the margins of war time events.

The war's impact did not take long to reach Moline's factories. In the directors' meeting on June 13, Brown learned that "we have been asked to figure [costs] on gun carriages and as a patriotic duty, may feel we must take on this work. We will be lucky to break even." Plans to construct a huge branch office building program that the board had approved six months earlier, including a four-story warehouse at Waterloo, went on indefinite hold. Still, Deere's domestic peacetime business continued and new product development work pressed ahead. Recalling the shortages of materials during World War I, Charlie Wiman, on July 9, "asked me to organize some means for getting the factories to adopt as far as possible the use of standard automobile sizes of rims and tires so it is possible to use old automobile tires on implements. The best size rim to use wherever possible is the 16 inch rim as that is standard for automobiles." Deere adopted this size very quickly and continued using it for years through the war and afterward.

On Brown's November 13 visit to Waterloo, Bill Fraher, Elmer McCormick's assistant engineer, "promises [Brown would see] an S.X. tractor for November 25 meeting. McCormick showed me a model and layouts of machine gun turrets mounted on a Model A tractor." Brown saw the machine on November 25 when "several points about drawbar and implement attachment holes were discussed." (As with the previous experimental F.X., the R.X. disappeared from Brown's diaries without a trace.)

Deere found itself balancing civilian agricultural production against increasing U.S. government contracts with some difficulty. Brown reported that on February 12, 1941, the Waterloo factory produced 321 tractors in three shifts, its highest output to date. Deere's

BELOW: *For an engineer, Theo Brown was a very capable artist. His diaries are full of blends such as this, where he has illustrated the front end of the new styled Model H, along with notes about the weather, his wife's visit to her mother, and their dinner plans that same evening.* Theo Brown Diaries, Special Collections Library, George C. Gordon Library, Worchester Polytechnic Institute

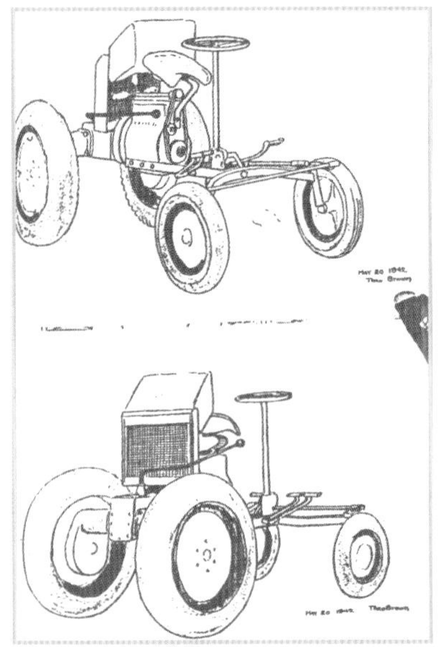

1940 sales had topped $84 million with net income of $12.2 million. For comparison, first-ranked IHC's sales from all divisions was $274.6 million with net income of $23.2 million; Allis-Chalmers for the first time crept ahead of Deere in gross sales, at $87.1 million, but it earned just $5.1 million net income. (In mid-June when Brown happened to meet Allis' tractor division manager, Harry C. Merritt on a train, Merritt confided that "their tractor division is the only end of their business that makes any money. Their tractor division volume is 60 to 65 percent of their total volume.)

The balancing act between government contracts and agricultural machinery production began to represent significant numbers. By early April 1941, the board reported "Deere & Company has war contracts for about $18.5 million for differentials and transmissions in tanks." Not even a week later, the board approved another production variation for Waterloo's Model H. Again, the Two-Cylinder Club's research revealed the decision from April 11, 1941:

"To meet the demand from the field for high clearance adjustable tread front wheels on the Model H tractor, we will adopt an "HWH" tractor similar to the present AWH and BWN tractors. To obtain additional clearance under the rear axle, we will change the rear wheel with tires from 7-32 to 8-38." This changed the angle of attitude, visually, of the tractor, from nose-up with the HW or HN, to nose-down with the HWH or HWN.

Farmers could vary the front axle width by 12 inches. Waterloo engineers completed one prototype, similar to the HN. Public announcement and production came about two months later. On May 27 engineering published the decision to produce the HNH narrow version. Production for these two series continued only through mid-1942.

At the end of 1941, Henry Dreyfuss and his designers and engineers had caught up with the Model G. Plans inside Deere & Company intended that the company would

Theo Brown's diary steadily reported the progress of World War II. It was a subject that was on everyone's lips. At a monthly meeting of the Farm Equipment Institute (FEI) advisory standards committee on Friday, September 12, 1941, Charles E. Frudden of Allis-Chalmers approached him. Frudden wanted to talk to Brown "of an idea he has of conserving materials during this national emergency. He proposes leaving off starters from tractors to save the copper, zinc, etc., also save chromium by painting tractors grey for the 'duration,' and other eliminations. He has not mentioned it to anyone else." Brown promised to talk with Frank Silloway about Deere's thoughts. "It seems to me to be a most constructive idea."

It was a prescient conversation. On November 13, the Chicago Tribune reported that while the farm equipment industry "has been whirring along [through 1941] at about 121 percent of its 1940 production rate," the Office of Production Management (OPM) proposed cutting output to 80 percent of its 1940 level for 1942. The industry hoped that the 80 percent figure would apply only to new domestic production and new products. It lobbied to retain 100 percent output for repair parts and export manufacture.

introduce the new version early the next year. As the year drew to a close, Brown conceived a small single-row tractor. He based his idea on reversing the direction of travel of Moline's small LA model. His notes for November 13, 1941, described the operator sitting ahead of the engine rather than behind it. He went further in the next few days, pushing his wartime frugality. He envisioned a simple single-row cultivator that used a motorcycle with an outrigger wheel. Unfortunately, the war caught up with everybody early one morning in December.

Pearl Harbor Changes Everything

December 7, 1941, was a date that would "live in infamy" in Moline as well as in Hawaii and Washington. The events at sunrise in Pearl Harbor shaped corporate policies for all American manufacturers for the next three years. For Deere, its styled Model G appeared with a manual starting system as its predecessors did. Deere shipped the tractor on steel wheels and it held off introducing the new long-anticipated six-speed transmission. The transmission and electric system used too many metals that were precious to the war effort. Raw materials costs would have been prohibitive, even if supplies had been available.

As it was, the federal government reasoned that with raw materials and other product shortages in effect, annual price increases might represent an avoidable hardship to domestic consumers. Deere and others could not raise prices to cover improvements to existing productions. They could publish a higher price only for a new model. Changing the designation of a vastly improved, Dreyfuss-styled, Model G to "GM" allowed Deere to recover the costs of all the improvements.

The plans for the 1942 Model G included Dreyfuss's sheet metal work as well as rubber tires, electric lights, and self-starter and the new six-speed transmission. Deere delivered very few that were so fully equipped. At the same time, however, the company introduced the GN (single front) and GW (wide front axle). Farmers could order rear axles that provided tread width as great as 104 inches.

Keeping the Home Farms Working

For farmers throughout the United States, Brown continued work on his own prototype reversed-and-revised LA, now designated the Model 101. He watched it do field work in mid-October against an LA and an Allis-Chalmers Model B. "The new tractor has many advantages," he wrote on October 24, "the perfect vision for cultivating, ease of getting on and off tractor, position of operator out of dirt. The only disadvantages seemed to be that of handling levers of towed implements." Elmer McCormick, as chairman of the Power Farming Committee and a long-time admirer of Brown's ideas and innovations, reported to the board the next day. "Though this tractor does not in its exterior appearance follow the conventional line, it might be a forerunner of a new design of tractor. The machine has sufficient merit to warrant further development work."

Six months later, the 101's radical looks still provoked strong responses. At the April 27, 1943, quarterly directors meeting, Brown showed his new tractor. "They all said it was so

OPPOSITE: *One of the great frustrations of Theo Brown's life was his inability to get his cherished Model 101 compact tractor into production. The idea came to him in November 1941. Over the ensuing months, his notebooks are filled with variations on his ideas. This concept used the engine from the Model LA. Deere built numerous prototypes and thoroughly tested each one.* Theo Brown Diaries, Special Collections Library, George C. Gordon Library, Worchester Polytechnic Institute

In early March 1942, as Deere geared up to take on war time production that produced 500 M-3 tank transmissions and differentials each month and 400,000 75-mm shells, Charlie Wiman told the directors about Deere's newest order "for 3,184 MG1 crawler-type tractors designed by Cleveland Tractor Company for the Air Corps. They are to haul bombers and service them. They weigh something like 6 or 7 tons and sell for $7,600. We are to make 1 in October and then in a year reach 25 a day. It is a big job that will keep 3000 men busy." It prompted Wiman in late April to propose merging Cleveland Tractor with its small and medium-size Cletrac crawler line, with Deere. The board was unenthusiastic. Two months later, on June 19, Wiman resigned as president of Deere to serve in the U.S. Army as a Colonel. He was assigned to the tank and combat vehicle division, industrial service and production, in the ordnance department. He never forgot his middle name was Deere. The company's wartime production soared to 1,500 tank transmissions a month, and 10,000 of the 75-mm and 90-mm shells each month. The initial order came through for 2,100 of the Cletrac bomber tugs. Deere soon contracted for bomber fuselages and ship superstructures for the Navy. By late July, Brown estimated the volume of materiel production for all of 1942 would top $200 million.

revolutionary they would have to get used to it but thought it offered real possibilities." When Wiman himself got to operate it in early June, he confessed to Brown that when he initially saw the 101 idea, he didn't think much of it, but "today he was very enthusiastic. He liked the appearance of the tractor, particularly the rear view, also the handling, lift, cultivating."

Colonel Wiman's insistence on continuing civilian product development during the war kept Deere's engineers and its plants well-occupied. The company had two projects in the works. The first tractor would come in immediately after the war ended, and as with all the models before, it would provide the ground work for the transitions ahead. The other, a machine moving now through the design stage, offered a development so significant that it would change the thinking about every tractor that was yet to come.

OPPOSITE INSET TOP: *Brown referred to his concept for the Model 101 tractor as the "all visibility tractor." The sight-lines he drew here make this apparent. He imagined the tractor as a single row cultivating machine. These drawings from November 18 and 19, 1941, and show the machine in its earliest incarnations.* Theo Brown Diaries, Special Collections Library, George C. Gordon Library, Worchester Polytechnic Institute

OPPOSITE INSET BOTTOM: *Once the idea of tractor "styling" engaged Deere's engineering department, a number of inventors had ideas. Here, on March 18, 1938, Theo Brown has added sheet metal to shroud the engine sides on the Model A, complete with a fairing that partially covers the belt pulley wheel.* Theo Brown Diaries, Special Collections Library, George C. Gordon Library, Worchester Polytechnic Institute

OPPOSITE: *Brown was a fiercely loyal Deere company man. Through his career, he earned more than 100 patents and hatched thousands of ideas, including this one, on February 26, 1940, for a new company trademark or dealers' logo. His diary entry on July 29, showed the official version and noted that the "trademark [was] adopted by Deere & Company Board of Directors, July 30."* Theo Brown Diaries, Special Collections Library, George C. Gordon Library, Worchester Polytechnic Institute

The Experimental Meetings,

Written by Theo Brown
1920s through 1940s

(During Brown's final years with Deere, he took a number of writing assignments from Charlie Wiman. In addition to the history of Deere's tractor development, he produced a paper for Deere's public relations department on how tractor design came about at Deere & Company.)

"Before the advent of the general purpose type of tractor there was not the need for the same close cooperation between the various factories of a company like Deere & Comapany as exists today. Unlike the tractor, the horse is not subject to changes in design. His general anatomy remains constant. The horse is taken as is, and horse drawn equipment is designed accordingly.

"When the general purpose type of tractor was brought out 20 odd years ago, the complete mechanization of the farm became possible. The added clearance under the tractor body and the variable wheel tread made it practical to plant, cultivate and harvest row crops with tractor power. It was possible to mount a cultivator on a tractor in a manner in which the operator guides the cultivator as he steers the tractor.

"To mount a cultivator on a general purpose type of tractor means that attaching points must be provided on the tractor. Here then came the need for the cultivator designer and the tractor engineer to get together to work out the problem. It was soon recognized that the success of this general purpose type of tractor depended on how well the integral implements performed.

"A Deere & Company Power Farming Conference was held during February 1929, attended by 46 factory managers and experimental men. In January 1931, a 'Power Farming Committee' was appointed by Col. Wiman to study the whole subject of power farming and particularly general purpose tractors and integral equipment. Members of this committee were Elmer McCormick, Lou Paradise, Harold White and Theo Brown. The idea was to keep the various experimental departments alive, as to what was going on in the power farming field, to learn the other fellows' problems, to rub shoulders with the experimental [staff] in other plants and to bring out the necessity for close cooperation between implement and tractor engineers. The first get together was in December 1932, the last meeting in 1944.

"During this period of years, new models of general purpose tractors and new models and types of integral equipment have appeared. All these changes created new problems as to how the integral equipment has to be attached and detached with the least effort and time.

Friday, March 18, 1938

"To care for this problem, a 'Quick Detachable' committee was appointed. Later, a 'Wheel Committee' has aided in keeping down the number of different wheels and the quality of design. Later still, when hydraulic control came into the picture, a committee, under the chairmanship of Wayne Worthington, was promptly appointed.

"Not only did this need for cooperation between our own factories exist, but the need was apparent for some form of cooperation between members of the industry. The lack of any standardization as to draw bar locations and power take off locations on different makes of tractors, was causing untold complication when trying to attach the different makes to tractors to power-take-off-driven implements. The Advisory Engineering Committee of the Farm Equipment Institute Safety Committee took this matter in hand. Deere is represented in this committee by Elmer McCormick, Bill Coultas and Al Johnson. This committee is now working on the standardization of remote cylinder dimensions for hydraulic control so that different makes of tractors and implements equipped with hydraulic control can be used together.

"This then gives a brief resume of what is the background for these meetings. The one word 'cooperation' expresses it."

—Theo Brown, September 30, 1947

CHAPTER 16

1943–1954

ENTER DUBUQUE, WELCOME THE M

PREVIOUS: 1946 MODEL D
Deere's steadfast Model D was among the last of its old series tractors to receive Henry Dreyfuss's attention. The first styled D appeared in April 1939. Deere kept the D in production through June 1953.

RIGHT: *Over its life, the Model D engine grew from 6.5-inch bore to 6.75-inch bore although Waterloo engineering didn't change the 7.0 inch stroke. Deere announced the end of production in early 1953 but demand continued even after the plant had committed the space. This forced Waterloo staff to assemble the final 92 of the 1953 models on a city street along side the mill shop.*

World War II forced diversity on Deere & Company. Alongside tractors, tank engines, and military crawlers, the company produced artillery shell casings. When the war ended, the U.S. government asked Deere to continue with that and other projects as well.

This signaled to Charlie Wiman the need to increase capacity. Land around the Waterloo facilities largely was spoken for. The board already had made commitments for the remaining space available in Moline. So it looked outside the immediate area. Criteria included "navigable water" on which to bring raw materials in and to ship completed products out. The board selected Dubuque, Iowa, and Wiman convinced them in January 1945, to seek outside financing for an ambitious $30 million project of land acquisition and building construction.

The new plant opened two years later. Within six months, the Dubuque factory was manufacturing Deere's new Model M tractor. Wiman had insisted that the experimental department continue developing new products for peacetime even as the war continued and reduced supplies of raw materials had substantially curtailed the company's own agricultural equipment production.

The other impetus for this pressure to expand facilities and update the product lines came from Michigan again. Henry Ford had returned to tractor manufacture in 1939. This time he arrived with a strong advantage. Scotsman Harry Ferguson's ingenious three-point hitch had made Ford's small 9N tractor into an industry giant. Ford replaced the 9N in 1942 with the Model 2N (for the

OHN DEERE
D2890R

OPPOSITE: *Automobile designers attempt to fill the wheel wells with big tires to give the sense of power. They should take note of Deere's styled D with its 13.5-28 rear tires. With this size rubber, the D sold for $1,445 in 1946.*

same fiscal reasons that led Deere to introduce the GM). The Ford-Ferguson tractor flummoxed Deere's engineers and product specialists.

Ford offered it only as a standard-front low-clearance model. There were no narrow- or wide-front variations. Ford made clear he had no plans for tricycle fronts or high-crop models either. Yet his small tractor could do 50 percent more work per hour than its competitors. It outsold Deere by the same margin.

Theo Brown learned that in California Ferguson's hydraulic control made Ford's N series the best-selling tractor in the state. "Ford has stolen the show with his tractor with hydraulic power," he wrote during a visit there. Towed implements needed broad headlands to swing around as they reversed direction. Ferguson's integral plow and hydraulics on Ford's tractor let operators maneuver tightly. This increased their yield per acre on California's expensive farm land. Broad headlands were a luxury few California farmers would accept.

ABOVE: *Deere made its effective on-board hydraulics standard equipment on these styled D tractors. Electric starting and lights remained optional.*

California was "the hydraulic state," as Brown learned on a later trip. Visiting dozens of farmers throughout the vast farming regions, he saw countless homemade adaptations using Ge-Be hydraulics to operate scrapers, wide disk harrows, chisel plows, and even a Case combine. After visiting one 12,000-acre farm, and seeing another that stretched 4 miles long and 1 1/2 miles wide, Brown understood the labor-saving efficiency that hydraulic power brought to big-scale farming. Hydraulics permitted operators to set, operate, and lift implements weighing much more, and covering more ground, than they could handle by mechanical levers. Tractor makers responded with stronger engines running larger hydraulic pumps through additional hydraulic cylinders; this expanded the work potential of each tractor, implement, and operator. Working many rows at once enabled California farmers to achieve huge crop output using fewer machines even on the vast farms Brown visited.

Brown continued development testing on his one-row cultivating tractor. He already had fitted it with the next generation of Emil Jirsa's Powr-Trol experimental hydraulics. By July 15, Brown had four prototypes testing. Elmer McCormick and Wayne Worthington each spent a day cultivating in small corn, alternating between Brown's prototype and an Allis-Chalmers Model B. "They felt the idea of the new tractor is sound, that is, in placing the man to the front. It makes for a much better cultivating job. They both felt that the very best engineering talent should be used in making a final design." In the nomenclature of Deere's experimental department, Brown's prototype now had a designation, the Model 101. By September 1944, as the war's appetite for men and material continued, Brown pushed for a 1946 introduction of his new machine. The board agreed to continuing "the engineering in a very vigorous manner and [giving] Nordenson at the Tractor Company the job. We all want the 101 to be as near perfect as possible before it is put on the market."

Working hard to get his tractor into production, Brown tried a new innovation during a demonstration in late October. He attached a small spring to the steering handlebar so that this kept the front wheel pointed inward toward the wall of the furrow.

"By having the corners of the field rounded on about a 50-foot radius, the tractor ran without an operator. It seemed to work very well and ran several hours by itself. We measured the distance around the field at seven-tenths of a mile. The tractor pulling a 16 inch single bottom integral plow made a round trip in 9 1/2 minutes or 4.4 miles per hour, which means plowing an acre an hour rather than 3/4 acres per hour."

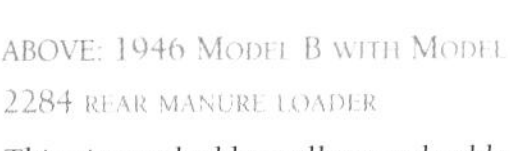
ABOVE: 1946 MODEL B WITH MODEL 2284 REAR MANURE LOADER
This rig worked by pulleys and cables off the tractor's belt pulley. The operator lowered the boom to horizontal and ran the forked shovel outward, scooping manure as it went. California collector Dax Kimmelshue found and restored this labor saver.

RIGHT: *Theo Brown and his colleagues never stopped imagining tasks Deere's tractors might perform. In 1939, the implement division introduced these rear-mounted manure loaders. The operator moved the material by scooping it up, swinging the boom around over a spreader or to another location, and dumping the hinged shovel.*

Immediately after Charlie Wiman resigned from Deere to serve in the U.S. Army ordnance department Deere's board elected Burton Peek as its new company president. Peek, another Theo Brown fan, led the next quarterly directors meeting. Throughout the session, Peek referred to the machine either as the full-vision tractor or "the Theo Brown tractor." It was, he said, "Deere's first tractor specifically designed for implements." However, even though Wiman was no longer in Moline, he communicated regularly with Brown. Brown wrote that Wiman wanted to see the Model 101 with 12 to 14 horsepower and "to be sold for as low a price as possible [so] it will find the small farmer and market gardener and be a second tractor on large farms." Later in the fall, Wiman encouraged Brown to provide 14 1/2 horsepower and get a four-speed transmission to

ABOVE: *The only way this machine could work was with its rear pedestal planted hard onto the ground to stabilize the tractor as the loaded shovel swung around on the boom. Deere advised operators to place heavy counterweight on the tractor front end as well.*

1950 Model MT

Charlie Wiman hoped the Model M would challenge Henry Ford's new N-series tractors. He assigned Willard Nordenson, father of the successful L and LA models to create the machine in the new Dubuque factory. Dubuque introduced the tricycle version MT in 1949.

ensure a suitable transport speed. He suggested Brown go to Salinas, California, to watch his machine undergo further tests.

Return to Peacetime Production

After the war ended, Waterloo engineering restored the Model G to its original build specifications with electric start and rubber tires, equipment that had been standard issue up until the day after Pearl Harbor. Deere dropped the M suffix from the tractor's designation as well.

Waterloo introduced a variation on the G in March 1950. The new high-crop GH gave the normal GW wide-front model an additional 14 inches of ground clearance. Waterloo specifically intended the GH for sugar cane growers in the southeast. Deere shipped 73 of the GH models to Louisiana branches for sale and distribution while another 46 went to Florida.

Waterloo manufactured the final Model G in February 1953. Between May 1937 and December 1941, it had produced nearly 11,200 unstyled versions. From January 1942 through March 10, 1947, it manufactured 9,920 war-time GM tractors, and from March 7, 1947, until February 19, 1953, Deere assembled another 41,530 styled Gs in all variations, bringing total output to around 64,642 tractors. For the Model H, production began October 29, 1938, and ended February 6, 1947, after manufacturing approximately 60,116 tractors.

At this same time, Deere & Company continued upgrading and up-rating its venerable Model D, and the A and B as well. Unstyled narrow-front- and wide-front-axle Model As appeared in 1935, and in 1937, the company introduced a Hi-Crop version on each front

end. The next year Model As got styled with each version continuing in production beneath Henry Dreyfuss' handsome sheet metal. At the same time, Deere introduced the four-speed transmission. In 1941, the six-speed transmissions replaced the four, and a new 5.5x6.75 inch engine increased overall displacement.

Deere brought out the styled version of the D in 1939. It added an optional electric generator, starter, and lighting. The Model B, introduced with a 4.25x5.25-inch engine on a short frame, stretched 5.5 inches in 1937 and added narrow- and wide-front models and hi-clearance versions almost at the same time. In 1938, the company replaced the tin work with Dreyfuss's styled versions, and engine stroke grew from 5.25 to 5.5 inches. The six-speed transmission appeared in 1941 as with the other models, but in 1947 the entire tractor grew again. Overall length stretched another 6.8 inches to 132.3 inches and height increased from 56 to 59.6 inches. Shipping weight rose from 2,880 pounds to 4,000, some

One common complaint that dealers heard was that operators had a hard time getting onto the M tricycles. With rear tread adjustable from 54 inches down to 38, it's easy to see how farmers wondered where they were to set their feet.

JOHN DEERE
JOHN DEERE

of which came from the addition of electric starting. Engine displacement jumped up to 4.69x5.5 inch bore and stroke. Where Model B frames formerly had been cast, Waterloo engineering now stamped them out of pressed steel forms. This offered greater rigidity and improved overall quality.

Dubuque Tractors Move the Benchmark

Willard Nordenson's success in bringing the Model L and LA into production earned him another tractor assignment and then a promotion. At Moline, Nordenson had devised and developed the prototype S.X. tractors and he led the team that brought them into production as Deere's Model M. Charlie Wiman was very pleased with Nordenson's efforts. In 1946, a year before Deere opened the Dubuque tractor works, Wiman named Nordenson to be the new plant's engineering manager.

As Nordenson had done with the L, he mounted the M's two-cylinder engine upright. Its crankshaft ran parallel to the direction of travel. Mike Mack, Waterloo's former director of the product engineering center, theorized that "Nordenson just decided to do his thing, and by making it vertical, it set it a little bit apart, somewhat of a departure from the traditional." The engine burned gasoline only, running at 1,650 rpm.

Deere & Company hoped the M would be the perfect foil for Ford's N-series. To compete directly with the Ford, Deere introduced the M first in a standard front general-purpose utility tractor only. But its power rating created a market that its standard front end didn't completely fill, and at the beginning of 1949, Dubuque introduced the M Tricycle, Model MT. Nordenson's engineers then produced an adjustable wide front, a tricycle dual-wheel front and a single front wheel configuration. What's more, Dubuque engineer Dan Hall expanded the capabilities of Theo Brown's long-awaited hydraulic lift, the Touch-O-Matic. Deere had only just introduced the Brown/Hall system on the Model M, and the MT offered a duplicate cylinder to provide lift control for left or right side implements independently of each other, something the Ford-Ferguson system did not.

The Touch-O-Matic was a fully integrated hydraulic cylinder system control unit that could raise, lower, or set implements to working depth. It had taken nearly a decade to develop and perfect it. Brown and his staff labored through dozens of incarnations and variations on their way to success. New ideas along the way earned Brown more than a dozen new patents.

The tractor engine's crankshaft drove the hydraulic pump. This provided hydraulic functions whether the tractor was moving or not. Operators could precisely place cultivators or plows at the head of a row and set their working depth before moving forward. A large lever that engineering staffs nicknamed "The Liquid Brain," stuck out of the transmission case. This lever operated in a quarter-circle arc to control the hydraulics.

Seating position and comfort had been a Dreyfuss concern from the start of his relationship with Deere. For the Model M, the industrial designers took their ideas further. Dreyfuss was very concerned that farmers frequently stood while the tractor was moving. Was it a matter of stretching tired leg muscles? Or was it simply for better visibility in tight maneuvers?

INSET: *This was another factor that made getting on or off the MT a challenge. Support chains for the 3-point hitch sat close to the high rear-mounted belt pulley. Despite these problems, Deere sold nearly 30,500 of these tricycle models between 1947 and 1952.*

OPPOSITE: *The Model M used a 101 cubic inch "square" engine, with bore and stroke equal at 4.0 inches. At 1,615 rpm, this developed 18.2 horsepower at the drawbar and 20.5 horsepower off the belt pulley. The tricycle M, or MT, sold for $1,200.*

ABOVE: 1950 Model MI

At the end of a long day, Don Merrihew's shed awaits the arrival of his MI. Deere introduced industrial versions of the M in 1949 and continued to manufacture them until mid-August 1952.

RIGHT: *The M and its industrial sibling introduced Deere's new hydraulic Touch-O-Matic hitch and implement system. On agricultural tractors, this system replaced Henry Ford's and Harry Ferguson's 3-point hitch as the system of choice.*

Dreyfuss devised a telescoping steering column with a full 12 inches of travel. A sharp twist to a collar ahead of the wheel locked it or released it. In its forward position, it cleared room for the operator to stand and lean against the wheel without being pinched. At the longest extension, it allowed the comfortable bent-arm steering style most farmers preferred. The seat also received attention and this marked the next step in care and concern for operator comfort and fatigue. Dreyfuss made the seat adjustable forward and aft to accommodate taller or shorter users. The farmer also could inflate a small air bag inside the seat to cushion the bouncing or accommodate the tractor's side tilt or list during plowing. Dreyfuss angled the seat forward slightly so operators used their legs to hold them into the seat. This left the thighs unsupported, which encouraged blood flow so the legs didn't fall asleep.

Brown's 101 Full-Vision Tractor

Brown forged ahead with his radical midengine prototype Model 101. In one demonstration after another, he heard "the 101 stole the show." During a dinner following one successful field trial, a number of the observers told him, "They hoped Deere would put this tractor on the market soon and 'be first for once instead of following.'"

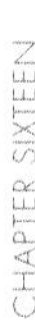

Waterloo's Quik-Tatch Debuts

The Quik-Tatch was another engineering development that Deere premiered on the M. This was the "QD" system that Theo Brown, Elmer McCormick, Willard Nordenson, and other engineers had devoted nearly a decade to investigating, imagining and trouble-shooting through one idea after another. Reading Brown's diary makes it clear that some concepts moved slowly through Deere's product review procedures. Others gained higher priority when competition loomed. IHC had pioneered its own "Quick Detachable" rapid implement mount-and-dismount system on its Farmall F-12 models for 1937.

Deere's system earned its engineers another handful of patents. The resulting system worked best with a new line of tools and implements that Brown and his staff specially designed for it. (It proved very difficult to retrofit couplings to existing implements so they would align properly.) It reduced implement hook-up time from hours to minutes. With a tractor in the hands of an experienced operator and its implements properly set up, the operator could attach or remove Deere's integral two-bottom plow in two minutes. A mower, including attachment to the PTO, took only 10 minutes to mount or disconnect. Deere's sales brochures claimed the system was so foolproof that it even was possible to unhook and leave the implement "in the field when coming to the house for lunch or at the end of the day."

Just as Willard Nordenson had done with his compact L and LA tractors, he mounted the two-cylinder engine vertically in his M models. A six-volt Delco-Remy system provided ignition, starting, and electric lighting.

Brown installed an air-cooled Wisconsin four-cylinder engine into one of the prototypes in late January. In early July, he conceived an industrial and shop version of his creation. The next day, July 11, 1944, he heard from Weaver Tractor Company, a major Deere-Caterpillar dealer in Woodland, California, near Sacramento. A. S. Weaver himself wrote Brown telling him that after seeing the demonstration, "We would have no hesitancy in placing an order with you for fifty, which we would expect to sell all inside of a year's time."

Brown found an affordable four-speed transmission for his 101 and he perfected its hydraulic controls. The day after Wiman returned to Deere from the Army in late September 1944, he came to drive the new tractor. Wiman pronounced himself "delighted and tremendously impressed," and he judged the tractor "wonderful." Wiman ordered one sent to his Tucson ranch for winter testing. He wanted to compare it to the prototype that Maxon had developed and to the other prototypes from Waterloo. "He thought that the #101, as the one with the most promise, should be there too," Brown noted on November 27.

Two days later Henry Dreyfuss spent all morning restyling the sheet metal and redesigning the 101's seat and its position. Throughout the afternoon, Brown, Wiman, Charley Stone (now head of production for all Deere products), McCormick, and Nordenson conferred about the new machine. They established a manufacturing cost of $321. Nordenson wanted some decision "as to what field this tractor should fill."

For most applications, industrials ran on 5.0-15 front tires and 9.0-24 rears. To improve operator comfort, Jim Conner at Henry Dreyfuss's office devised a telescoping steering column that offered 12 inches of travel.

Wiman challenged Nordenson. "How would you feel if Allis-Chalmers has a tractor as far along as this?" Brown reported the conversation in his diary, concluding, "Wiman and Stone seem to have more vision about the possibilities than the others." Yet Wiman's question was apocryphal. His vision was far-sighted.

Enter the 102, Wither the 101

With the 101 not yet approved for production, Brown had another idea in late March 1945, for a convertible tractor. On this machine, similar to his 101, the operator sat on the engine. However, here the drive wheels straddled the engine. Frame support tubes projected out the front and back. The operator could insert the steerable wheels into either end of the tractor, depending on the job requirements. Front steering worked best for plowing and harvesting. Cultivating would be easier with rear steering. Besides adjustable track, this tractor also could provide an adjustable wheelbase. Brown designed the new machine around Ford-Ferguson hydraulics and lift controls.

As though he sensed that production of his 101 would never happen, Brown began pulling back from the prototypes. Between the director's meeting on November 29, 1944, and the next on February 27, 1946, there are only three entries referring to his tractor while it had occupied pages and pages of his diaries during 1944. The first instance refers to his patent on the tractor's design, while the second discusses field tests with another air-cooled Wisconsin engine equipped with a self-starter. "Did well," he wrote. On January 2, 1946, in his neat print rather than his narrative cursive, he outlined weight specifications for the 101 (tractor alone, 2,115 pounds, tractor and cultivator, 2,435 pounds).

On February 27, he was resolved. "Here is what I think we should do with the #101 and tools before we let go entirely. . . ." The seven items on his list amounted to fine-tuning the implements. He had developed this tractor as far as he could go. It began to affect his health and by summer, Wiman sent him off for another long vacation.

In September, when Brown returned, the 101 was alive again. Wiman had assigned Nordenson to move ahead and Nordenson had given it to Bill Cade (Brown's nephew who worked in engineering at Dubuque) and two other engineers. Wiman "said he thought the 101 would be on the market in 1948 and would be needed by that time."

Brown was past 65 by now. Wiman was pleased at Brown's rest and relaxation during the long summer because he wanted the engineer back working "even if I only come to the office one hour a week."

By early October, Nordenson, Dan Hall, and Bill Cade had found ways to mount all the hydraulic mechanisms and, after testing, they were encouraged by the tractor's performance. Nordenson "thought the M tractor would be more in demand as a tricycle tractor and the 101 would come in as the big volume 4-wheel tractor. I do hope so," Brown wrote. "It seems to me it should some day set the design for 4 wheel small tractors."

A week later, October 11, 1946, Brown and Wiman went to Dubuque for the groundbreaking of the new Dubuque Tractor building. This new structure would house all tractor manufacture to be transferred from Moline. Wiman pulled Brown aside.

"There were only 2 tractors Wiman said he was crazy about, the W.X. (diesel) and the 101," Brown wrote that night. By mid-October, Brown finally was able to answer the question that Nordenson had posed two years earlier: For fields of use, Brown envisioned a general-purpose model 101, a low center of gravity model for mowing and haying, and an industrial and shop model. On New Year's Day 1947, he listed production of the 101 in its three configurations as three of the six wishes he held for the next year. Through the next year, however, Brown's revised version, the 102, occupied more of his time than the 101.

On March 12, 1947, Brown noted that "the first M tractor minus power control came off the line today at Dubuque." By mid-March he had one of his 102 prototypes running. He had incorporated Ford-Ferguson hydraulics and hitch elements. He used "remodeled" Ford running gear to operate the cultivator rigs ahead of the front wheels.

Deere gave the Ms a four-gear transmission that offered these industrials a top speed of 12 miles per hour. In low gear, the 2,695 pound tractors could pull nearly their own weight, 2,329 pounds.

During their quarterly meeting in late July 1947, the board voted to increase the Dubuque plant's size by 50 percent (adding some 320,000 square feet) and to enlarge Waterloo by about 30 percent. Their goal was to take Waterloo up from 250 to 325 a day, and Dubuque from 50 up to 150 tractors a day. (For comparison, Brown noted that IHC production was 600 a day, Ford's was 400, Allis-Chalmers manufactured 220, Case 150, and Massey-Harris produced between 35 and 50 tractors each day.)

On September 9, Brown wrote, "Herman Altgelt started in my department today. He has taken out over 100 patents. I think he will be a real addition to Deere & Company talent." Altgelt filled the position that Wiman had hoped to offer Jesse Lindeman nine months earlier.

While Altgelt's arrival excited him, two months later, on Wednesday, November 5, Brown read news that stung him. Charlie Wiman had confronted a reluctant Willard Nordenson three years earlier in late November 1944, wondering what would happen to Deere if Allis-Chalmers had a machine similar to Brown's 101 as far along in development as Brown's was. Brown now knew that Allis-Chalmers *did*.

"Milwaukee; November 4 (AP)—The Allis-Chalmers Manufacturing company will begin production early next year of a new type of farm tractor in a Gadsden, ALA., plant recently leased from the war assets administration.

"W. A. Roberts, executive vice president of the tractor division, said today the machine was designed especially for use on family-size farms. The engine is mounted in the rear and the operator has unobstructed view of the ground working tools mounted on the frame of the tractor ahead of the operator."

"It seems too bad," Brown wrote alongside the small newspaper clipping, "that we can't get the #101 tractor along faster and not come out with credit for a full vision tractor."

For Brown it only got worse. The next day, Massey-Harris announced its new Pony, a compact four-cylinder 12-horsepower tractor weighing 1,450 pounds. In Brown's view, it was Willard Nordenson who slowed progress. "Had quite a talk with Charley Stone about the 101 tractor. Am discouraged at the lack of enthusiasm Nordenson has shown. Suggest we have some users of this tractor tell Nordenson what they think about it."

The following April, Stone reported that Dubuque had computed costs on Brown's 101 tractor at about 15 percent less than the Model M, roughly $85 to $88. "He said the saving was more than he expected. The plan now is to make a survey for the demand for their tractor and to come to a definite decision by October. It is impossible to do much now as the M, MC and MT [design changes] must have priority. Also some work will be done on a small M to compare costs. Bill Cade [Brown's nephew working for Nordenson at Dubuque] said Nordenson told him that work on the 101 was to be laid aside for the present. I can't understand not at least doing some designing even if actual construction has to wait."

"The *Farm Implement News* out today carries a full account of the new Allis-Chalmers 'G' tractor which has seat ahead of the motor," Brown wrote on the night of April 29, 1948. "It is claimed to be the greatest development since the advent of the Farmall tractor.

"Since I thought of the front seat tractor 6 1/2 years ago, I can't help being somewhat discouraged to see my idea coming out first by some other company and their getting all the credit.

"Deere & Company are most conservative and sometimes it is hard to find new ideas I work out put on the shelf until years later."

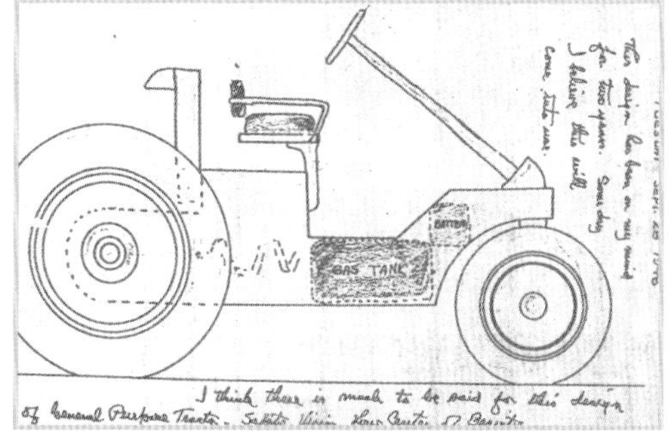

After several years of experimenting with his "all-visibility tractor," the idea evolved into what Brown called his "Low Down" tricycle tractor, dated September 28, 1948. He had worked much of his career on designing safety into tractors and implements. This low-center-of-gravity concept was intended to give otherwise top-heavy tractors much better stability and provide operators easier access. Theo Brown Diaries, Special Collections Library, George C. Gordon Library, Worchester Polytechnic Institute

October came and went along with Charley Stone's promise for decision. Wiman, Stone, and Duke Rowland examined Brown's year old work and evaluations on the reconstructed Ford and asked for an additional six copies of the report. As the fiscal year ended, Brown reported Deere's sales volume was more than $307 million. The company manufactured 76,000 tractors in fiscal 1948, paying its 26,000 employees an average wage of $1.56 per hour, or $59.85 a week. Brown never mentioned the 101 again.

Over the next few months, Brown revised his sketches of the Ford-based Model 102 tractor, creating one in late November with a center pivot, as a kind of early articulated concept.

"This working out new ideas that are somewhat in the future," Brown wrote on April 12, 1949, "is rather discouraging for when our implements and tractors as we build them are in demand, no one relishes the idea of change. Yet I feel strongly that our present line of tractors will be out of date before long. . . ."

CHAPTER 17
1943–1949

JOHN DEERE
MC

IF NOT CLETRAC, THEN WHY NOT LINDEMAN?

PREVIOUS: 1952 Model MC *The MC was Deere's successor to Lindeman's BO crawler. Theo Brown and Dubuque chief engineer Willard Nordenson got Lindeman to engineer the new M crawler just as he'd done with the BO models. Then Deere acquired Lindeman.*

RIGHT: *Just as it is on M standards and M tricycles, the belt pulley is nestled just below the operator's seat even on the MC. Deere made 12-inch wide track shoes standard equipment although it offered 10s and 14s as options.*

Crawlers had frustrated Charlie Wiman. In early 1941, Frank Silloway had reported to the directors on the "Deere-Caterpillar tie-up in California." Silloway told the board, "It had worked out admirably. There has been some criticism but the advantages are way ahead of any disadvantage." Deere finished producing 2,251 Cletrac MG1 crawlers for the Air Force on October 23, 1943. It had been easy and profitable manufacturing for the Air Force. Yet, despite Wiman's sales efforts, the board had been unwilling to take Cleveland Tractor under its umbrella.

As Waterloo wound down production on the BO, it still shipped chassis to Lindeman. His great success in marketing the small crawlers for orchard use and then for construction applications finally awoke the board to the need to continue crawler development. Perhaps now, Deere was ready to take it in-house.

Roughly a month before Waterloo delivered the last BO chassis to Lindeman's Yakima factory, a prototype arrived. Jesse Lindeman and his brothers had received drawings earlier. They knew what to expect. The prototype was a question from Dubuque: Would this M tractor convert to a crawler as easily as the BO had done? They wanted Lindeman to develop and test a prototype.

"Well, we converted the M to the MC for them. They followed what we had done, except in the final drive," Lindeman remembered Nordenson's engineers and their clever changes. "They did a cost-cutting deal. We had to piece in our final drive like Caterpillar and everybody else. The inner piece and then the new gear went onto the outer side.

JOHN DEERE

"Well, those boys made one casting and it was open at the bottom. You just put the gear up into the bottom. It was a lower cost deal, and a better lineup too. That's where experience beat genius!"

Around that time, in mid-October, Wiman was in Dubuque to break ground for factory expansion that would house all tractor manufacture Deere transferred from Moline. At that event, Wiman confided a plan to Brown.

He "was going to try to get Jesse Lindeman to come to Moline as my assistant and gradually work into my place." Wiman said this would allow Brown to take the entire summer off each year.

On December 11, 1946, Brown's diary reported that the board voted to buy Lindeman Power Equipment Company for $367,000. "Jesse Lindeman is a genius in creative thinking and it was mentioned that he might be another 'Theo Brown.' Charlie Wiman was very enthusiastic to get their company and even more so to get Jesse. I hope he, in time, will take my place."

For the next seven or eight years, Lindeman was a regular feature around Moline. He steadfastly resisted the permanent position and relocation Wiman had hoped he would accept. Jesse was an innovator and Wiman still valued and wanted his ideas. Deere's engineering efforts stumbled over draft control and the hydraulics that kept a plow at a preset depth. Waterloo and Dubuque engineers all favored adapting the Ford-Ferguson three-point hitch, a system Lindeman had thoroughly investigated. While it had problems, engineering hoped to resolve them by the time Ferguson's hitch patent expired. Then Deere immediately could offer its improved version of Ferguson's technology.

After a long week of winter field testing in Texas in February 1951, Brown concluded "The big question seemed to be: What value has draft control? Jesse has probably had more experience with Ford than anyone else. He says that in some cases such as in field cultivators, draft control is a real advantage while for some other implements draft control would be a detriment. And too, the proper adjustment of the amount of draft is not clear to the average operator. In other words, it is not a foolproof mechanism." Brown and Lindeman each had devised their own systems. Both worked better at maintaining depth and resisting side movement on hillsides. Lindeman visited Deere test farms almost monthly to observe and revise his own system. He also made suggestions for the Waterloo and Dubuque versions. He and Brown became close friends, often dining together at the end of long days spent watching inferior systems frustrate everyone present.

It wasn't until 1954 that Deere relocated all the Lindeman Yakima operations and many of their 422 employees to the Dubuque Tractor Works facilities. On the final day of operations, Wiman made the last of his regular visits to Yakima, to Lindeman, to Jesse and his brother, Joe.

"He arrived after I'd walked through the whole factory, saying goodbye to everyone. I was told he was outside in a big car, waiting to see me," Lindeman recalled. "We sat and

OPPOSITE: *Deere manufactured the first MC on March 3, 1949, at what had been Lindeman's plant in central Washington state. Orchard growers especially in the sandy soil in central Washington came to like the new MC as much as their old BO crawlers.*

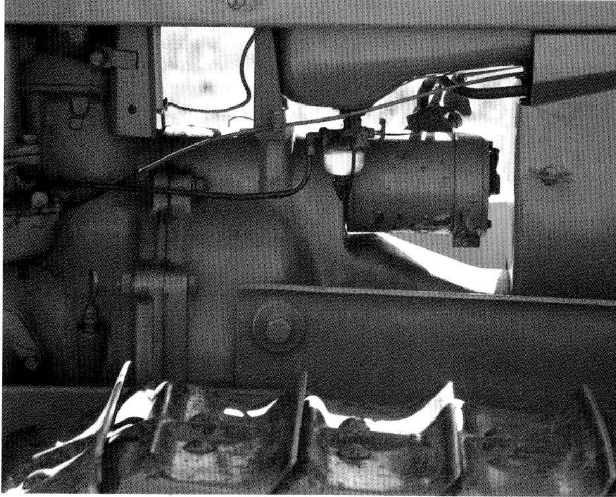

ABOVE: *Willard Nordenson's engineers at Dubuque looked at what Jesse Lindeman had devised to convert an M standard into a crawler. They took everything except Lindeman's final drive. Nordenson created a simpler, less costly system and Deere put the tractor into production.*

NEXT PAGE: *By the time operators got their MCs to their fields the machines had been thoroughly tried and tested. At Deere's Texas farm, engineers created a course complete with steep hills and big rocks, a far cry from the terrain this farmer traveled between the vines on his vineyard near Napa, California.* Deere & Company Archives

"Let me tell you a little about 'genius,'" Lindeman said with a hearty laugh. "The day of the prototype test, Colonel Wiman came out all the way from Moline to see the first new MC. He was always really interested in the tractors. We had pulled the new tractor outside. It would only go around in a circle.

"When we went from the wheel tractor," Lindeman explained, "we had a small pinion because we were driving a big diameter rear wheel in order to get roughly the same speed out of the tractor. The procedure was we had to cut the ring gear and the sprocket wheel. We had to speed it up because of the smaller sprockets.

"Well, they put one of the regular sprockets in there and one of the new sprockets. One on one side, one on the other.

"So all it would do is turn left! So here we were. The Colonel was coming in the train station right now and we were trying to figure out why this tractor would only go left all around the yard!

"It was *not* funny until after we figured it out. Then we had a big laugh about it," Lindeman continued. "But we didn't tell the Colonel about it for some time."

The next morning, Wiman got a chance to try out the new Model MC and to compare it directly with the BO-Lindeman." After running the MC, Wiman climbed back on a BO. Portland Branch manager Pat Murphy got on the MC and Wiman challenged him. Lindeman laughed at the memory.

"The Colonel, in his dark fedora, was really tickled because he outpulled the new MC crawler! He was on one of ours, a BO, and he outpulled the new MC!

"We had cut the wheel ratio in the wheel tractors easily in half. Both of them would slip in their tracks. But the BO would slip less! We did that for all of them. And that was the trip the Colonel came out to buy the plant."

talked for more than an hour, just sitting there. He wanted to know about everyone, how they were, how they'd be. And how I was." Lindeman went silent for a moment.

"I used to go back to visit and I probably saw the Colonel four visits out of every five. I'd go back there, or down to his Tucson farm, just to keep an eye on things. At the last minute I decided not to move back there but I ended up in the engineering department anyway. Colonel Wiman's secretary used to call me 'Jess-ey'. One day she said, 'Well, Jessey, I hear Colonel Wiman is going to make you a board member!' But you know, he never did." Perhaps it did not happen because Lindeman chose not to move to Moline. Possibly others on the board were less enthusiastic than Wiman about the "outsider."

"The plant closed out here and there was nobody working in it, just Orie Durland [Lindeman's chief engineer and good friend] and me. Going back there to Moline, they had two experimental farms and we used to spend almost all our time there. They used to call us their 'idea men.'

"The Colonel never drank too much, but he loved to support a men's party. Get four or five or six of his key people and go out.

"We go back there and sometimes it was just an excuse for a big banquet," Lindeman laughed again. "So everybody'd go and get half tight.

"And the ideas would flow like water."

LEFT: *The low slung crawler stood just 50.5 inches to the top of the radiator, 5.5 inches lower than M standards and tricycles. With 12-inch tracks it measured 67 inches wide.*

BELOW: *An era ended and Jesse Lindeman took a moment to pose for a photo. He had more-or-less perfected the Deere crawler. As this, the last of his Model BO-Lindeman conversions got ready to clank off the line, he must have wondered about his future. He went on to develop the successor MC. Then he sold his company to Deere and watched as his machinery and his employees all moved east.*

CHAPTER 18
1949–1954

NOT THE FIRST DIESEL,

JUST THE MOST EFFECTIVE ONE

It was the biggest tractor they had built so far. It was their most powerful. And it was the one that took the longest time to get right.

Deere introduced its diesel-powered Model R at their dealer show in Manitoba, Canada, in June 1949. Like nervous parents, product engineering and marketing department staffs always worried if they had gotten the new machine right. It wasn't long before the company knew just how "right" they'd gotten it.

PREVIOUS: 1949 MODEL R DIESEL *Diesel engine technology had challenged dozens of tractor and truck manufacturers. Deere invested some 66,000 hours in field-testing its 16 diesel prototypes to ease starting challenges and eliminate operating bugs throughout the 1930s and 1940s.*

RIGHT: *Deere's six-gear transmission gave the Diesel R a top road speed of 11.5 miles per hour and phenomenal pulling power in lower gears. While the tractor weighed 7,400 pounds, in its Nebraska University tests, it tugged 6,644 pounds in first gear.*

Earlier, between April 19 and April 28, Deere kicked off the 1949 Nebraska state tractor testing session with Model R serial number 1358. In 57 hours of engine operation, testers reported one single repair. During the warm up run, a glass sediment bowl in the fuel-line broke. Engineers replaced it. Testers reported no other repairs or adjustments performed during the duration of the test itself. They recorded a maximum fuel economy of 17.63 horsepower-hours per gallon of fuel.

Deere was not the first to offer a diesel. Others had tested them at the Lincoln campus test site. The first had been nearly 17 years earlier in June 1932. Caterpillar brought its Model 65 "Diesel" to the university. The "rated brake horsepower" tests then reached a maximum of 74.73 horsepower. This set a Nebraska test economy record of 13.87 horsepower-hours per gallon. The next year Caterpillar's "Diesel 75" beat its own previous record with 83.34 horsepower and 14.62 horsepower-hours per gallon.

Deere's development of the diesel engine began soon after it and Caterpillar enacted their trade and marketing agreements. Deere's customer demand for more power was part of the motivation. Yet the stories of diesel development that slipped out of Waterloo and Moline brought

This was Deere's biggest tractor yet, and the company's most powerful. When Deere introduced it in Manitoba, Canada in June 1949, they set a new benchmark for what wheeled tractors could do.

about a return of rumors of the change from two cylinders to more. It reached a frenzy toward the end of 1936.

Deere & Webber sent a letter to their dealers, "Bulletin No. 11," dated December 23, 1936:

"Under the date of June 27, 1930, we issued a bulletin to all of our dealers reading as follows:

"We are again receiving reports, originating no doubt from competitive tractor salesmen, stating we were coming out with a four-cylinder tractor.

"This is propaganda, pure and simple, and there is nothing to this claim. . .

"WE ARE NOT MAKING A FOUR CYLINDER TRACTOR, NOR ARE WE EVER THINKING OF MAKING ONE." (Capitals are theirs).

Yet developing additional power through the diesel was not so simple. The gelatinous nature of the fuel in cold temperatures made starting very difficult under those conditions.

Throughout 1936, Waterloo engineering worked on a procedure to start the engine on gasoline and run it until warm. Then the operator would switch fuel supplies over to diesel. By 1937, engineers were experimenting with a higher-voltage electric starting system, 24 volts. Even that was not enough power to heat the fuel and start the engine in the cold. Elmer McCormick's staff tried various combustion chamber shapes in order to produce the required high compression. They needed something like 16:1 compared to 4:1 for the kerosene engines. By mid-1940, engineers had sufficiently sorted out the combination of problems and they produced the first of the W.X. prototypes. These eventually became the Model R.

Between 1941 and 1945, McCormick's engineers thoroughly tested and evaluated eight W.X. prototypes at test farms at Laredo, Texas, in Minnesota, and on Charlie Wiman's ranch in Tucson, Arizona. Waterloo engineering assembled five more during 1945 and another eight in 1947. By this time McCormick's staff had answered the question of the starting procedure. They devised an opposed two-cylinder gasoline "pony" engine with an electric starter. This resembled a system that Cat's diesels introduced in 1931. Operators ran the pony to warm up the diesel engine block and fuel. Once temperatures met a certain level, the gasoline engine propelled the starter for the larger diesel main engine.

1950 Model R Diesel

Deere's metal cab was a factory option for the big diesel. Dual wheels came from dealers. Deere interrupted its diesel development program during World War II.

Waterloo involved Henry Dreyfuss with the W.X. from the start. With the massive cooling required for the twin 5.75x8-inch cylinders, the fan tended to suck field debris into the radiator grille mesh. Dreyfuss set the angle of its corrugations at what easily could be swept clear by a farmer wearing gloves.

It established a style that customers would recognize through the next decade. The only drawback was that with mesh screening up front, operators had to watch their driving. The vertical crown piece that Dreyfuss introduced on styled As and Bs had protected farmers from front impacts. It served as a bumper as well as a "design element." Yet Dreyfuss abandoned it on the big R.

Deere manufactured the first diesel R in January 1949. On January 12, it shipped that tractor to Wolf Point, Montana. Its cold weather starting abilities got an immediate test in Montana's subzero winter. Elmer McCormick never got to see his production W.X. drive off the line. He died of a heart attack on September 12, 1948, at age 58. He had been Deere's chief engineer at the Waterloo Tractor Company for 17 years. Two weeks later, the board appointed Wayne Worthington as head of research at Waterloo, the stepping stone to the chief engineer position.

ABOVE: 1952 MODEL RI-EXPERIMENTAL Michigan industrial collector Don Merrihew knew he had something unusual on his hands when he found this experimental industrial model R. He found brazings on the front end to accommodate an American Tractor Equipment (ATECo.) bulldozer blade when Deere worked with the idea of wheeled road construction machinery.

RIGHT: *These were big tractors whether they wore green or industrial yellow paint. Measuring 147 inches overall, they rode on 14.0-34 inch rear tires and 7.50-18 inch fronts.*

JOHN DEERE
DIESEL
R
JOHN DEERE

After dozens of attempts to ease starting, Deere's engineers settled on the idea of using a small electric-start gasoline "pony" engine to turn over and preheat the diesel before it cranked the 416 cubic inch big twin to life.

A Time of Transition

Charlie Wiman reluctantly approved Theo Brown's retirement. Brown left on November 1, 1952, but not before Wiman exacted a promise from the 74-year-old engineer that he would serve on the John Deere Advisory Committee. "Of course," Wiman wrote to him, "I may and likely will request that you undertake a particular special assignment from time to time."

Deere's Model R ended production on September 17, 1954. Waterloo had assembled something approaching 21,300 tractors. The giant R had developed 45.7 horsepower on the drawbar, 51 horsepower on the belt pulley. The two-cylinder engine, in its many sizes,

In 1893, German engineer Rudolf Diesel invented the engine that the world named for him. Caterpillar learned of the engines years later from shipyards on nearby San Francisco Bay. Cat spent years perfecting the diesel for tractor applications before introducing it in 1931. It clearly led the path for others to pursue. Deere was known for the overall operating efficiency and economy of its "stove top fuel" tractors. Engineers and the board knew it could not afford to ignore the diesel, no matter what the difficulties might be in its development.

The difficulties were numerous.

Before the end of 1935, International Harvester Corporation introduced its WD-40. It was the first diesel-powered wheeled tractor. With its introduction, IHC issued a challenge to its competitors. Deere's board quickly committed resources to develop the diesel engine for its own agricultural products. Waterloo produced a handful of diesel engines, the "PX" series, that engineers installed in modified Model D tractors. Waterloo and Moline engineering tested these thoroughly through the late 1930s and into the early 1940s. While the company competed vigorously with IHC, Deere's association with Caterpillar still was excellent at that time. This was due largely to Frank Silloway's ongoing encouragement of Cat's unique product.

California's soil conditions made it a natural market for Caterpillar's crawlers. But a lesser market existed within Caterpillar's market-base for wheel-type tractors around the farm. Silloway had opened the door. Caterpillar supported the notion. Cat went further and answered some of its skeptical dealers who worried that Deere's two-cylinder engines did not follow the trends of other makers. Caterpillar themselves had just introduced a two-cylinder diesel. This development encouraged Silloway and he seized the moment. He had hoped to decrease Deere's exclusive dependence on agricultural tractors. Silloway wanted to increase the company's portion of the growing industrial tractor trade. Through shared efforts in retailing, marketing, and even research, this could come about.

for all its power, despite its exceptional longevity, had revealed its limitations. It showed its age. Protests that the branch sales staffs had issued at the end of 1936, and that the factory had echoed the following spring, no longer reverberated 18 years later.

Waterloo had a new series of tractors ready to replace the alphabet designations. For Deere, the production letters sequence stopped at R. Numbers were coming. In the next few years, they would grow from tens to hundreds. Soon after that, as designations multiplied again, they were joined by radical changes in engines as well.

CHAPTER 19
1949–1955

HN DEERE

THE ALPHABET ENDS

WITH MULTIPLES OF TEN

PREVIOUS: 1954 MODEL 40 HC *Deere manufactured this, the first high crop Model 40, on August 27, 1954. The machine benefited from its new engineering, providing farmers with 32 inches of axle clearance while standing only 67.1 inches to the top of the radiator.*

RIGHT: *Problems with Dubuque's Model M forced Deere to accelerate its development and introduction of the Model 40 replacement. Having acquired almost all of Lindeman Equipment Co. in house, Deere produced the first crawler with three lower track rollers in November 1952.*

The dramatic sheet metal changes that Henry Dreyfuss produced for the diesel Model R established the look that Deere followed through the 1950s. This new appearance hinted at the engineering developments that Waterloo and Dubuque had accomplished beneath the skin as well.

The evolution began with the Model 50 to replace the B, the 60, replacing the A, the Model 70 for the G, and the new 40 for the M. It didn't end until the new Model 80 replaced the R. This was a three-year period that encompassed a farm wagon full of improvements and advances.

But, to back track briefly, even as the big diesel R first appeared in 1949, one question arose yet again: Should the company re-examine its 25-year devotion to two-cylinder engines? Power was the consideration here. Needing more of it was the motivation.

Deere provided a proliferation of electric accessories. The tractors had starters, lights, and better instrumentation. Waterloo and Dubuque handled this easily with a more powerful generator and a larger battery. But hydraulics was a different matter. Emil Jirsa and his colleagues at Moline had created a system called Powr-Trol. It required a pump that Jirsa ran very efficiently off the engine. Operators now called on their tractors to do more and more work. Visionary implement designers such as Theo Brown, Irishman Harry Ferguson, and IHC's Bert Benjamin had ably directed farmers toward this goal. It took more power simply to run the hydraulic pumps that raised and lowered ever-larger attachments.

Deere's two-cylinder engines challenged physics and chemistry. There is an absolute limit to the distance across a piston face that engineers could make a spark travel to ignite a fuel mixture

ABOVE: *Standard width track shoes were 12 inches with 10-inch and 14-inch sizes optional. The crawlers weighed 4,000 pounds, almost 1,000 more than Model 40 row-crop versions before adding the blade.*

RIGHT: *Deere produced only 284 Model 40 high crops in 1954 and 1955. These used the 100.5-cubic-inch twin with 4.0 inch bore and stroke. They developed 22.9 horsepower on the drawbar and 25.2 off the flywheel at 1,850 rpm.*

evenly and efficiently. Deere's diesel bought the company a little time. But Dubuque, Moline, and Waterloo engineers, as well as Deere's board already had faced the future: The diesel gave their two-cylinder engines only another decade of life at the most.

Charlie Wiman had seen other manufacturers while he served as an Army ordnance colonel. This exposure made him more visionary. By the time he returned to Deere from the war, he was willing to accept risks. Now he advocated more cylinders. Nordenson's engineers at Dubuque, anxious for new challenges, encouraged the Colonel. They reminded him that Nordenson already had mounted the engines in the Model M tractor vertically. This represented a change in thinking and engineering from Deere's previous big tractors. The recumbent two-cylinder engine had lain there, horizontal, longitudinal, unchallenged, since Louis Witry first positioned the side-by-side twin onto the Waterloo Boy chassis almost 40 years earlier.

Board member L. A. "Duke" Rowland argued for patience and caution. Rowland had joined the Board in 1942; six years later it named him manager of the Waterloo Tractor Works. This Englishman knew his own mind and had little reluctance expressing it. Rowland impressed Wiman, and the board named Rowland a vice president in 1947.

Rowland argued that the time and effort needed to bring Deere's diesel to production had been long and expensive. While Dubuque or Waterloo might not need the 12 years it

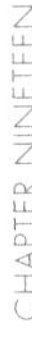

took for the R to do its next project, developing a four- or six-cylinder engine certainly would take more than a year.

Rowland was not Deere's champion of expensive and complicated progress. While he had board approval for it, there is no coincidence that Rowland had authored Deere's official 1936 factory denial of a switch to four- or six-cylinder engines. This came two months after Deere & Webber's branch issued their bulletin repudiating competitors' rumors in December 1935.

The Model R introduced the concept of separate fuel supply for each cylinder (fuel injectors in the case of the diesel engines, carburetors for the others). Mixing the fuel and air this close to the intake valves permitted greater precision in blending the two. Horsepower output rose slightly. Nordenson carried this technology over into the new tractors that Deere introduced in 1952.

1953 Model 50

Deere introduced this tractor to replace the long-lived Model B and brought it out first as a row-crop tractor with the V-wheel front end. A host of innovations appeared with these models including Duplex carburetion, live power-take-off (PTO), "cyclonic fuel intake" to better mix gas, and air prior to combustion, and improved Powr-Trol hydraulic depth control.

JOHN DEERE
70

The company launched the Model 50 and 60 first. Deere offered both of these as row-crop versions. Farmers could order the Model 60 from the start as a hi-crop. Deere had adopted "Live" power-take-off from several of its competitors. This improvement first appeared on the 50 and 60 series. "Live" PTO meant that the power-take-off shaft rotated independently of tractor motion and used its own independent clutch to disengage it. This allowed machinery to continue working even at the end of the row where the tractor had to stop and maneuver through a turn.

Within the two-cylinder engine, Deere engineers had designed a new combustion chamber. Engineering papers referred to it as "cyclonic fuel intake." Modifying the intake valve venturi induced a cyclone-like swirl that mixed the fuel much more completely. This further increased power and improved economy whether the engine fired on gasoline or distillates. It appeared as well on the newly offered liquefied propane gas (LPG) for the Model 60 in 1954 and in 1955 for the 50.

This better-mixed combustion tended to run cooler. Still, engineering gave the cooling system a major overhaul even though it remained hidden behind the Henry Dreyfuss stylish grille. Until the number series began, Deere had not used water pumps but instead it relied on the thermosyphon system for cooling. This had served Deere tractors adequately since the days of the Waterloo Boys. With the Model 60, 50, 70, 40, and 80, Deere now pressurized the radiator and pumped the coolant. A thermostat controlled the radiator louvers. This relieved the farmer of the need to crank them manually to adjust air circulation through the radiator.

The optional rear exhaust was a Henry Dreyfuss innovation. He maintained that the vertical pipe blew fumes in the operators' faces, blocked their forward vision and assaulted their hearing. He once posted a note in his New York office that promised a case of Chivas Regal Scotch whisky and a night in the nearby Waldorf Astoria with a famous actress to the first designer or engineer who could get the exhaust off the hood and keep it there. The rear exhaust option routed the gases through a series of bends and curves. Eventually the fumes and noise blew out beneath and behind the rear axle. Despite slightly reducing the tractor's ground clearance, Dreyfuss accepted the risk of collapsing the pipe mounted below the belt pulley in exchange for the benefit to operator's lungs and hearing. Deere promoted this for work in and out of low-opening doorways in barns and sheds

In 1953, the Model 70 appeared. This was nearly 20 percent stronger than the Model G that it replaced. The Model 70 and 80 introduced power steering to America's farm tractors. Engineer Chris Hess designed a system that pumped hydraulic fluid past a vane-type cylinder. This turned the vertical front steering shaft. When the company introduced the 70, the hydraulic Powr-Trol system had one-third more capacity and power than Deere had provided on the Gs. As with the 60 and 50, engineering upgraded the electrical system from 6 to 12 volts. The Model 70 Diesel again claimed the Nebraska test economy record in 1954 at 50.4 horsepower with 17.74 horsepower-hours per gallon. The V-4 gas starting engine displaced 19 cubic inches.

1954 Model 70 HC

While 50 series models replaced the Bs, and 60s updated the As, the 70s increased Model G performance by nearly 20 percent. The 70-series high-crops such as Tony Dieter's tractor here, loomed high over the landscape, whether it was California cotton fields, Louisiana cane plantations or here in a friend's Iowa pasture.

JOHN
BE CAREFUL

ABOVE: 1955 MODEL 50

Wide-front 50s offered adjustable tread width from 48 to 80 inches and at the rear, these long axles allowed farmers to stretch width from 62 to 98 inches. Power steering made maneuvering these models much easier.

LEFT: *A federal court judge refused to renew Harry Ferguson's patents on his 3-point hitch, calling it too useful an improvement to protect beyond a single term. Deere, and its Los Angeles affiliate Killefer, quickly developed and introduced the model 9-02 that turned Deere's Waterloo-designed hitch into a quick attachment 3-point connection.*

Troubles with the M Hurried Introduction of the Model 40

The Model 40 was Deere's next numbered addition to the 1953 tractor line. This replaced the Model M. The substitution was complete throughout the entire lineup. As early as the summer of 1950, however, Deere knew that it had problems with the M series. Tractors had not met sales expectations. By the fall the scope of the situation had become clear.

"At an all day meeting of Branch House men and factory men," Theo Brown wrote in his diary on a snowy Wednesday night, November 8, 1950. They had gathered "to try to find out what the reason is that models M and MT tractors do not sell."

The terminology, "not sell," clearly is a matter of interpretation. By the end of its life, Deere had produced something close to 87,812 of the M tractors. This far exceeded the Model H production of 58,263 and the G's roughly 64,000 models. Model As, Bs, and Ds each had sold in the hundreds of thousands. Deere had very high expectations for the market demand for the M.

LEFT: 1956 MODEL 60 ORCHARD
One observer has described them as Buck Rogers at 6 miles per hour. Of course, they are working tools, carefully designed to function superbly in fruit and nut tree orchards and groves but in perfect condition as Walter Keller's example is, they almost are sculptural works of art.

OPPOSITE TOP: 1955 MODEL 70 WITH DEERE MODEL 22 COTTON PICKER
Innovative engineering inspired Deere's harvester works to mount both single and double row cotton pickers on 60 and 70 series tractors and run the machines in reverse at up to 3.5 miles per hour. The raised operator platform gave drivers great visibility and was necessary to clear the harvester head.

OPPOSITE: *Iowa collector Larry Maasdam's overhead hopper held 1,200 pounds of picked cotton, blown upward by the Air-Trol harvesters. Deere developed its first mounted cotton harvester prototypes on Model GP tractors as early as 1929.*

"The branch house men were very frank in saying the M and MT were not satisfactory. Dealers and customers don't like them. Hard to get on and off. Equipment not satisfactory. A basic change in design is necessary with low center of gravity. The Ford tractor is way outselling us and a tractor more or less like the Ford seems to be what is wanted.

"The apparent failure of the M and MT tractors to appeal to the trade and the difficulty of selling them has caused much concern to Deere & Company. With an investment of 18 million at Dubuque, this is serious. I had felt for a long time that this type of tractor is passé. The Ford seems the tractor it's hard to compete with."

The new 40 series, as well as all the other models in the new number line, were much easier to enter or exit. Platform redesign and new fenders allowed room ahead of the rear wheels

RIGHT: 1956 LANZ BULLDOG MODEL D2402 VINEYARD
Along with Lanz Mannheim came its subsidiary operations near Madrid, Spain, called Lanz Iberica. After acquiring Lanz, Deere's presence in Europe swelled during the next several years.

ABOVE: *Lanz introduced this vineyard model in 1956, by narrowing up front and rear track and lowering operator position slightly. The low-mounted horizontal, longitudinal single-cylinder engine helped stability.*

OPPOSITE: *With its single shank ripper blade stuck deep into the ground, the Model 40 standard got a good workout. Introduced in 1953, the 2,750 pound tractor sold new for $1,521 in its last year of production, 1955. Deere manufactured standard front end models also as medium high clearance V-versions for vegetable growers and H versions as high crops.* Deere & Company Archives

to climb on or off the tractor. Nordenson's staff also had succeeded in lowering the tractors' center of gravity. Much of Brown's developmental hitch, his implement line, and his hydraulic system for his development 102 went into production. Dubuque offered Nordenson's 40 series as a Standard, Hi-crop, Tricycle, Wide (two-row utility), Utility or Crawler, and it added a "Special" 40C (using a V designation for cotton/sugar cane applications).

The Model 40C improved traction and operator comfort over the MC. Nordenson made four track rollers standard equipment instead of the MC's three, and offered five as an option. This also substantially improved track and drive gear durability. The 40C continued the legacy that Jesse Lindeman established. However following Deere's "consolidation" of Lindeman's operations during the lifetime of the MC, every 40C was born in Dubuque.

The 80 was the final new model in the series in 1955, and it retired the R. The Model 80 took a good, big, strong tractor and made it better, bigger, and stronger. Waterloo increased its power output by one third. The transmission added a sixth forward gear. As with the Model 70, Deere delivered the 80 with power steering.

The 40 through 80 series tractors provided power over a broad spectrum. The 7,850-pound diesel 80 peaked at 61.8 drawbar horsepower drawbar/67.6 belt pulley horsepower belt. The LPG Model 70 produced 46.1 horsepower and 52 horsepower, weighing 6,335

Deere's devotion to Ford's implement lift frustrated Brown greatly. His revised, next-generation Model 102 now was a radical-looking Model 202. It had a lower center of gravity than any tractor in production anywhere in the world. It was almost effortless to get on or off. It had performed well in every field test. The hydraulic system he and Herman Altgelt had devised always worked better than Ford's.

"At 10 this morning [November 20, 1950], our department showed our three #202 tractors with all integral equipment including breakaway bottoms, disc plow, lister, field cultivator, corn cultivator and front end bedder. What we tried to show was we have something better than Ford so we should not copy him."

Wayne Worthington, Waterloo's design manager, showed Brown an assessment he had written for the board. "The 202 was a great step in advance and the tractor we finally design must have many of the features of the 202," Worthington told him. The next day, Wiman invited Brown and Altgelt to a meeting in Dubuque with Worthington, Duke Rowland, and Charley Stone. "It is the first time we have been asked to such a meeting."

In the 202 at last, Brown felt that Product Development, Stone, Worthington, and everyone else would see "that the 202 embodies features that look to the future and are desirable." But it was not to be.

Willard Nordenson, Dubuque's chief engineer, was strangely missing from every demonstration that included Brown's 202. As the man responsible for the M and MT, he and his assistant Barrett Rich had their hands full figuring out what went wrong and how to fix it soon. Brown and another 170 Deere executives and engineers witnessed the first showing of Waterloo's 50 and 60 series tractors on Monday, June 2, 1952. Introductory demonstrations are similar to Broadway stage play openings complete with hundreds of opportunities for something to go wrong and embarrass engineers and bosses. It was another seven weeks, at another introduction on July 31, before Nordenson sought out Brown. Brown recalled the conversation in his diary that night. It was the first time in more than a year that Nordenson had spoken to Brown candidly. Pressure from the board had dictated his actions.

"He confessed that he was required to use Ford equipment, and so the adoption of the three-point hitch for the M & MT tractors was an expediency. He was impressed by the fact that the designer of implements has to know his business."

pounds. Next down was the Model 60 LPG: 38.1 and 42.2 horsepower in a tractor weighing 5,300 pounds. Then the LPG Model 50 stepped in peaking at 29.2 and 32.3 from a tractor that weighed 4,435 pounds. The "little" 40C weighed in at 4,669 pounds in Lincoln, Nebraska, for its tests in early September 1953. It pulled 4,515 pounds in low bear, nearly its own weight. The little engine that could did. It rated 20.1 horsepower on the drawbar and 24.9 on the belt.

But these numbers were good only until 1955 or 1956. Then, not only did the specifications go up again, but so did each model number.

Lyle Cherry, Deere's general sales manager, introduced the Model 60 and 50 on June 11, 1952. His detailed and lengthy comments are quoted in the *Two-Cylinder "Collector Series" Volume One*. During his presentation to the branch salesmen and managers, he pointed out all the features of these two new models. "Gentlemen," he said, wrapping up his remarks, "I believe you will agree with my opening comment that never before has any manufacturer presented new tractors with so many outstanding improvements over current models."

However, Cherry knew what Dubuque and Waterloo had coming next. With a little bit of imagination, one almost can imagine Cherry adding to himself one more thought.

"And fellas, you ain't seen nothin' yet!"

CHAPTER 20

1955–1959

BETTER
AND BETTER

Power Steering is important. Rear exhaust is beneficial. Fuel economy records are desirable. Still, the primary function of agricultural tractors is to pull tools through the ground or across it. Farmers used slightly more than 1 million tractors in 1935. In 1955, the Agricultural Census reported 4.35 million wheeled and crawler tractors in use. From this perspective, Harry Ferguson's three-point hitch had thrown Deere and all its competitors for a loop.

PREVIOUS: 1958 MODEL 320 STANDARD #1
Brent Liebert's 320 Standard was the first 320 produced on June 25, 1956. The club of 320 collectors is somewhat limited in membership as only 3,083 more 320s in all variations followed this one out the door.

RIGHT: 1956 MODEL 320 STANDARD
Float Ride Seats adjusted to accommodate drivers of widely different sizes and weights. Push button electric starting brought ease of operation that rivaled contemporary automobiles.

It was not merely the success of his hitch that caused troubles. Ferguson's system clearly had an impact on Ford's N series sales over other tractors. It was the engineering efficiency and the fact that Ferguson had patented his clever idea for use on Henry Ford's tractors that plagued the competition. Ferguson's and Ford's success was that this three-point hitch took a small, standard-front lightweight tractor and endowed it with performance characteristics of a larger heavier machine by using the laws of physics. It was stunningly simple for farmers and engineers to understand once they saw a demonstration. That, too, was a source of great frustration to everyone else. Because *that* signified that anything similar to it, close in appearance or function, was liable for a lawsuit charging patent infringement. Everyone else's version of Ferguson's three-point hitch had to be more complicated.

Deere was no exception. Most everyone played along fairly until the 17-year original life of Ferguson's patent ran out. At that point, a federal court judge refused to renew it. He ruled that Ferguson's three-point hitch was too important to agriculture to remain under patent protection. As the date approached when Ferguson's invention entered the public domain in 1953, each company

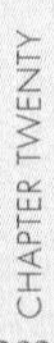

JOHN DEERE

RIGHT: *Deere's 20-series hinted at styling and engineering to come over the next five years. Touch-O-Matic hydraulics and Load and Depth Control 3-point hitches made the tractor a delight to use in tight quarters and on smaller farms.*

redesigned its own hitch to take advantage of Ferguson's ingenious linkages and his automatic draft control.

Deere, again, was no exception. Its answer was "Custom Powr-Trol." Waterloo and Dubuque engineers had introduced the earlier Powr-Trol system on the Model R. It did not automatically accommodate the range of tractor movements over the ground. The operator needed quick reactions to lift or drop the plow when the nose of the tractor dropped or rose up. Deere prepared to incorporate this "Load-and-Depth Control" into its current tractors. This new system offered operators their choice of precisely controlling implement height or depth. They could instead allow the system to adjust working depth automatically in coordination with tractor motion. At this point, Deere had enough major and minor changes to satisfy its product planners and marketing people. To take advantage of the sales potential of these improvements, they designated the new models as the "20" series.

There were many other improvements. Theo Brown's Quik-Tatch system now would rapidly couple ever-larger implements to Deere's Load-and-Depth Custom Powr-Trol. The operator's seat, already equipped with a low back rest for lumbar support, incorporated a slightly higher seat back and it added arm rests, now available in logo yellow as well as black. For the farmer climbing into the driver's seat on a sunny afternoon in August, the more reflective yellow was a welcome change from heat-absorbing black vinyl.

Deere introduced models across the complete range. The 320, 420, 520, 620 and 720 appeared in early to mid-1956 with the 820 following soon after. The 420s continued the entire line of Model 40, tractors including the crawler and Hi-crop version. While the tractors resembled the previous series from a distance, Deere's sales department had asked Henry Dreyfuss for some new styling.

Dreyfuss knew of other developments working in Moline and Waterloo. The scope of these projects prohibited much investment in current production. Yet this huge new project, Deere's new tractors code named OX and OY, was behind schedule in its overall development. The executive committee of the board reluctantly rescheduled its launch from 1958 to mid-1960. The directors agreed they needed something now to keep customers from going elsewhere for the next shiny new tractor. The board accepted that these changes could be mostly cosmetic.

Jim Conner, the Dreyfuss partner in charge of the John Deere account, recommended painting the engine cover's side panels in yellow. This would contrast with dark green block letters for the John Deere name and lighter-weight script numbers for the model designation. These would appear on an angle down near the base of the radiator's side panel.

1956 Model 420 HC

The 420 high crop is uncommon enough (just 420 produced) without adding in the optional All-Fuel usage engine option. What makes this more unusual is that it was one of 13 so-equipped models initially shipped to John Deere's distributor in South Africa. The green side-panels give it away as an export model.

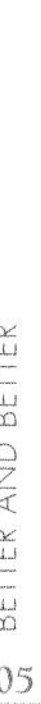

ABOVE: 1958 MODEL 320S
The gas-engined 320's used Deere's 100.5-cubic-inch upright twin with 4.0-inch bore and stroke. This compact engine, carried over from several previous models, benefited from improvements and, at 1,650 rpm, it developed 22.4 horsepower at the drawbar and 24.9 off the PTO (belt pulleys were optional by this time).

RIGHT: *Deere's Model 320 high clearance model was known as the Southern Special. Intended for vegetable farmers in east Texas and southern Louisiana, Deere fitted these tractors with Model 420 S front axles and rear wheels to increase ground clearance in a cost-effective manner.*

JOHN DEERE
320

1958 Model 520

Deere offered the 520 as a tricycle, row-crop dual front, adjustable wide front, and this single front starting in mid-July 1956. It ran on a 6.50-16 front and 9.5-42 rear tires.

As Deere prepared the 20 series models for introduction, the board learned that not all of OX and OY work was tardy. Waterloo gasoline engine development specialist John Sandoval had been experimenting with cylinder head and combustion chamber designs. His work yielded so many benefits to performance and fuel economy that Deere introduced some of them on the 520, 620, and 720 models introduced in 1956.

The Twenties become the Thirties

In 1958, Conner trimmed back his vertical side panel. He eliminated the horizontal green bar and gave the engine cover panel a diagonal cut to further expose the engine. The tractor name remained in the same typeface, but he changed the new "30" series numbers to shadow-style. He positioned them squarely onto the sheet metal near the top of the radiator. For the sales staff, these differences were bold enough to point out to customers. If it were not for paint and appearance, it would have been difficult otherwise to differentiate the 20-series tractors from the new 330, 430, 530, 630, and 730 models from the outside.

Conner and his colleagues continued performing modifications to sheet metal and to instrument and control lever placement. The "30" series was a further visual tune up for what Waterloo was developing behind the scenes.

When Deere introduced the 830 in mid-1958, the dealers, branch staff, and the fortunate farmers invited to the premier recognized that "this is just about as good as it gets." Deere and Dreyfuss had advanced the art and science of hydraulic draft-controls, engine breathing and combustion, operator comfort and general ease of operation farther than any other maker. More than a decade after Charlie Wiman asked Theo Brown to look into the idea of a cab for the tractor, Waterloo introduced a weatherproof steel cab with good visibility and good ventilation.

What's more, Deere had perfected the diesel engine to the highest art: at the end of 1959, a review of the top five Nebraska test performers in terms of power and fuel economy,

With gas, all-fuel, and liquefied propane gas (LPG) available, this gas version was the most powerful. The 189.8-cubic-inch engine used 4.69-inch bore and 5.50-inch stroke and at 1,325 rpm, it developed 34.3 horsepower on the drawbar and 38.6 on the PTO.

using *any* fuel, counted five Deere tractors. The sixth-place Volvo was 0.75-horsepower-hours per gallon out of fifth. First place went to Deere's frugal Model 720 at 17.97 horsepower-hours per gallon at 56.66 belt horsepower.

By the middle of 1960, Deere had manufactured more than 1,450,000 two-cylinder tractors. The tractor division had achieved breathtaking success. In 40 years, tractors had gone from the single most dreaded topic of boardroom discussion to the corporate profit leader.

Loyal farmers, discontent when crop prices fell, weather confounded them, or when their machines failed to live up to expectations, had long since come to know and respect John Deere's tractors. With their power and reliability, their ease of service and comfort, Deere gave its loyal users everything they wanted.

Yet throughout his life after the war, Charlie Wiman had come to understand human nature. If Waterloo or Dubuque offered people something more, they'd want it. If Deere

OPPOSITE: 1958 MODEL 620 LPG ORCHARD

The 620 models stretched 135.25-inches long, measured 86.6-inches wide and, with the operator shrouding and the higher LPG fuel tank, sat 64-inches tall, 2-inches lower than a 620 standard. Deere carried the 620 orchards on during 630 production, deciding against building any 630 Orchard models.

ABOVE: *Looking more like a green Batmobile than a slow moving tree-and-branch-saving farm tractor, this propane model is one of 247 orchard 620s that Deere manufactured.*

RIGHT: *Propane was a very popular tractor fuel through the 1950s until the demand for diesel became more widespread and ultimately eclipsed it. While the LPG models with their higher compression developed 34.3 drawbar horsepower, gas models produced 33.6. There also was a significant price benefit to LPG in those days as well.*

and Dreyfuss made current production look old and seem out of date, future products would seem essential. It would take a huge leap to do this. Wiman, the visionary, who had died in 1955, already had forced the issue. Barely 200 other individuals in America knew that the company already had jumped.

If any tractors ever could be called "beautiful," they might be Deere's Model 530 and 630. With these machines, Dreyfuss' staff produced a truly *stylish* tractor. They installed its automobile-style dash panel at the end of a flipped-up cowl. They mounted the steering wheel flatter, more like an automobile as well.

"One thing we introduced was the Human Factor seat," Jim Conner recalled. "One of my first assignments when I started with Dreyfuss was to work on the Lockheed Electra in 1953 and 1954. We worked very closely with Dr. Janet Travell on the airplane seats." Dreyfuss had learned of Travell's research at Harvard University Medical Center. Best known as President John Kennedy's back specialist, her less visible work dealt with human engineering in a manner similar to Dreyfuss' own ideas. She had determined not only how to heal injuries to the lower back, but she understood what caused them initially. She had developed ideas about how to avoid them in the first place.

"When Henry got Travell in to do a study of tractor seats and to work with us, she went out to Waterloo to drive tractors. She turned up," Conner began to laugh, "in the field, on the morning we were going to do this, wearing green slacks and a yellow top."

JOHN DEERE
620

RIGHT: 1958 MODEL 820 WITH HANCOCK MODEL N8 ELEVATING SCRAPER

The powerhouse 820 used Deere's massive 471.5-cubic-inch diesel twin with 6.125-inch bore and 8.0-inch stroke. At 1,125 rpm, the big machine developed 69.7 horsepower on the drawbar and would pull more than 8,600 pounds. Self-loading scrapers helped the tractor keep moving by lifting the soil into the scraper bed.

BELOW: 1959 MODEL 430 HC

While 430 standards hunkered down at a modest 56 inches from the ground to the top of the radiator, the high crop models raised the nose another 12 inches. Front and rear track was adjustable from 54 to 84 inches and the high crops weighed 3,400 pounds.

Placing the tractor operator right over the rear driving wheels was the initial problem. This rear end, often fitted with extra wheel weights for improved traction, offered no suspension compliance other than tire flex to soften impacts that traveled straight up the operator's spine. The "Float-ride" seat, developed from Travell's recommendations and introduced on the 20 series, got a shock absorber of its own on the largest of the 30 series tractors. No other manufacturer matched the operator comfort this seat provided.

"It had an interesting innovation. Dr. Travell knew that as your stature increases, your legs get longer and you want to be further away and your arms are longer. She figured out an angle—about 27 degrees—so that the seat went up and down on an inclined track. And we developed a suspension with springs and dampers—shock absorbers—that could be adjusted for the weight of the operator. And, it had a memory." Conner was amused by the technological marvels on their tractors that took automakers another two decades to adopt.

ABOVE: 1959 MODEL 430 I MODEL F3

Deere manufactured just 53 of these industrials using the Holt forklifts. An option for the industrials was a clutch-type "direction reverser," perfect for the stop-and-go-back-and-forth industrial operations of a forklift.

630
JOHN DEERE
Power Steering

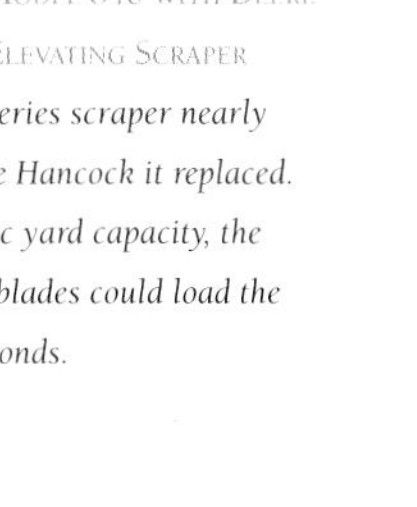

OPPOSITE: 1959 MODEL 630 HC
The high crops and all 630 models used Deere's 302.9-cubic-inch twin of 5.5-inch bore and 6.375-inch stroke. Running at 1,125rpm, the engine developed 44.2 horsepower at the drawbar and 48.7 horsepower off the PTO shaft.

LEFT TOP: 1960 MODEL 840 WITH DEERE MODEL 400 ELEVATING SCRAPER
Deere manufactured just 63 of these machines in 1958, mated to Hancock scrapers. In 1959, Deere took production in house at Waterloo and began manufacturing its own scrapers, producing at least 600 more of these combinations in 1959 and 1960.

LEFT: 1960 MODEL 840 WITH DEERE MODEL 400 ELEVATING SCRAPER
Deere's 400-series scraper nearly duplicated the Hancock it replaced. With 7.5 cubic yard capacity, the chain-linked blades could load the cart in 45 seconds.

RIGHT: *Deere designed this combination so that the scraper was an integral part of the tractor. Engineering set the scraper hitch point over the rear axle for traction as well as maneuverability.*

LEFT: *Without a figure to give it scale, it's hard to imagine the size. This combination is 33 feet long and weighs 23,400 pounds. Rear tires are 18.00-26s. Indiana collector John Craig found this giant earth mover and restored it together with Steve Mellott.*

BE CAREFUL
540 RPM PTO
CUSTOM
POWR-TROL

Articulated Four-Wheel Drive Answers the Big Power Question

At the turn of the century, farmers in the northern plains states needed massive steam or gasoline traction engines pulling 8-, 10-, or 12-bottom plow gangs to open up virgin prairies. The farmers who worked that country operated over vast acreage. Small tractors that suited farmers in the central Midwest and the eastern states never were too useful to those in the Dakotas, who just used more of the tractors and wore them out sooner.

By the late 1950s, Douglass and Maurice Steiger in Fargo, ND, had assembled their first four-wheel-drive tractor using parts from Euclid earthmovers. Their system got the then-enormous amount of horsepower—238—to the ground without wasted wheel spin. The brothers incorporated a pivoting, or articulated, body as a way to steer the tractor while running on full power. They had their first tractor running in 1958.

At that same time, Deere's engineers faced the identical challenge. As the Steiger brothers had done, Waterloo reached similar conclusions, even to using an outside supplier diesel. In 1959, Deere introduced its 8010 using a 215-horsepower six-cylinder. 425-cubic-inch GMC supercharged engine. It was the first articulated four-wheel-drive tractor offered by any full-line company. The company intended the tractor more as an evaluation machine than a consumer product, so it limited production and distribution to handful of copies.

Deere never offered the 24,860-pound 8010 to the University of Nebraska for testing. It might have forced the university to recalibrate its instruments. Deere followed the 8010 in 1960 with the improved 8020 model, which it offered more widely for sale. Deere kept the 8020 in production into 1964.

LEFT: 1959 MODEL 630 HIGH CROP

Among the work that Deere engineers and Dreyfuss designers were most proud of was their combined efforts to simplify the rear end of the tractor while also making it safer. Deere's quick-detach 3-point hitch system and its clearly labeled and logically located Powr-Trol hydraulic couplings sped up field work for operators.

CHAPTER 21

1953–1961

JOHN DEERE

DEERE BRINGS THE FUTURE TO 1960

PREVIOUS: 1960 MODEL 4010 DIESEL #1
Deere had introduced the squared fenders and dual headlights on its 1959 30-series models. The New Generation models came in this row-crop configuration as well as adjustable wide-fronts, utilities, and single narrow fronts.

RIGHT: *Henry Dreyfuss Associates designer Jim Conner got involved early in Deere's development process for these new models. Dreyfuss emphasized "human factors" that made the tractors fit the operators better and, by influencing instrument, control, lever, and pedal placement, make the machines work more logically and safely.*

"The two-cylinder tractor was the essence of simplicity," Bill Hewitt observed. "The good farmer could do a lot of the repairs on it. If he needed to have the valves ground, or the cylinders bored, all he had to do was remove the engine block and take it into the dealer. There were already other people's cylinder blocks which had been ground. These were waiting for immediate transfer." Hewitt knew this perspective was crucial to understanding Deere's tractor history. "Those were the kinds of things that kept tractors running, because the two-cylinder model was so easy for a normally talented farmer/mechanic to keep running."

As Deere & Company approached its 100th anniversary in 1937, Bill Hewitt neared graduation from University of California at Berkeley. He had majored in economics. The native San Franciscan then went east to Harvard for business school. But he returned home when he came up short of funds to continue grad school. After the World War II, Lt. Commander Hewitt returned again to California. He entered the farm machinery business, managing a territory for a Ford tractor distributorship.

In 1948, he married Patricia "Tish" Wiman, Colonel Charlie Wiman's daughter. A few months later his father-in-law offered him a job. Hewitt was someone "with a bright future." He already was a part of the Deere family.

Hewitt exceeded expectations. He learned rapidly and rose quickly through the company. Starting as a San Francisco branch territory manager, he became the branch's assistant manager and then its manager. He learned the business and the company from Ben Keator, a man of proven perception. Keator, along with Pat Murphy, had led Lindeman into the Deere family.

1960 Model 3010 Diesel #1

Deere's New Generation of Power startled most of its loyal customers. John Deere tractors with four and six-cylinder engines were things most thought they'd never see.

Wiman watched Hewitt, but the Colonel didn't pave his son-in-law's way. Hewitt earned a reputation for sensitivity, grace, even-handedness, intelligence, and fairness. In a company such as Deere, these were virtues that also were part of the company legacy. In 1954, Wiman was gravely ill. Still, he wished others to nominate his successor. Keator did just that. His letter to the board, quoted by Wayne Broehl in *John Deere's Company*, glowed:

"We should have a young man—this is most important—who is a leader, who knows the business and has a vision for the future of our line, who is cognizant of the problems to be met and how to handle them. . . . He has youth, he is smart, catches on to things quick, and has vision, enthusiasm, and courage to get things done. . . ." Keator summed up, "Bill is a very dignified and personable man and you would go a long way before you would find his equal for that job."

The curved engine hood resolved appearance problems, but it raised other questions. If the tractor ran on a side hill, was the operator capable of using all the controls comfortably and safely? Jim Conner and senior partner Bill Purcell made a trip to study one of the current production tractors.

"We made a whole bunch of photographs of Bill working the controls," Conner explained. "A lot was still unchanged from the old Model B. Bill went through all the motions. From those photos we began to figure out from our knowledge of ergonomics all the things we needed to change.

"One was to make the angle of the steering wheel less vertical. Location of the pedals. Location of the levers." All this work was aimed at the new tractors. But Conner and Purcell developed this very early. When the board slipped the introduction to 1960, Waterloo incorporated many of these improvements onto Deere's 30-series tractors, to keep them alive and appealing.

"We cleaned up the operators platform, we relocated controls and instruments, narrowed the cowl at the back even more with the cast iron cowl and instrument pod, for greater visibility while the farmer was cultivating. We introduced flat fenders with hand grips and headlights." Their quad headlights reiterated automotive styling of the day.

Conner retired in 1987 after 35 years with Dreyfuss. Conner's and Dreyfuss' relationship with Deere were part of the reason such advances were possible.

"We never took the design problem and ran home with it and did it all up and brought it back and said, 'This is it! This is the way it's going to be.' Everything we did was on a cooperative and mutual basis.

"The interesting thing about Bill Hewitt was that he took a personal interest in all the products. If we were showing a new prototype, he would come. He would check it out pretty thoroughly. If he had comments he would walk up to Henry or Bill or me. He had a good aesthetic sense and his impressions were quite valid, really right there."

Wiman's health deteriorated further. On June 22, 1954, he created the position of executive vice-president, setting up his succession. He nominated Hewitt. The board agreed unanimously. Not quite 11 months later, Wiman died on May 12, 1955. On May 24, the board elected Hewitt as Deere's sixth president. He was not quite 41. Hewitt recalled that time almost four decades later.

"My predecessor had already started the design work for the New Generation of Power four- and six-cylinder tractors. That was a momentous change, this New Generation of Power. Up until then most of the improvements were 'improvements' that modified existing design. The 'improved' design came out and later it was improved. But each time it was modifications.

"There was a meeting," Hewitt recalled, "The senior engineers, some board members, and the Dreyfuss design people couldn't quite believe that Deere & Company was willing to start fresh, with a 'clean sheet of paper,' as they called it. One of the engineers asked if that meant they didn't have to carry anything over to the new tractors. The chairman thought and said, 'It might be good if the tractors were still green and yellow.' Let me tell you, that silenced the room for a moment."

The four cylinder diesel displaced 254 cubic inches with 4.125-inch bore and 4.75-inch stroke. At 2,200 rpm, the engine developed 52.8 horsepower at the drawbar and 59.4 horsepower off the PTO shaft.

Deere spent most of a decade devising and developing these new tractors. With engineers given a mandate to start fresh to create the best machine possible, Deere chairman Charlie Wiman did ask them the retain the green and yellow paint scheme.

"The Waterloo people," Jim Conner began, "had already come up with a design and a kind of mock-up tractor when we got into this." Conner, a design partner with Henry Dreyfuss, had joined the firm in 1952. While he had some design responsibilities on the number series tractors, he was the man in charge of design for the New Generation tractors.

"Wisely, at Waterloo," Conner continued, "they had taken a task force out of the group concerned with day-to-day engineering, and removed them to a separate place to work on the new tractors. The 'Falls Avenue Annex,' at Falls and Knoll Avenue, was a vacant grocery store that the company rented. This prototype mock-up was of interest to us as a kind of starting point, but we all quickly discarded it.

"It had a narrow-angle V-6 engine in it. I don't know if they ever built running engines. It was pretty slim but still the valve covers protruded into the line of sight. There were no doubt other considerations too, because the V-6 engine went away rather soon."

Waterloo engineering's Merlin Hansen managed Deere's New Design Group that began its work in the grocery store before moving in 1955 to the "tin shed." This was Deere's first steel building erected on the site of the new engineering design and test facility southwest of town.

Hansen's assignment came early in 1953. It seemed to present a conundrum: "To give the farmer more tractor for equal or less cost, and to ensure that it would do more work with less effort on the part of the operator." This left plenty of room for interpretation because his assignment included producing a complete power range of machines.

Hansen conferred with Wallace DuShane, in charge of overall design, John Townsend, the diesel engineer, and John Sandoval, in charge of gasoline engines. Together they set targets of 50 and 70 horsepower for the two models they would introduce in late 1957 for the 1958 model year. Hansen looked into the future, searching for power requirements beyond the 35-horsepower industry average at that time. When he met with Vernon Rugen to discuss transmissions, they agreed to offer a broader range of speeds than before. They wanted to package it in a smaller casing and make it easier to shift than previous models.

Waterloo's development nomenclature labeled these new machines the OX (70-horsepower version) and OY. It would be up to the Deere Name & Numbering Committee to give these models their final designations before introduction. The New Design Group agreed that the 70 horsepower OX would be its primary development target. Engineers settled on configuring the new tractor along Model 70-720 dimensions. When Vernon Rugen devised a planetary final drive assembly nearly 11 inches shorter than what Deere used on the 20 series models, Hansen and DuShane reduced the wheelbase and shortened the tractor.

The question of power output involved Waterloo engineers and it brought in the Dreyfuss designers as well. Henry Dreyfuss pointed out that Deere's (and every manufacturer's) propane fuel tanks protruded through the sheet metal hoods. He asked the engineers to consider finding a different location. One of their more radical decisions placed the fuel tank vertically in front of the radiator. This put inches back into the

JOHN DEERE
8010
DIESEL

LEFT: 1960 MODEL 8010
This machine broke new ground for Deere. The company's first articulated four-wheel-drive measured 19 feet 10 inches in length on a 10 foot wheelbase. It weighed 26,450 pounds.

INSET: *Deere selected GMC's two-cycle 6-cylinder 425-cubic-inch diesel with 4.25 inch bore and 5.00 inch stroke to power this machine. At 2,100 rpm, this supercharged titan developed more than 150 horsepower at the drawbar, good for a 21,000-pound towing capacity.*

ABOVE AND OPPOSITE: *It was Deere's biggest 3-point hitch to date. In fact it was the company's largest tractor. It road on 23.1-26.00 tires on all corners.*

tractor's wheelbase and length, but it improved visibility for cultivating and other front tool bar work.

Dreyfuss' concerns always were the "human factors:" How do they make any project more operator-friendly? As Conner explained it, "Engineers are machine oriented; the goodness of Dreyfuss' work is how the human interfaces with the machine." For Dreyfuss, this meant more safety, more comfort, more efficiency, and more convenience.

Jim Conner worked with Deere's Dan Gleeson on chassis, seating, and controls decisions. When they got Christian Hess involved, his concerns for implement hitches led them to reposition the operator seat nearly 12 inches forward and 12 inches lower than on the 720 and 70. As Merle Miller explained this in his book, *Designing the New Generation John Deere Tractors*, this location allowed more room for the hitch components. It shifted the operator further forward, nearer the middle of the tractor. This move yielded a smoother ride. The forward position enabled designers to provide access to the operator's platform

1961 Model 3010 Gas
The handsome front end of the New Generation tractors left small slots for cooling above a strong solid casting that also served as a front bumper for careless operators. Main cooling air came in through side vents.

from either side of the front of the tractor as well as by stepping over the seat from the rear. Gleeson and Conner added steps and handholds on the front side of the platform.

New Generation, New Power

Engines represented critical considerations for these new tractors. As Miller pointed out, "Farmers often have strong emotions when it comes to their tractors. The performance of the engine is a strong influence on the farmer's opinion. For many operators, the engine is what gives the tractor its personality, its character, its spirit." Personality, character, and spirit are not quantifiable measurements. Hansen and his team could not dial these into the new engines using rudimentary computer-aided design programs. Yet engine power or its torque, its ease of starting in cold or hot weather, and its reliability and durability, are elements that they could engineer into a powerplant. In addition, Hansen and engine designers Townsend and Sandoval wanted to create engines that shared as many parts as possible. That proved to be an enormous challenge; in the end, the OX and OY used only the same piston and connecting rod.

Before growing to four and six cylinders, Sandoval and Townsend produced two vertical, in-line diesel two-cylinder engines and one gasoline version. Each had a 3.75-inch

bore and 4.375-inch stroke. Townsend settled on the Roosa Master rotary diesel fuel-injection pump. This is a common system that Ford, Allis-Chalmers, and International Harvester all have used on their diesel engines. The question of cylinder numbers and configurations arose next.

The New Design Group determined it would consider an in-line four, a 60-degree V-four, a 45-degree V-four cylinder and another in-line four with an overhead camshaft. Marketing pointed out that many of their competitors had an in-line four. Hansen and his engine team moved on immediately. The first engine Sandoval completed was a gasoline 45-degree V-6 of 3.75-inch bore and 4-inch stroke. Sandoval mounted both intake and exhaust manifolds inside the V. The results encouraged the engineers who quickly made several additional four- and six-cylinder gasoline V-engines. These had only the intake inside the V. According to Miller, their width and the manufacturing costs, coupled with

1961 Model 1010-C
Agricultural Crawler
Deere introduced the 1010 series in 1961 as a compact tractor providing "A man's work at a boy's pay." The Ag crawler, meant especially for vineyard and orchard work, supplemented an industrial model for dozing and excavating.

1962 Model 4010 H

Wisconsin collector Walter Keller found an extremely unusual high crop. It left the Waterloo production line with a gas-engine, the only one produced in 1962. Consigned to engineering, it worked on Deere's test farms.

structural and vibration problems, doomed these six prototypes and the V-configuration.

From there, the engineers advanced through four versions of in-line four- and six-cylinder engines. Gasoline and LPG engines settled at a 4-inch bore and stroke. Townsend continued hunting for a suitable configuration for his diesel. At 4.125-inch bore and 4.75-inch stroke, Townsend was content. Sandoval's innovative cylinder head and combustion chamber design already had provided benefits early in the program. Deere's board had chosen to incorporate some of the improvements into production 20-series models starting in 1956. Gas and LPG engines for the OX and OY got 12-volt electric systems while the diesels needed 24-volts.

Among their more clever design innovations, Sandoval and Townsend designed the engine blocks so oil lines were inside the casting and all fuel lines were external. Contaminating engine oil with coolant or fuel can be disastrous. No fuel leakage could dilute the lubricating oil and damage the crankshaft and main bearings.

The New Design Group planned five different transmissions. These ranged from a basic synchronized gear transmission to a power shift with eight forward speeds and three reverses. As Miller reported, the engineers agreed that new transmissions must transmit 25 percent more power than before, cost no more to manufacture, and fit in a smaller package. Hansen and Rugen considered adding torque converters. They knew that tractor operators do not shift in sequence like truck or car drivers. Instead farmers shift to keep torque consistent. Hansen concluded that "the torque converter was both unnecessary and undesirable for agricultural use."

The scope and scale of development proved larger than engineering had anticipated and it took longer than Deere's board had hoped. In late 1957, the executive committee met and agreed to postpone introduction of this new series to the summer of 1960. It removed the pressure from an engineering staff that might release something not quite ready.

Harold Brock, Deere's new director of research, knew that experience intimately. As chief engineer for Ford Motor Company's tractor division, he had watched his engineers

1962 LANZ MODEL 700 VINEYARD
John Deere-Lanz produced these diesel vineyard models from 1962 through 1965. With 50 horsepower, they were the most powerful tractor in the line up.

JOHN DEERE-LANZ
700

slave frantically to complete the company's landmark Select-O-Speed shift-on-the-fly transmission. The board had imposed a deadline for introduction. The Select-O-Speed offered ten forward speeds and two reverse. It had problems that led Brock to conclude it was not ready for production. Yet at least one member of Ford's board succeeded in bullying the other directors into pushing it into service. Brock argued vigorously for delay. For his resistance, the board transferred him over to the truck division, and eventually out of Ford. Soon after, Deere hired the experienced engineer.

Hewitt and Hansen were more patient. They wanted a power shift transmission as anxiously as Ford did. But even months after introducing the Select-O-Speed, Ford's engineers had no clue how to fix transmissions that might fail in the field after as little as six or eight hours of use. Deere stepped back.

Ed Fletcher and Wilbur Davis both tackled hydraulics for the OX and OY. Deere's tractors previously used "open center" hydraulic systems. These allowed hydraulic fluid to retreat to reservoirs while trapped oil held the cylinder's piston in place because valves closed. This system worked well for operating a single-cylinder hydraulic system. Deere's engineers envisioned operators of the new tractors needing separate raise-or-lower capabilities for front and rear or left and right sides. This might require two or more cylinders. Fletcher and Davis concluded that the more expensive but quicker-responding closed center system was what the OX and OY needed.

With the added weight on the tractor and its capability to lift and carry larger heavier implements, Ed Fletcher paid special attention to the brakes. He devised a radically new system. Traditionally, Deere had placed brake drums on differential shafts. These rotated much more slowly and with a fraction of the torque of the drive axles or the final drives. Fletcher relocated the brake discs within the differential onto the final drive sun pinion and applied a hydraulic boost. This low-torque placement provided much greater stopping ability with Deere's new power brakes.

"Hitches were more than a means of lifting and carrying an implement," Miller wrote. "The links and their attachment locations permitted the implement to follow the tractor

ABOVE LEFT: *Despite the newness of the machine, it still was simply a working machine, meant for mundane jobs as well as glamorous photos. The operator here on the 3010 Row Crop hoists manure into a John Deere spreader. The front loader is Deere's Model 35.* Deere & Company Archives

ABOVE: *John Deere's D-Day New Generation introductions included an industrial equipment launch as well. This dramatic view under the Model 50 Backhoe mounted on a 1010 crawler showed a 1010 wheel loader with 710 front bucket, and dealers enjoying the amusement-park atmosphere.* Deere & Company Archives

OPPOSITE: *As part of the Deere world family, these 700-series models used Deere's Model 2010 diesel engine coupled to Lanz's 10-speed transmission. Henry Dreyfuss' office did the styling.*

over small hills and through depressions or swales. . . . Designing the hitch geometry involved a compromise considering several important characteristics, which included lift capacity, hitch sensing, transport clearance, implement penetration, hill-and-swale and contour operation." The system Christian Hess and Wilbur Davis devised blended the best of Theo Brown's work with the greater potential of closed-center hydraulics. Hess had spent years working with Brown on hitch geometry and design, first to get around Harry Ferguson's three-point system, and then to tame and improve it.

The New Design Group developed "Styling Objectives" early on in the conception phase of this project. Most significantly, these objectives demanded that:

"The styling should not dictate the tractor design. The styling should be functional.

It should be a clean design, not having parts projecting beyond the basic sheet metal.

The rear of the tractor should be simplified in appearance.

The tractor should be more compact for its power.

The underside of the tractor should appear plain, with the frame alongside the engine to provide implement mounting points."

For Dreyfuss designer Jim Conner, these were goals he had sought consistently to advance his previous designs for production tractors.

"Our approach was not streamlining," Conner explained. "It was to make a nice-looking tractor where everything had its reason for being.

"The curved hood started with the New Generation tractors. Henry proposed and stuck to the idea of making the tractor hood one piece. 'They do it for automobiles,' he said. 'They stamp the entire roof of a car!' [This grew into a "no-visible-joints" recommendation that became a New Design Group policy rule.]

"He had a reason. There were a lot of tire and wheel options on these tractors. Sometimes you had bigger wheels in the front so the tractor would be pointed uphill. Sometimes it would be the other way, pointed downhill. We never could tell what the buyer would want for his particular operation.

"By having a curved line on top," Conner continued, "you couldn't so easily tell that the tractor was leaning one way or another. And later, with the Sound-Gard cabs, we tapered the cab roof and windows. So there was no longer any vertical or horizontal reference line in the side profile. It didn't look funny or like it was broken when it was tilted down or up in the field!"

Such detail seems inconsequential until compared with the competition. Dreyfuss understood that most tractor purchases involved the whole family. Buyers might consider Deere's tractors the mechanical equal to IHCs or Fords. However, if Deere's looked better, less "funny," in the field pulling plows or running home down the road for dinner, that factor might cinch the sale.

Engineers and designers agreed that one element of Dreyfuss' success with Deere & Company was communication. Keeping everyone, engineering, manufacturing, sales, marketing, and President Bill Hewitt in the flow of information and allowing them equal access at every stage, eliminated problems on the eve of production. "We can't do that," or "We don't have tools which can stretch this metal or bend that piece" were disasters that never occurred. Hewitt's close interest and involvement meant that approval came from the top down. All the steps necessary from the prototype demonstration through product manufacture to introduction and after-sale service in the marketplace represented no surprises to, or from, anyone involved.

Unless they were intentional.

Deere certainly intended a big surprise on D-Day, August 29, 1960.

That Monday more than 100 airplanes from 75 cities delivered nearly 6,000 John Deere dealers and spouses to Dallas, Texas. They came to see what seven years work had created. The next day, when Bill Hewitt opened the back door of the convention center and the faithful spilled out, they saw $2 million worth of Deere's New Generation of Power. The company's Name and Numbering Committee had settled on Model 4010 for the six-cylinder OX series and 3010 for the companion four-cylinder OY models. Waterloo Tractor Works displayed 136 tractors, and 324 supplementary implements, tools, wagons and combines came from Deere's other plants. They spread across a 15-acre parking lot next to the Cotton Bowl stadium.

Deere wasted no time getting the full complement of crop versions designed as it developed the New Generation of Power models for 1960. Here in Culican, Mexico, Deere tested new 4010 Diesel High-Crops with border disks that banked soil against the tomato plants. Deere & Company Archives

There had been some leaks. Some dealers knew in 1959 that there was a new tractor, even that it had more than two cylinders. But this new lineup was not what they expected. And they loved it.

CHAPTER 22
1961–1982

JOHN DEERE

THE QUEST FOR MORE POWER

AND MORE FEATURES

The New Generation of Power reached farmers everywhere by 1961. Deere introduced tractors ranging from the 80-horsepower six-cylinder diesel 4010 (the OX,) through the four-cylinder 3010 (the OY prototype series) and down to the 35-horsepower gas or diesel four-cylinder Model 1010. Merlin Hansen had met his nearly impossible assignment to "give the farmer more tractor for equal or less cost, and to ensure that it would do more work with less effort on the part of the operator." The production 4010 developed the power of a Model 830 yet it almost fit inside the dimensions of the smaller 730. The 3010's introductory price was in line with Deere's suggested retail price for its earlier 70 and 720 models.

PREVIOUS: 1964 MODEL 1010 ORCHARD
Gas 1010s ran with a five-forward-gear transmission offering speeds from less than 2.6 miles per hour up to 16.9. Orchard versions weighed just about 4,150 pounds.

RIGHT: 1965 MODEL 4020 H - LPG
Deere's new 4020 introduced not only more power but a more effective way to use it, with the long-awaited Power-Shift transmission that offered operators all 8 forward gears without needing to stop to shift. This was one of just 4 high-crops with the new transmission in 1965, and one of only 19 powered by propane gas.

By 1962 Deere had supplemented the lineup with the 5010 (code named the OZ through its development stages). This was a 100-horsepower, six-cylinder, two-wheel-drive tractor rated to pull seven plows. In addition, Dubuque offered an orchard and grove version of the small 1010 and of the 55-horsepower four-cylinder 3010. But once again, neither Waterloo nor Dreyfuss chose to rest on their newly earned laurels.

One year later, Deere organized Flight 63, to bring the same dealers to Waterloo. Sales had slackened slightly and Deere management had two goals for this promotion effort. The board gambled that giving distributors a tour of the factory and showing them new tractor models on the production line might spark their initiative. If that wasn't enough, the board hoped that introducing two new models might energize branch sales staffs. Waterloo's engineers increased the power of the 3020 from 59 to 65 horsepower out of the four-cylinder engine. It raised the already

JOHN DEERE
4020

1964 Model 2010-I

While the Keller family business is construction, most work around the home place and museum is more tractor oriented though needs arise to move concrete block. Waterloo produced its own forklifts for the industrial 2010 chassis.

1964 Model 1010 Orchard

Based on Deere's 1010-Utility models, Waterloo added full rear fenders and combination running-board/branch deflectors behind the front tires.

No Longer Runner Up

The New Generation lineup brought Bill Hewitt's ambition to reality. Deere had sold 23 percent of the farm tractors in the United States in 1959, the next-to-last year of its two cylinder models. By January 1964, the company's market share had reached 34 percent. It took Hewitt less than a decade to achieve his goal. Ironically, just as he never noted the date when he set his sights on being number one, no one recorded the day in 1963 on which Deere had shed the runner-up title. While IHC sold $665.4 million, Deere soared far beyond them with $762 million in sales for 1963 with profits of $48.4 million. Deere even surpassed industry heavyweight Caterpillar in sales for 1963. Deere had become the largest farm equipment manufacturer in the world.

Barely six months later, but not timed to coincide with any sales accomplishment, Deere held another celebration at Moline. It opened its new Administrative Center in June 1964. Finnish architect Eero Saarinen had designed the striking building just before he died in 1961. His associates completed his plans to use unpainted steel girders as exterior structural and design elements. Saarinen had selected the steel material, called Cor-Ten, because it would rust quickly and its deep red color would blend into the rolling site. A number of engineers found it ironic. Historian Wayne Broehl quoted one who said, "We've been warning farmers against rust for 120 years, now we are building a big rusty building."

1963 Model 110 Lawnmower
Deere's Horicon Works, producing Deere's grain drills and other planters, got caught in the agricultural market slump in 1960. It began looking for new products. In 1963 Horicon launched the Model 110 Lawn and Garden Tractor. Power came from a Kohler single-cylinder engine.

respectable 4020 six-cylinder from 84 to 91 horsepower. To get the power to the ground, Waterloo provided an optional Power Differential Lock.

Upgrades and Improvements Became Standard Procedure

In 1965 Deere upgraded the 5010 to 5020 nomenclature as Waterloo raised output by 10 percent from 121 to 133 horsepower. In 1969, it increased output again to 141 horsepower. Still, the competition for power continued. Deere offered the 4020 and 3020 with optional hydraulic-powered front-wheel drive, called Front Wheel Assist, FWA. This was not a true four-wheel drive, but it provided a significant increase in traction. With modifications inside the engine, engineers increased output again to 96 horsepower for the 4020 and 71

JD
JOHN DEERE
JOHN DEERE

for the four-cylinder 3020. Waterloo achieved another generation of power when it introduced turbochargers on the diesel 4020 models, renumbered as the 4520 in 1968 with 122 horsepower. The 4320 arrived in 1971 with 115 horsepower, and the 4620 superseded the 4520, now with 135 horsepower. These looked virtually identical to the first New Generation tractors except that Waterloo fitted the FWA models with smaller front tires that were chevron-patterned versions of the rears. Engineering substantially reinforced the front axle housings in front of and around the differential casing.

In 1968 Deere introduced replacements for its big articulated four-wheel-drive 8010 and 8020 models. These came from Wagner Tractor Company of Portland, Oregon. It was an advantageous arrangement for both companies at the time. Wagner's primary market, the Pacific Northwest logging industry, was in a recession. Wagner faced laying off many of its employees. Waterloo engineering had encountered delays in developing its replacement four-wheel drives. Moline contracted with Wagner. Deere would take all the Wagner's agricultural (WA) production of its two largest machines, the 178-horsepower WA-14 and the 220-horsepower WA-17 for 1969 and 1970. Deere's agreement left things open after that. Wagner painted its two giants in Deere Green and Yellow.

By 1970, Deere had its own tractor called the 7020 ready for introduction and it ended its relationship with Wagner. Waterloo's new machine was less powerful, with 145 turbocharged horsepower, but it was more technologically advanced. Deere introduced the 7020 in 1971; it remained in production through 1975 when Deere intercooled the turbocharged fuel-mix. This brought another technology and a substantial power boost to farm fields. Called the 7520, this high-tech model arrived with 175 horsepower in 1972.

OPPOSITE: 1966 MODEL 445
This was Argentina's version of Deere's Model 435. Deere's board built a factory at Rosario in 1957 and the first tractors appeared in 1958.

NOT EVERY INNOVATION WAS POPULAR

Six years into the life of the New Generation, at approximately its halfway point, the Dreyfuss team's efforts with human factors produced one of the least popular options Deere ever introduced. Getting the farmer to accept it was perhaps Deere's most difficult marketing chore. The company tried making gifts at trade shows. Recipients left it behind. Finally, this new system required an unprecedented corporate giveaway.

Farmers understood the logic behind a rollover protection system (ROPS). They steadfastly believed the need for it never would happen to them. Engineers, insurance institutes, and educators knew better. Starting right after World War II, in the late 1940s, Nebraska tractor test chief Lester

BELOW: *The Rosario factory produced a tricycle, row-crop utility, an orchard, and this vineyard model starting in 1963. These small tractors used two-cycle two-cylinder GM diesels manufactured under license.*

IN-1-5
OUT-2-6
N
OUT-3-7

ABOVE: 1967 MODEL 2020 ORCHARD *Deere produced fewer than two dozen of these orchard models. The 2020 line appeared in 1965. The factory offered either gas or diesel engines.*

Larsen began dramatically demonstrating the risks of tractor rollover. He used a Deere Model B that university engineers had fitted with a protective frame. Larsen and colleague Jack Steele rolled the tractor about 300 times in 10 years. Each time the tractor went over, they crushed a dummy whose head was a glass jar filled with water and catsup. The name "Jughead" became popular far beyond the tractor safety world.

At Deere, safety had been a concern dating from Theo Brown's early efforts to cover rear PTO shafts. In mid-1959, engineer Roy Harrington and product development manager Charles Morrison fabricated Deere's first ROPS, with seat belts, on an OY New Generation 4010 prototype. New Generation chief engineer Merlin Hansen understood that if Deere disguised safety improvements (that no farmer ever asked for) as a sunshade (that many had requested), the customer might even pay for it. Deere introduced its Roll-Gard structure in 1966. Even with its sunshade-style roof, it met few takers. Bill Hewitt recalled the resistance and the steps Deere took to make the safety device more appealing to the invincible farmers.

"We made a significant contribution to operator safety and comfort," he began. "Most tractor operator fatalities occur when the tractor rolls over. To install a proper roll bar would add five hundred or eight hundred dollars to the cost of the tractor. But instead of paying eight hundred dollars more for a Deere tractor, they would buy another tractor from someone else. Because farmers, being human, knew that they didn't need a roll bar.

"So," Hewitt explained, "we decided to give all of our engineering specs to each of our competitors. They wouldn't have to go through the process of testing and developing [their own] on the agreement that they would make roll bars standard equipment and we would make them standard equipment.

OPPOSITE: *The tricky transmission linkage takes some getting used to. Operators sit low behind sheet metal protecting them from overhanging branches.*

1969 Model 820 Vineyard

The swept-back front axle and this roll-over hoop were part of the equipment for the narrow vineyard tractors delivered in France, such as this one.

"Because we couldn't sell the things in any quantity to justify our investment in them, we gave away our engineering." Hewitt paused to let the significance sink in.

By 1966, Hewitt no longer was content to be runner-up in any category in any way. Deere no longer was runner up to IHC or any other agricultural equipment manufacturer in the world. Hewitt had made a gesture that reinforced Deere's commitment to safety and its dedication to "human factors" in a way rarely duplicated in American business history. He gave away to Deere's runners-up nearly six years and many millions of dollars worth of research that Waterloo, Dubuque, and Moline engineering and Dreyfuss designers had performed in the interest of operator safety.

"Everybody then adopted roll bars," Hewitt laughed. "Then the cabs came in with glass and air conditioning. The roll bar was incorporated and we couldn't make them fast enough."

1970 Model 3020 FWA

Hydraulic power front-wheel drive first appeared in 1968. This was not a true-4-wheel drive. The liquid hydrostatic connections allowed power transfer to the ground without the traditional gear bind-up that solid linkages exhibit. This unusual tractor also has Deere's Power Shift, the console, and the new Power Weight-Transfer hitch.

Jim Conner picked up the story from the Dreyfuss perspective.

"When we started on the Generation II tractors, the brief we worked out together was to make the Roll-Gard and the cab integrated. So that the structure of the cab was strong enough to take a roll over. That was the beginning of the Sound-Gard cab."

Conner was proud. Its appearance, testing, development, and its introduction to Deere's engineers were at his direction.

"We decided that we were going to do the best cab possible with all the safety features, all the human factors features that a cab could have: rollover protection, sound insulation, heat insulation, operator insulation from vibration and dust, air conditioning, pressurization so the air goes out, does not get sucked in, improved vision, easy entry and exit, flat platform, the second generation of the Travell-designed seat. That cab on the Generation II tractors just blew everybody away."

JOHN DEERE
7020

LEFT: 1970 MODEL 7020
Turbocharging arrived at the farm field with the arrival of Deere's 7020. The big 6-cylinder 404-cubic-inch engine used 4.25-inch bore and 4.75-inch stroke. At 2,200 rpm, this engine developed 127.8 drawbar horsepower and an impressive 146.2 horsepower off the PTO.

The SoundGard received the engineers' blessing. Once Waterloo put it in production, Deere offered it on the four Generation II "30-series" models that Waterloo introduced in New Orleans on August 19, 1972. The updated cab inspired a new name for Deere's tractor engineering as well, the Sound-Idea line. Deere celebrated the cab's noise-blocking capabilities when interior sound levels on the Model 4230 registered only 83 decibels, dB(A) at full load. This was quiet enough that Deere's cassette stereo radio became a frequently selected option. But the Sound-Idea name referred equally to the "soundness" of the entire tractor's concept, from operator comfort through the nearly life-long durability of Deere's new hydraulic oil operated-and-cooled Perma-Clutch.

The appearance of the tractors changed slightly with Dreyfuss's next-generation hood concept.

"The down sloping hood," Conner explained, "which came out on the 1972 tractors, from a design standpoint, had a couple things going for it.

"One, to let it slope downward gave you better visibility over the nose. Two, it gave you more space under the back of the hood to get 'stuff' in, because there is always more 'stuff' that needs to be in there. So we brought the back up, front down and curved the top. Now, there was no longer a 'horizontal' horizon line to look at, to sight along. It picked up what we started with the tractors in 1960."

The Name and Numbering Committee moved this 30-series ahead from the New Generation as well. The new Model 4030 offered 80 horsepower, the 4230 offered 100, the

OPPOSITE: *The 7020 that Deere tested at Nebraska University weighed 18,495 pounds with dual tires all around and pulled almost 9,000 pounds at more than 5 miles per hour. Deere fitted 18.4-34.0 tires as it left the factory.*

JOHN DEERE

LEFT: 1971 MODEL 4620 PFWD
Deere's engineering raised the bar with this model. It already had turbocharged several of its tractors but the 4620 series introduced intercooling to the mix. Intercooling used an air or water cooled radiator to chill the fuel-air-mix, making it denser and therefore more potent.

4430 produced 125 horsepower, and the 4630 rated 150 horsepower at the PTO. Deere made Synchro-Range transmissions standard equipment, connected by the Perma-Clutch, the innovative hydraulic wet-plate clutch. For the farmer needing even more power, the articulated four-wheel drives boasted 175 horsepower from the 8430 and 225 from the 8630.

From the Model D to the present day, engineers had watched farmers' fuel preferences. By the mid-1960s, when work began on the 30-series, Waterloo decided it would limit production to diesel engines exclusively for these models. At the end of 1973, Waterloo ended gas engine production.

Across the United States the early 1970s witnessed a huge jump in the farmer's net income. Farm sizes expanded even as the numbers of farm owners decreased. Chemicals controlled weeds, insects, and other pests, and they also enhanced crop yields and accelerated

OPPOSITE: 1971 MODEL 1520 ORCHARD
This was the big brother to Deere's compact three-cylinder Mannheim-built 820. Deere first intended these solely for European use but America's small farm owners soon grew interested when they recognized this fit in perfectly between the relatively too-small 1020 and the too-large 2020.

JOHN DEERE

TOP: 1973 DEERE 10-SPEED BICYCLE
Rod Groenewald, the Executive Director at San Diego County's Antique Gas & Steam Engine Museum has always been an enthusiastic bicyclist. But when he saw this one, he grabbed it, knowing it was one of the few Deere products he easily could lift up and set into his truck.

harvests. This was the beginning of an era where, as Willard Cochrane described it in *The Development of American Agriculture, A Historical Analysis*, "The technological strategy for increasing crop productivity involved the adoption of plant varieties with a high yield potential, increasing the plant population per acre, and feeding those plants all the commercial nutrients they could use efficiently." Tractor operators raised or lowered fewer two- and four-row cultivator rigs and instead ran higher speeds carrying sprayers or spreaders with arms swung wide to cover six or eight or more rows.

This was still chemical agriculture's early days, however, it suggested that growers had more control than ever before. Hybrid seeds enabled farmers to plant the best versions of their crops for their soil and moisture conditions. Between 1970 and 1980, average

LEFT: 1972 MODEL 4020D
By 1971, the Model 4020 diesels were nearing the end of the line. Deere manufactured 4020s from 1964 into 1972. The 404-cubic-inch engine developed 83.1 horsepower at the drawbar and 93.8 off the PTO.

OPPOSITE: 1972 MODEL 3020 H
This was the last gasoline-engine high-crop produced at Waterloo. With a Power Shift Transmission, Roll-Over Protection system, and console, this machine spent most of its life working among tomato plants at one of Campbell's soup and juice operations.

ABOVE: 1974 MODEL 4230 LOW PROFILE *This replaced the Orchard and Grove designation within the Generation II line up. These 4230s were the second model up the power range, using the 404-cubic-inch six and producing 83.9 drawbar horsepower and 100.3 off the PTO shaft.*

OPPOSITE: 1973 MODEL 4030 WITH DEERE MODEL 48 FRONT LOADER *Deere introduced the Generation II models with the new, improved Sound-Gard cabs in 1973. This 4030 was the smallest of the series, using the 329-cubic-inch 6-cylinder engine developing 67 horsepower at the drawbar and 80.3 off the PTO.*

wheat yield per acre increased nearly 10 percent, from 31.8 bushels to 34.1; corn jumped from 80.8 bushels per acre to 103.1, cotton from 436.7 pounds per acre to 497.7, and potato yields rose from 226.3 hundredweight to 271. Larger incomes enabled owners to replace aging equipment. Demand for Generation II tractors forced Waterloo to expand its production facilities. It built an additional engine manufacturing plant as well.

Deere upgraded its entire tractor line in mid-1975 with the introduction of its 40-series. This range began with the 40-horsepower three-cylinder diesel Model 2040 manufactured at Deere's Mannheim, Germany, plant. Mannheim also provided the three-cylinder 50-horsepower 2240 and the six-cylinder 80-horsepower 2860 that appeared in early 1976. The midrange four-cylinder 60-horsepower Model 2440 and 70-horsepower 2640 came from Dubuque.

ABOVE: 1975 MODEL 8430
Mountain Environmental's big articulated 4-wheel-drive idles while Brett Lucking loads lime into the Gehl Scavenger behind it. The 22,810 pound tractor used Deere's 466-cubic-inch six. At 2,100 rpm, it developed 155.6 drawbar horsepower and 178.2 horsepower off the PTO shaft. It runs here on dual 20.8-34.00 tires.

ABOVE RIGHT: 1979 MODEL 4240
In 1978 Deere launched a new legend in its Iron Horse series, the 40-series of row-crop tractors. Powerful, economical to operate and strong, these machines moved the benchmark. Deere advertised them as "The new Iron Horses with More Horses and More Iron."

OPPOSITE: 1977 MODEL 8430
Junior Hein of Glidden, Iowa, pulls an Earthmaster 14-foot model 1165 disc across harvested corn fields in central Iowa. Nebraska University Tests revealed that these dual wheel models could pull 8,133 pounds at 5.8 miles per hour, making fairly short work of this quarter-section field.

Deere named its bigger tractors in the 40 series the Iron Workhorses. These powerhouses appeared in 1977 as 1978 models. The smallest, the Model 4040, used an all-new 404-cubic-inch diesel that developed 90 horsepower on the PTO. The rest of the series used the 466-cubic-inch block. Deere's Model 4240 produced 110 horsepower, the turbocharged 4440 put out 130 while Deere rated the big 4640 with turbocharger and intercooler at 155 horsepower. The biggest of these was Waterloo's 4840 with 180 horsepower and the Power Shift transmission as standard equipment. Deere's promotion for these Waterloo models claimed "more horses from more iron."

For big power, nothing beat the four-wheel-drive 180-horsepower 8440 and the 228-horsepower 8640. These articulated models offered optional front and rear hydraulic differential locks for really tough traction conditions and as many as four remote hydraulic cylinder outlets. Deere's new single-lever operation Quad-Range transmission got all that torque to the ground and then operators discovered that tires limited traction. Dual- and triple-wheel configurations appeared on large farms throughout the Midwest and West.

The nature of the tractor market changed between 1965 and 1980. The U.S. Census reported that while there were 4.79 million tractors on farms in 1965, there were only 4.32 million in 1980. By the end of 1980, 1 percent of the farms in the United States (the largest ones) produced 25 percent of the nation's food. A smaller number of farmers ran much larger operations with ever more powerful machinery.

New styling on the hoods marked the obvious difference between the early 40-series and the "New Profiles in Performance" midrange models that appeared for the 1980 model year. The hoods sloped up more noticeably to the dash that incorporated an electronic instrument panel. Model designations changed only with the 80-horsepower Mannheim six; it became the 2940. Mannheim engineering offered each of its tractors

JOHN DEERE

1981 Model 2240 Orchard with Deere Model 145 Front Brush Rake

with Deere Model 145 Front brush rake The 179 cubic inch 3-cylinder diesel developed 40.2 maximum drawbar horsepower and 50.9 off the PTO shaft. The 8-forward gear transmission offered speeds from about 1.9 miles per hour up to 17.5 and the 5,895 tractor could pull or push nearly 3,000 pounds.

OPPOSITE: 1980 Model 4440 with Deere Model 567 Round Baler

This model sat in the middle of the Iron Horse herd, developing 108.6 drawbar horsepower and 130.6 off the PTO. The operator is baling corn stubble.

with optional mechanical front-wheel drive (MFWD). They moved the front differential to the side and mounted the tie-rod ahead of the front axle. This reduced the risk of damaging young plants.

Deere's Generation II tractors put power at the finger tips of the farmer. Mechanical and hydraulic engineering provided unprecedented output and performance. Dreyfuss' human engineering offered unmatched sophistication. Generation II put the competition a generation behind.

LEFT: *A Model 4520 Standard kicks up dust with its John Deere two-way, four-bottom plow slicing through corn stubble in flat lands. Equipped with its insulated cab, its front ended is loaded with counter weights. This machine is working!* Deere & Company Archives

OPPOSITE: 1981 MODEL 4640
In Iowa and Nebraska, corn harvest can seem endless to farmers and visitors alike. Here the dual-wheeled 156.3-PTO-horsepower 4640 waits its turn to unload while the Deere Model 8820 Titan II combine augers its own hopper into the waiting semi. The "HydraCushioned" seat and more sound-deadening materials built into the Sound-Gard cab make long hours in the Iron Horses more easily endured.

This is one weary and worn out Model 4520, sitting cabled and blocked to the ground at Deere's proving grounds. With its roll-over-protection canopy removed, its current purpose is unclear. But the presence of the white dynamometer car in the background suggests that this machine just went through hard testing. Deere & Company Archives

CHAPTER 23
1983 AND ON

INTO THE PRESENT,

INTO THE FUTURE

PREVIOUS: 1990 MODEL 4555
Kicking up a swirl of dust behind it, this new line 55-series tractor pulls an H&S Hi-Capacity rake behind a Deere mower through corn stubble in southwestern Iowa. The 55-series first appeared in 1988 and Deere rated this 4555 at 155 PTO horsepower.

RIGHT: 1985 MODEL 4450 CASTOR ACTION/MFWD
True four-wheel drive systems can bind up the front axles in tight turns. Deere devised a system called Castor Action mechanical front wheel drive. In this, the front wheels lay over 13 degrees off vertical as they turn. This "cuts" the turn the way a motorcycle does and gives the tractor the same 50-degree turn capability of comparable 2-wheel-drive models.

Starting in the late 1960s, Deere's experimental researchers investigated every kind of alternative fuel and power source it could try. Gordon Milar, head of engineering research, supervised assembly of a gas turbine-powered earth scraper. But this technology caused problems that Deere could not solve economically. After going so far as to construct their own gas turbine in 1969 and installing it in a modified Model 5020, they concluded that gas turbines were not fuel efficient. By 1973, Mideast politics had begun to influence the economies of the world. Availability of gasoline was no longer a sure thing. Deere shelved the turbine project and engineering looked back to diesel engines. Still, the company experimented.

Deere acquired rotary engine rights in 1984. The early 1980s brought on an agricultural depression so severe that Deere went after any means of diversification. Encouraged by Department of Defense and U.S. Marine Corps funding to develop a compact wheeled or rubber track troop carrier that could be air-dropped with first wave invasion troops, engineering became intrigued with the idea of engines that worked well on any low-grade fuel. In those days rotary engines notoriously had problems with seals. However, a research partner, Rotary Power International, in New Jersey, had solved this problem.

Deere installed one of Rotary Power's three-rotor 80-horsepower engines in a Model 2950 and performed the full range of tests. In a test recorded by video camera, the engine ran first on gasoline, then heating oil and eventually salad oil. The only appreciable difference was the density of the exhaust and, according to observers, the aroma of the exhaust. It sounded like

JOHN DEERE
2755

an Indianapolis racer. Dreyfuss senior partner Bill Purcell was present for a later round of tests.

"It was a fascinating project," Purcell recalled, "but it was probably defeated for environmental reasons as much as any other. Fuel economy is of great importance to the farmer, it is usually his largest single expense after the equipment itself, and the rotary emissions were not clean. In some countries of the world, that would have been a problem."

Deere stuck with diesels. Engineering steadily increased the engines' output and improved their economy even when the economy outside Deere had halted.

In 1982, Deere introduced its 50-series. These ranged in power from the Mannheim-built 45-horsepower three-cylinder 2150 and 50-horsepower 2255 orchard and vineyard models, up to the 300 PTO horsepower articulated four-wheel-drive Model 8850. This used a new turbocharged, intercooled V-8 designed and manufactured at the new Waterloo engine plant. Deere now considered 100 to 190 horsepower its midrange and for the five new models in this series and introduced a new 15-speed powershift transmission that boasted a 7 percent fuel economy improvement.

ABOVE: 1992 MODEL 2755 *To provide high clearance yet ride level, operators fit these with 13.6-38.00 front tires and 13.6-48.00 rears. Because much vegetable harvesting in California is hand-labor, these tractors have Hi-Lo transmissions, doubling the number of forward gears to 16 and providing a creeper, or slow-walking pace travel speed of less than 3/4 miles per hour.*

LEFT: *These tractors were international in their heritage. With engines produced at the Mannheim plant, Deere assembled the tractors at its Saran, France, factory. Engineering rated these tractors at 76.6 PTO horsepower.*

770

OPPOSITE: 1994 MODEL 770 WITH DEERE MODEL 70 FRONT LOADER
By 1994 Deere offered eight smaller agricultural tractors up to 40 PTO horsepower. This 770 has the optional hydrostatic or power front-wheel drive and Deere rated these 3-cylinder tractors at 20 horsepower off the PTO.

LEFT: 1996 MODEL 7600
Following the New Generation in 1960, then Generation II and on to the Iron Horse models, Deere again updated and upgraded its tractor line up with The New Breed of Power in 1992. Engineers relocated the upright exhaust pipe to a position near the windshield post to minimize its intrusion in the operator's field of view.

Deere also offered its innovative Castor/Action mechanical front wheel drive (MFWD) on all the models starting with the Mannheim four-cylinder 55-horsepower 2350, up through Waterloo's six-cylinder intercooled 190-horsepower 4850. This system added 13 degrees of front wheel caster, or rake, to facilitate extremely tight turning. By laying the front tires over in a turn, similar to what a motorcycle does, Deere's tractors could carve a smaller circle, something otherwise impossible with four-wheel-drive tractors whose drive gearing binds up in acute angles.

Deere returned to specialty crop manufacture with the low-profile 2750 for orchards, the high-clearance 2750 "Mudder" for California vegetable farmers working with bedded crops, and a series of wide-tread models on the 2350, 2550, 2750, and 2950 chassis for other vegetable and tobacco growers. New SoundGard bodies were even quieter than ever, measuring 73.5 dB(A) under full load.

The 55-series arrived in time for Deere's 150th company birthday in 1987. Again, the Mannheim line filled in midpower-range models, stretching from the three-cylinder 45-horsepower 2155 through the turbocharged three-cylinder 2355N with 55 horsepower, specially configured for orchards and vineyards. Deere renamed the 2755 "Mudder" and its companion 2955 as high-clearance models. An optional 96-inch wheel track turned these models into California vegetable specialists. Waterloo added its own vineyard model, the 2855N at 80 horsepower. Many California wineries ordered these with MFWD to pull 1- and 2-ton grape wagons up and down hills during harvest.

BRENT
540
JOHN DEERE
9100

In January 1989, Deere sent its dealers to Palm Springs, California, where it introduced the big 55-series machines. These appeared as the 105-horsepower Model 4055, the 120-horsepower 4255 offered as a high crop, as well as standard or MFWD model. The lineup stopped at Deere's first 200-horsepower row-crop model, the 4955. Each of these used Waterloo's 7.6-liter in-line six-cylinder diesel with redesigned intake and exhaust valves and ports and new seven-hole fuel injection nozzles. All models but the 4955 used the 16-speed Quad-Range transmission and Deere's Perma-Clutch. The big tractor came standard with the 15-speed Power Shift.

ABOVE: 2001 MODEL 9300T
Numbers tell the tale: this powerhouse weighs 39,000 pounds and it rides on 7,992 square inches of tread. That puts 4.9 pounds of pressure per square inch onto the soil, about the impact of a 20 pound infant standing on your bare feet.

OPPOSITE: 1998 MODEL 9100
This 28,380 pound tractor will bend to a 42-degree angle to steer tightly around the yard or the fields. Its 496-cubic-inch 6-cylinder engine developed 260 PTO horsepower with its turbocharger and intercooler. Deere made its 12-speed transmission standard and offered an optional 24-speed PowrSync version.

Deere's biggest tractors, the new 60-series, premiered in Denver prior to the Palm Springs winter introduction. Deere offered a 200-horsepower articulated four-wheel-drive Model 8560 as an alternative to its row-crop 4955. Articulated power ran up as high as a monstrous 14-liter Cummins turbo diesel for the 322 PTO horsepower Model 8960. Waterloo engineers moved the air intake stack and the exhaust and switched to a one-piece upper windshield. These two changed greatly improved forward visibility. The 60-series designation filtered down to Waterloo's row-crop version beginning in 1991. Models designated as 4560, 4760, and 4960 replaced the 4555, 4755, and 4955. These represented innovation in an atypical fashion. The new models offered no upgrade or improvement in horsepower output. But the other changes, updates, and modifications convinced sales and marketing staffs that these were, indeed, new models.

For decades Deere engineers and Henry Dreyfuss designers had labored to eliminate the blind spot that the air intake and exhaust pipe caused tractor operators. With the new 60 series, the forward view got much clearer. Waterloo mounted the air intake under the hood and gave it easy access through an opening side panel to clean it or change the element. It relocated the exhaust pipe to the front right pillar of the SoundGard cab.

Engineers and designers reconfigured the SoundGard entry with a larger platform, two handrails, and steps that adjusted to accommodate frame mounted equipment or crops. Optional exterior lighting not only illuminated the steps but also fully flooded the entire 360-degree circle around the tractor making night crop transfer from combines or to waiting trucks easier and safer.

Deere brought back Theo Brown's original rear axle width adjustment system, though it was much updated. Still, all an operator needed to do was jack up the rear wheel.

JOHN DEERE
FULL
ADD

After releasing the locking bolts and securing the jacking screw, the operator put the tractor in gear and watched as the wheels racked from a 60-inch tread out to 134 inches or back in.

ComfortGard cabs replaced SoundGards and those who had suspected Waterloo's engineer experts of slacking on the job fell silent in 1992. The company's new 6000 and 7000 series, their "All New Breed of Power," brought new power and new sophistication to mechanized farming. New in-line six-cylinder turbocharged diesels delivered as much as 38 percent more torque starting with the 66-horsepower Model 6200 all the way up to the 145-horsepower 7800.

The 70-series articulated models delivered even more. With at least 250 horsepower on hand in the 8570 and more than 400 available in the big 8970s, Waterloo engineers made good use of new electronics. Their remarkable Electric Engine Control system electronically adjusted valve timing to add as much as 25 more horsepower beyond the tractor's advertised output. This could occur only when the engine speed dropped below 1,900 rpm and sensors detected lugging. The extra power and torque would propel the tractor through the tough load. As engine speed reached 2,100 rpm, timing would return to normal and power would slip back to rated output. Deere called these models "Power Plus." It heralded its 1994 powerhouse 8000 series as "21st Century Technology Today."

In the late 1980s, Deere saw a need to further enlarge its tractor manufacturing capabilities. It acquired land and designed and constructed a large plant at Augusta, Georgia. Its first products emerged in 1992, as the Thousand Series, the 5200 with 40 horsepower, the 50-horsepower 5300, and the turbocharged 5400 model rated at 60 horsepower. With these tractors, Deere adopted another Theo Brown goal of easy access to the operator's platform. Engineers set the seat and the console-mounted controls and instruments further forward, a move accomplished by relocating the fuel tank behind the seat. This let designers put steps on both sides of the steering wheel.

Waterloo and Mannheim continued to update models for Europe and the United States through the mid-1990s and they changed the entire lineup to the Thousand Ten Series for 1998 and the Thousand Twenty Series for 2000 and 2001. These included models from an 18-horsepower 4010 in 1996 to the 450-horsepower Model 9520 in 2003.

Never short on innovation, Deere & Company startled the agriculture and construction worlds in late 1996 when it introduced a rubber-tracked model as part of its big tractor lineup for sale in 1997. Jim Nogorka, an Australian engineer working in Deere's experimental projects, fabricated the prototypes. Deere produced four-wheel-drive and belted versions of each model, from the 160-horsepower 8100 through the 225-horsepower 8400. The rubber-belted crawlers got a T suffix following their model number.

Deere proceeded cautiously with development of its new models. It announced its 9000 series four-wheel drives in 1996 with the 9000T series crawlers appearing for sale in 1999.

OPPOSITE: *Deere calls these "All new power on tracks," and its promotional brochures refer to them as "land locomotives." That's not much exaggeration, with 360 horsepower and standard 24-speed Powr-Sync transmissions with Hi-Lo powershift, the 30- or 36-inch wide 106-inch long tracks get massive pulling power with minimal soil compaction.*

JOHN DEERE
6410

Deere's entire lineup continued up the counting progression in 2001 when all its lines reached the new Twenty Series. These new tractors look far into the 21st century for styling cues and engineering technology. Stronger engines, hydraulics, and hitches, better brakes, tighter maneuverability, virtually negligible soil compaction with its tracked models, unsurpassed operator comfort and sophistication are the characteristics of Deere's latest tractors.

ABOVE: 2002 Model 4610-L

It gets stares anytime another farmer sees it. Yet for California almond and walnut farmer Dax Kimmelshue, the tiny front wheels were the only way to get the nose down enough to clear his low hanging trees. These special front low-profile tires are 20.5 - 8.0s while the rears are 12.5L-16.5s.

LEFT:

The low clearance model is designed specially for farmers working in orchards and groves. Unlike orchard models decades ago, Deere no longer encloses rear tires or operators inside sheet metal. The exhaust, however, is carefully routed out below the operator platform foot step.

Ninety Years and Counting

When William Butterworth reluctantly and almost secretly brought tractors into Deere's lineup, he was the last of the full-line implement manufacturers to accept the new technology and the new risks. Charlie Wiman, who loved tractors as they continually led his profit statements, came to embrace risks, bringing to the company countless patents for new innovations. He pulled Deere nearer to its competition by encouraging Theo Brown and Elmer McCormick, Henry Dreyfuss, Willard Nordenson, and Merlin Hansen. Wiman saw the future and knew it would need a much better tractor. He seized the tractor and pushed it. As Theo Brown said, "Charlie Wiman is the only one who seems to have the vision." But regrettably, he didn't live to see his New Generation come before the public.

That challenge, that responsibility, that legacy, and finally that success fell to his successor and son-in-law, Bill Hewitt. During Hewitt's 37 years with Deere, the company pioneered many ideas. Hewitt led Deere & Company out of the United States and into the world. He found new customers and new markets. His engineers created new products for them. He delivered to Deere's domestic tractor owners what his predecessors had promised would never come, four- and six-cylinder engines. Almost immediately after their introduction, the customers flocked to the New Generation with a devotion and enthusiasm unexpected and unparalleled in American industry history.

OPPOSITE: 2002 MODEL 8520T
Charles Erickson keeps pace with his son Todd in the combine as they harvest corn in southern Minnesota. Most row-crop configuration track tractors run an 88-inch tread width. Deere offers 16, 24, or 30 inch tracks.

LEFT: *These tracks run 89 inches on the ground and the steering wheel operates an electro-hydraulic-controlled differential that slows one side while speeding up the opposite track. As the tractor pivots, it flings corn shucks everywhere and the tracks can squeeze some onto the large drive wheels.*

"Always though, we preserved the principles," he explained. "They don't change. Integrity doesn't change. Certain methods change, to adapt to changing forces that surface themselves in the passage of time. . . ."

For Deere & Company, one "force" was a phone call from Hewitt's father-in-law, Charles Deere Wiman, to offer him the chance of his life. For Hewitt and Deere & Company the "force" was a sheet of paper. At the bottom of the page was a line that now can be written in green ink:

"Not content to be runner up."

Deere has persevered. While its products have not all been perfect, the company has scored more often than it has missed. Nearly all the companies it once competed against are gone, merged into acronyms or hyphenates, or submerged into other corporate identities.

Deere & Company celebrated the 200th anniversary of John Deere's birth in February 2004. For a company with a heritage as rich as this one, it is natural to sit back and reflect on past accomplishments, on nineteenth- and twentieth-century advances and successes.

What should comfort Deere's tractor owners and farmers is a certain knowledge. Somewhere in an office in twenty-first century Moline or Augusta, New York City, Mannheim, or Waterloo, engineers and designers are hard at work on computers, on paper, in their head. They are developing the twenty-second century technology that will go into Deere's tractors next year and beyond.

INDEX

SOURCES

150 Years of International Harvester; C. H. Wendel. Crestline Publishing Co. Sarasota, FL. 1981.

150 Years of J. I. Case; C. H. Wendel. Crestline Publishing Company, Sarasota, FL. 1991.

Activities of the SAE Tractor War Emergency Committee; A. W. Lavers. A paper delivered to the Society of Automotive Engineers, Washington, DC. September 23, 1943.

Agricultural Engineering; J.Brownlee Davidson. Webb Publishing, St. Paul, MN. 1921.

Agricultural Engineers' Handbook; C.B. Richey, Paul Jacobson, Carl W. Hall. McGraw Hill, New York. 1961.

Agriculture in the West; Edward L. Shapsmeier, Frederick H. Schapsmeier. Sunflower University Press, Manhattan, KS. 1980.

Agricultural Technology in the Twentieth Century; R. Douglas Hurt. Sunflower University Press, Manhattan, KS. 1991.

Agricultural Tractor, The – 1855-1950; R. B. Gray. American Society of Agricultural Engineers, St. Joseph, MI. 1975.

All In A Day's Work – Seventy-Five Years of Caterpillar; Gilbert C. Nolde. Forbes, New York. 2000.

Allis-Chalmers Farm Equipment 1914-1985; Norm Swinford. American Society of Agricultural Engineers, St. Joseph, MI. 1993.

American Agriculture – A Brief History; R. Douglas Hurt. Iowa State University Press, Ames, IA. 1994

American Farm Tractor; Randy Leffingwell. Motorbooks Publishing Co., Osecola, WI. 1990.

American Gasoline Engines since 1872; C. H. Wendel. Crestline Publishing, Sarasota, FL. 1983.

Benjamin Holt – The Story of the Caterpillar Tractor; Walter A. Payne. University of the Pacific, Stockton, CA. 1982.

Caterpillar; Randy Leffingwell. Motorbooks Publishing, Osceola, WI. 1993.

Century of Ford and New Holland Farm Equipment, A; Norm Swinford. American Society of Agricultural Engineers, St. Joseph, MI. 2000.

Comparison of Three Tractors; Glen Christoffersen. An unpublished paper. Ames, IA. 1953.

Corporate Reapers – The Book of Agribusiness; A. V. Krebs. Essential Books, Washington, DC. 1992.

Deere & Company's Early Tractor Development; Theo Brown. Deere & Co. internal publication. Moline, IL. 1953.

Designing for People; Henry Dreyfuss. Viking Press, New York. 1974.

Designing the new Generation John Deere Tractors; Merle L. Miller. American Society of Agricultural Engineers, St. Joseph, MI. 1999.

Design and Development of Engines for John Deere 3010 and 4010 Tractors; J.P. Townsend, D. E. Rudig. A paper delivered to the Society of Automotive Engineers, Milwaukee, WI. September 10, 1962.

Design this Day; Walter Dorwin Teague. Harcourt Brace & Co., New York. 1949.

Development of American Agriculture, The: A Historical Analysis, Second Edition; Willard W. Cochrane. University of Minnesota Press, Minneapolis, MN. 1993.

Diaries; Theo Brown while at Deere & Co. Moline, IL. On loan from Worchester Polytechnic Institute, Worchester, MA. 1913-1953.

Diary Notes – Talks with Henry Ford; Theo Brown. Unpublished typescript while at Deere & Co., Moline, IL. April 22, 1918 and other dates. On loan from Worchester Polytechnic Institute, Worchester, MA.

Encyclopedia of American Farm Tractors; C.H. Wendel. Crestline Publishing. Sarasota, FL. 1988.

Encyclopedia of American Steam Traction Engines; Jack Norbeck. Crestline Publishing, Sarasota, FL. 1976.

Farm and Garden Tractors; A. Frederick Collins. Frederick A. Stokes & Co., New York. 1920.

Farm & Power Equipment Retailer's Handbook; Leonard L. Wilson. National Farm & Power Equipment Dealers Association, revised edition, St. Louis, MO. 1964.
Farm Equipment Retailer's Handbook; Arch S. Merrifield. Farm Equipment Retailing, Inc., St. Louis, MO. 1953.

Farm Inventions in the Making of America; Paul C. Johnson. Wallace-Homestead Book Company, Des Moines, IA 1976.

Farm Machinery, Third Edition; Brian Bell. Farming Press, Ipswich, England. 1991.

Farm Machinery 1750-1945; Jonathan Brown. B.T. Batsford, London. 1989.

Farm Machinery & Equipment, Third Edition; Quincy Ayres, McGraw Hill, New York. 1948.

Farm Machinery Fundamentals; Marhsall F. Finner. American Puiblishing, Madison, WI. 1978.

Farm Power and Tractors, Fifth Edition; Fred R. Jones, William H. Aldred. McGraw Hill, New York. 1980.

Farm Steam Engineers – Pioneers in Rural America; Reynold M. Wik. Iron Men Album, Lancaster, PA. 1980.

Farm Tools Through the Ages; Michael Partridge. New York Graphic Society, Boston, MA. 1973.

Farm Tractors – 1915-1925 – I&T Collector's Series; C. G. Ewing, Randy Stephens. Intertec Publishing, Overland Park, KS. 1991.

Farm Tractors – 1926-1956 – I&T Collector's Series; C.G. Ewing, Randy Stephens. Intertec Publishing, Overland Park, KS. 1990.

Farm Tractors, 1950-1975; Lester Larsen. American Society of Agricultural Enginers, St. Joseph, MI. 1981.

Farm Tractors 1975-1995; Larry Gay. American Society of Agricultural Engineers, St. Joseph, MI. 1995.

Farm Tractors – A Living History; Randy Leffingwell. Motorbooks International, Osceola, WI. 1995.

Farm Tractor Milestones; Randy Leffingwell. MBI Publishing Co., Osceola, WI. 2000.

Farmers' Cyclopedia, Volume VII; various. United States Department of Agriculture/Doubleday, Page & Company, New York. 1915.

Farms and Farmers in an Urban Age; Edward Higbee. The Twentieth Century Fund, New York. 1963.

Ferguson – Inventor and Pioneer, Harry; Colin Fraser. John Murray, London. 1972.

Ferguson Implements and Accessories; John Farnworth. Farming Press, Ipswich, England. 1996.

Fitting People Inside a Machine; Henry Dreyfuss. Paper delivered to Society of Automotive Engineers, Los Angeles, October 5, 1944.

Ford and International Harvester: Competition and Development in the U.S. Tractor Industry 1918-1928; Jane S. Weaver. Unpublished thesis. Harvard University, Cambridge, MA. 1981.

Ford Farm Tractors; Randy Leffingwell. MBI Publishing, Osceola, WI. 1998.

Fordson, Farmall and Poppin' Johnny – A History of the Farm Tractor and Its Impact on America; Robert C. Williams. University of Illinois Press, Urbana, IL. 1987.

Ford Tractor Story – Part One – Dearborn to Dagenham 1917-1964; Stuart Gibbard. Old Pond Publishing, Ipswich, England. 1998.

Ford Tractor Story – Part Two – Basildon to New Holland 1964 to 1999;p Stuart Gibbard. Old Pond Publishing, Ipswich, England. 1999.

Full Steam Ahead – J. I. Case Tractors & Equipment 1842-1955; David Erb and Eldon Brumbaugh. American Society of Agricultural Engineers. 1993.

Grain Harvesters, The; Graeme Quick, Wesley Buchele. American Society of Agricultural Engineers, St. Joseph, MI. 1978.

Harvey Firestone – 1868-1938; James C. Young. Firestone Tire & Rubber. Akron, OH. 1939.

Henry Dreyfuss, Industrial Designer – The Man in the Brown Suit; Russell Flinchum. Cooper-Hewitt National Design Museum, Smithsonian Institution, New York. 1997.

Henry Ford and Grass-roots America; Reynold W. Wik. University of Michigan Press, Ann Arbor, MI. 1973.

Henry's Lieutenants; Ford R. Bryan. Wayne State University. Detroit, MI. 1993.

Historical and Current Developments in the Utilization of Tractor Power; Robert H. Casterton, Ober A Smith. A paper delivered to the Society of Automotive Engineers meeting, Milwaukee, WI. September 13, 1971.

Historical Perspective of Farm Machinery, A; Wendell M. van Syoc. Society of Automotive Engineers, Warrendale, PA. 1980.

History of Industrial Design 1919-1990 – The Dominion of Design, Volume III; Carlo Pirovano, ed. Electa, Milan, Italy. 1991.

History of the John Deere Industrial Equipment Division; Brian R. Alm. Deere Public Relations Department. Moline, IL. 1982.

How Johnny Popper Replaced the Horse; Donard S. Huber, Ralph C. Hughes. Deere & Co. Moline, IL. 1988.

Implement & Tractor – Reflections on 100 Years of Farm Equipment; Robert K. Mills, ed. Intertec Publishing. Overland Park, KS. 1986.

Industrial Design; Raymond Loewy. Overlook Press, Woodstock, New York. 1979.

Industrial Design – Reflection of a Century; Jocelyn de Noblet, ed. Flammarion/APCI, Paris, France. 1994.

International Harvester Farm Equipment Product History 1831-1985; Ralph Baumheckel, Kent Borghoff. American Society of Agricultural Engineers, St. Joseph, MI. 1997.

International Harvester Tractors, Randy Leffingwell. MBI Publishing Company, Osceola, WI. 1999.

International Harvester Tractors 1955-1985; Ken Updike. MBI Publishing, Osceola, WI. 2000.

Iowa Story – Iowan Invented Tractor; anonymous history of Froelich tractor. Iowa Development Commission Development Bulletin, February 20, 1950.

John Deere 30 Series Second Edition; J. R. Hobbs. Hain Publishing. Bee, NE. 2001.

John Deere – He Gave to the World the Steel Plow; Neil M. Clark. Deere & Co. Moline, IL. 1937.

John Deere Industrials; Brian Rukes. MBI Publishing Co. Osceola, WI. 2002.

John Deere Limited-Production & Experimental Tractors; Peter Letourneau. Motorbooks International, Osceola, WI. 1994.

John Deere Small Tractors; Rod Beemer. MBI Publishing Co. Osceola, WI. 2002.

John Deere Tractor Legacy; Don Macmillan, ed. Voyageur Press, Stillwater, MN. 2003.

John Deere Tractors, Randy Leffingwell.Motorbooks International, Osceola, WI. 1995.

John Deere Tractors and Equipment, Volume One 1837-1959; Don Macmillan. American Society of Agricultural Engineers, St. Joseph, MI. 1988.

John Deere Tractors and Equipment, Volume Two 1960-1990; Don Macmillan, Roy Harrington. American Society of Agricultural Engineers, St. Joseph, MI. 1991.

John Deere Worldwide – A Century of Progress 1893-1993; Don Macmillan. American Society of Agricultural Engineers, St. Joseph, MI. 1994.

John Deere's Company; Wayne G. Broehl, Jr. Doubleday & Co., New York. 1984.

J. I. Case Agricultural and Construction Equipment 1956 – 1994, Volume II; Tom Stonehouse, Eldon Brumbaugh. American Society of Agricultural Engineers, St. Joseph, MI. 1996.

J. I. Case – The First 150 Years; Michael S. Holmes. Case Corporation, Racine, WI. 1992.

Lanz Bulldog Tractors 1942-1955; Kurt Hafner. Kangaroo Press, Kenthurst, England. 1993.

Little Giants – John Deere Dubuque Works Tractors 1947-1960; J. R. Hobbs. Hain Publishing, Bee, NE. 1994.

Machines for Power Farming, Second Edition; Archie A. Stone. Harold E. Gulvin. John Wiley & Sons, New York. 1967.

Machines of Plenty; Stewart H. Holbrook. MacMillan, New York. 1955.

Modern Gas Tractor – Its Construction, Operation, Application and Repair; Victor W. Page. McClelland, Goodchild & Stewart, Toronto, Ontario, Canada. 1913.

My Forty Years with Ford; Charles E. Sorensen, Samuel T. Williamson. W.W. Norton Co., New York. 1956.

Nebraska Tractor Tests Since 1920; C. H. Wendel. Crestline Publishing. Sarasota, FL. 1985.

Number 101 Tractor – History and Development to January 30th, 1945; Theo Brown. Unpublished typescript. While at Deere & Co. 1945.

Oliver Farm Tractors; Herbert Morrell, Jeff Hackett. Motorbooks International, Osceola, WI. 1997.

Oliver Hart-Parr; C.H. Wendel; Motorbooks International, Osceola, WI. 1993.

The Open Door – Special Anniversary Issue – John Deere Horicon Works; Faith Meyer. John Deere Horicon Works, Horicon, WI. 1986.

Power Farming with Greater Profit; Anonymous. Deere promotional book. Moline, IL. 1937.

Power Test Timeline; Lorry Dunning. Unpublished. Davis, CA. 1998.

The Tractor – Its Influence Upon the Agricultural Implement Industry; Barton W. Currie. Curtis Publishing Company, Philadelphia, PA. 1916.

Traction Farming and Traction Engineering – Gasoline, Alcohol, Kerosene. James H. Stephenson. Frederick J. Drake & Co., Chicago, IL. 1917.

Two-Cylinder Collector Series Volume I; various. Two-Cylinder Club, Grundy Center, IA. 1991.

Two-Cylinder Collector Series Volume II; various. Two Cylinder Club, Grundy Center, IA. 1993.

Ultimate American Farm Tractor Data Book; Lorry Dunning. MBI Publishing, Osceola, WI. 1999.

Wheels of Farm Progress; Marvin McKinley. American Society of Agricultural Engineers, St. Joseph, MI. 1980.

Whereby We Thrive – History of American Farming 1607 – 1972; John T. Schlebecker. Iowa State University Press, Ames, IA. 1975.

Who Built America, Volume Two: From the Gilded Age to the Present; various. Pantheon Books, NY. 1992.

Yearbook of Agriculture; various. United States Department of Agriculture, Washington, DC. 1919.

Yearbook of Agriculture; Nelson Antrim Crawford, ed. United States Department of Agriculture, Washington, DC. 1927.

Yearbook of Agriculture; Milton S. Eisenhower, ed. United States Department of Agriculture, Washington, DC. 1930.

Yearbook of Agriculture; Milton S. Eisenhower, ed. United States Department of Agriculture, Washington, DC. 1932.

Yearbook of Agriculture – Farmers in a Changing World; various. United States Department of Agriculture, Washington, DC. 1940.

Yearbook of Agriculture – Power to Produce; Alfred Stefferud, ed. United States Department of Agriculture, Washington, DC. 1960.

Yearbook of Agriculture – After a Hundred Years; Alfred Stefferud, ed. United States Department of Agriculture, Washington, DC. 1962.

Yearbook of Agriculture – A Place to Live; Alfred Stefferud, ed. United States Department of Agriculture, Washington DC. 1963.

Yearbook of Agriculture – Farmer's World; Alfred Stefferud, ed. United States Department of Agriculture, Washington, DC. 1964.

Yellow Steel – The Story o f the Earthmoving Equipment Industry; William R. Haycraft. University of Illinois Press, Champaign, IL. 2000.

Interview with Jesse Lindeman, August 1992.
Interview with William Purcell, October 1992.
Interview with Bill Hewitt, October 1992.
Interview with Jim Conner, October, 1992.
Interviews with Harold Brock, October 1994, January 1995, April 2001.
Interview with Keith Rockey, Esq. December 1998.
Interview with Willard Nordenson, by Gary Olsen, 1982.